Environmental and Energy Policy
and the Economy

Environmental and Energy Policy and the Economy

Edited by

Matthew J. Kotchen, *Yale University and NBER,*
United States of America
Tatyana Deryugina, *University of Illinois at Urbana-Champaign
and NBER,* United States of America
Catherine D. Wolfram, *Massachusetts Institute of Technology and
NBER,* United States of America

The University of Chicago Press
Chicago and London

NBER Environmental and Energy Policy and the Economy, Number 5, 2024

Published annually by The University of Chicago Press.
www.journals.uchicago.edu/EEPE/

Subscriptions: For individual and institutional subscription rates, visit www.journals .uchicago.edu, email subscriptions@press.uchicago.edu, or call (877) 705-1878 (US) or (773) 753-3347 (international). Free or deeply discounted institutional access is available in most developing nations through the Chicago Emerging Nations Initiative (www.journals .uchicago.edu/inst/ceni).

Please direct subscription inquiries to Subscription Fulfillment, 1427 E. 60th Street, Chicago, IL 60637-2902. Telephone: (773) 753-3347 or toll free in the United States and Canada (877) 705-1878. Fax: (773) 753-0811 or toll-free (877) 705-1879. E-mail: subscriptions @press.uchicago.edu.

Standing orders: To place a standing order for this book series, please address your request to The University of Chicago Press, Chicago Distribution Center, Attn. Standing Orders/Customer Service, 11030 S. Langley Avenue, Chicago, IL 60628. Telephone toll free in the U.S. and Canada: 1-800-621-2736; or 1-773-702-7000. Fax toll free in the U.S. and Canada: 1-800-621-8476; or 1-773-702-7212.

Single-copy orders: In the U.S., Canada, and the rest of the world, order from your local bookseller or direct from The University of Chicago Press, Chicago Distribution Center, 11030 S. Langley Avenue, Chicago, IL 60628. Telephone toll free in the U.S. and Canada: 1-800-621-2736; or 1-773-702-7000. Fax toll free in the U.S. and Canada: 1-800-621-8476; or 1-773-702-7212. In the U.K. and Europe, order from your local bookseller or direct from The University of Chicago Press, c/o John Wiley Ltd. Distribution Center, 1 Oldlands Way, Bognor Regis, West Sussex PO22 9SA, UK. Telephone 01243 779777 or Fax 01243 820250. E-mail: cs-books@wiley.co.uk.

The University of Chicago Press offers bulk discounts on individual titles to Corporate, Premium, and Gift accounts. For information, please write to Sales Department—Special Sales, The University of Chicago Press, 1427 E. 60th Street, Chicago, IL 60637 USA or telephone 1-773-702-7723.

This book was printed and bound in the United States of America.

ISSN: 2689-7857
E-ISSN: 2689-7865
ISBN-13: 978-0-226-83572-3 (pb.:alk. paper)
ISBN-13: 978-0-226-83576-1 (e-book)

Environmental and Energy Policy and the Economy

EDITORS

Editor, *Environmental and Energy Policy and the Economy*
Matthew J. Kotchen, *Yale University and NBER, United States of America*

Editorial Board, *Environmental and Energy Policy and the Economy*
Tatyana Deryugina, *University of Illinois at Urbana-Champaign and NBER, United States of America*
Catherine D. Wolfram, *Massachusetts Institute of Technology and NBER, United States of America*

Relation of the Directors to the Work and Publications of the NBER

1. The object of the NBER is to ascertain and present to the economics profession, and to the public more generally, important economic facts and their interpretation in a scientific manner without policy recommendations. The Board of Directors is charged with the responsibility of ensuring that the work of the NBER is carried on in strict conformity with this object.

2. The President shall establish an internal review process to ensure that book manuscripts proposed for publication DO NOT contain policy recommendations. This shall apply both to the proceedings of conferences and to manuscripts by a single author or by one or more coauthors but shall not apply to authors of comments at NBER conferences who are not NBER affiliates.

3. No book manuscript reporting research shall be published by the NBER until the President has sent to each member of the Board a notice that a manuscript is recommended for publication and that in the President's opinion it is suitable for publication in accordance with the above principles of the NBER. Such notification will include a table of contents and an abstract or summary of the manuscript's content, a list of contributors if applicable, and a response form for use by Directors who desire a copy of the manuscript for review. Each manuscript shall contain a summary drawing attention to the nature and treatment of the problem studied and the main conclusions reached.

4. No volume shall be published until forty-five days have elapsed from the above notification of intention to publish it. During this period a copy shall be sent to any Director requesting it, and if any Director objects to publication on the grounds that the manuscript contains policy recommendations, the objection will be presented to the author(s) or editor(s). In case of dispute, all members of the Board shall be notified,

and the President shall appoint an ad hoc committee of the Board to decide the matter; thirty days additional shall be granted for this purpose.

5. The President shall present annually to the Board a report describing the internal manuscript review process, any objections made by Directors before publication or by anyone after publication, any disputes about such matters, and how they were handled.

6. Publications of the NBER issued for informational purposes concerning the work of the Bureau, or issued to inform the public of the activities at the Bureau, including but not limited to the NBER Digest and Reporter, shall be consistent with the object stated in paragraph 1. They shall contain a specific disclaimer noting that they have not passed through the review procedures required in this resolution. The Executive Committee of the Board is charged with the review of all such publications from time to time.

7. NBER working papers and manuscripts distributed on the Bureau's web site are not deemed to be publications for the purpose of this resolution, but they shall be consistent with the object stated in paragraph 1. Working papers shall contain a specific disclaimer noting that they have not passed through the review procedures required in this resolution. The NBER's web site shall contain a similar disclaimer. The President shall establish an internal review process to ensure that the working papers and the web site do not contain policy recommendations, and shall report annually to the Board on this process and any concerns raised in connection with it.

8. Unless otherwise determined by the Board or exempted by the terms of paragraphs 6 and 7, a copy of this resolution shall be printed in each NBER publication as described in paragraph 2 above.

Contents

Contents

Introduction

Matthew J. Kotchen, *Yale University and NBER,* United States of America

Tatyana Deryugina, *University of Illinois at Urbana-Champaign and NBER,* United States of America

Catherine D. Wolfram, *Massachusetts Institute of Technology and NBER,* United States of America

Welcome to the fifth volume of *Environmental and Energy Policy and the Economy (EEPE)*. The six papers that follow fit into the overall aim of the *EEPE* initiative: to spur policy-relevant research and professional interactions in the areas of environmental and energy economics and policy. The annual conference is hosted by the National Bureau of Economic Research (NBER), with participants from academia, government, and nongovernmental organizations.

This year's conference took place at the National Press Club in Washington, DC, with participants also tuning in online. We were fortunate to have a keynote presentation about climate and energy policy by Ben Harris, former assistant secretary for economic policy at the US Department of the Treasury. We are grateful to all the authors for their time and effort producing outstanding papers and helping to make the fifth year of *EEPE* a continued success.

In the first paper, Sarah Armitage, Noel Bakhtian, and Adam Jaffe start with the observation that newly scaled policy instruments focused on climate and energy are motivated not only by unpriced environmental externalities but also by innovation market failures. They review an extensive literature on innovation market failures, with an eye toward producing insights about the implementation of such policies in a climate and energy context. The paper will serve as a go-to resource for those looking for policy-relevant insights bridging the literatures on climate and innovation.

Richard Newell, William Pizer, and Brian Prest evaluate two methods of accounting for capital displacement in benefit-cost analysis. They

Environmental and Energy Policy and the Economy, volume 5, 2024.

illustrate how an approach based on the shadow price of capital is more solidly grounded in economic theory than the typical approach of using discount rates based on investment rates of return. Using theory and examples, they show how the approach is relatively straightforward to implement, and the paper has already had an impact on proposed revisions to the way the US government recommends conducting benefit-cost analyses of federal regulations.

Tihitina Andarge, Yongjie Ji, Bonnie Keeler, David Keiser, and Conor McKenzie provide a valuable contribution to the literature on environmental justice. Focusing on the Clean Water Act, they review all regulatory impact analyses since 1992 for insights about how environmental justice has, or has not, been taken into account. They also produce an original analysis of how the current configuration of water-pollution discharges across the United States affects different groups. The authors show that water pollution is more likely to affect households that are poor, White, and less educated. These patterns differ from those of air pollution, largely because most discharges take place in rural rather than urban locations.

Mark Curtis, Layla O'Kane, and Jisung Park contribute much-needed insights about employment transitions into and out of jobs most likely to be affected by decarbonization. They show that the number of transitions to "green" jobs is increasing rapidly, but the transitions from carbon-intensive sectors remain relatively low and the effects differ by location, worker age, and education. The analysis is important because policy makers often want such job-related information, and the authors leverage unique data sets and methods to provide the needed insight. This work also complements a paper in last year's *EEPE* volume that characterizes the set of green jobs emerging in the US economy.

Lucas Davis provides a detailed analysis of heat-pump adoption in the United States. Although evidence suggests that many energy-efficiency subsidies tend to benefit high-income households, Davis shows this not to be the case with heat-pump adoption, which many state and federal policies are seeking to promote. Heat-pump adoption is strongly correlated with geography, climate, and energy prices, and these are configured in a way that makes adoption uncorrelated with household income. Thus, heat pumps appear to offer an opportunity for subsidizing a low-carbon technology without favoring high-income households.

In the final paper, Robert Huang and Matthew Kahn examine the question of whether Republican-leaning states have a comparative advantage at generating green power. They find that Republican counties are faster at granting renewable energy permits because they have less strict zoning regulations. Republican counties also appear to have an advantage in wind generation due to lower land prices, lower population density, and higher wind speeds. In contrast, Democratic counties are more favorable for solar installations because solar panels are less land-intensive, and Democratic-leaning states provide more incentives for solar developers. These results provide insight about where energy transitions might be expected in the coming years.

Finally, we would like to thank Evan Michelson and the Alfred P. Sloan Foundation for the financial support that has made the *EEPE* initiative possible. We are also grateful to Jim Poterba, president and CEO of the NBER, for continuing to support the *EEPE* initiative, and to the NBER staff, especially Denis Healy, Rob Shannon, and Helena Fitz-Patrick. Planning is already underway for next year!

Endnote

Author email addresses: Kotchen (matthew.kotchen@yale.edu), Deryugina (deryugin@illinois.edu). For acknowledgments, sources of research support, and disclosure of the authors' material financial relationships, if any, please see https://www.nber.org/books-and-chapters/environmental-and-energy-policy-and-economy-volume-5/introduction-environmental-and-energy-policy-and-economy.

Innovation Market Failures and the Design of New Climate Policy Instruments

Sarah Armitage, *Boston University*, United States of America

Noël Bakhtian, *National Academies Board on Science, Technology, and Economic Policy*, United States of America

Adam Jaffe, *Brandeis University, and NBER*, United States of America

Executive Summary

Moving beyond the combination of adoption subsidies, standards, and (albeit limited) attempts at carbon pricing that largely characterized US climate policy over the past decade, recent climate-related legislation has transformed not only the scale of US climate activities but also the policy mechanisms adopted. Newly scaled policy instruments—including demonstration projects, loan guarantees, green banks, and regional technology hubs—are motivated not only by un-priced carbon externalities but also by innovation market failures. This paper maps the economics literature on innovation market failures and other frictions to the stated goals of these policy instruments, with the goal of focusing discussions about how to implement these policies as effectively as possible. The paper also discusses how program evaluation can help to illuminate which market failures are most relevant in a particular context and which policy instruments are most targeted to them.

JEL Codes: O31, O38, Q54, Q55, Q58

Keywords: innovation, climate, market failure, demonstration projects, loan guarantees, green banks, regional technology hubs

I. Introduction

Recent legislation in the United States has provided the opportunity to inject significant federal funding into policy instruments that have not been previously adopted at this scale in US climate policy. Moving beyond the combination of adoption subsidies, standards, and (albeit

Environmental and Energy Policy and the Economy, volume 5, 2024.

limited) attempts at carbon pricing that largely characterized climate policy over the past decade, the Infrastructure Investment and Jobs Act (IIJA) of 2021, the CHIPS and Science Act (CHIPS) of 2022, and the Inflation Reduction Act (IRA) of 2022 have transformed not only the scale of US climate activities but also the policy mechanisms adopted. These laws have appropriated or authorized significant funding for clean energy demonstration projects ($13.5 billion appropriated under IIJA and $5.8 billion appropriated under IRA), loan guarantees ($11.7 billion in appropriations, $350 billion in lending authority under IRA), green banks ($27 billion appropriated under IRA), and regional technology hubs ($11.5 billion appropriated under IIJA), among other programs.[1]

One common characteristic of these newly scaled policy instruments is that they are motivated not only by the presence of unpriced carbon externalities driving a wedge between private and social costs of emissions but also by innovation market failures. As has been well documented in the economics literature, these innovation market failures exacerbate and interact with the carbon externality in complex ways (Jaffe, Newell, and Stavins 2005). A particular feature of the newly funded policy instruments mentioned above is that they all target the middle of the technology innovation process, after early-stage research and development (R&D) but before widespread deployment. During this middle phase, new technologies are tested at larger scale and integrated into existing infrastructure, and new business and financing models are developed and validated. Without intervention, this phase of the innovation process may proceed too slowly relative to the social optimum, or not at all—as a result of nonappropriable knowledge creation, financial frictions, or coordination failures. (Fig. 1 maps these newly scaled policy instruments and innovation market failures to Technology Readiness Levels, which are defined in table 1.)

Furthermore, key features of these policy instruments are motivated by concerns not traditionally thought of as market failures, such as fostering economic development in disadvantaged regions, creating new jobs in ways that address equity objectives, addressing historically unequal burdens of pollution from fossil fuels, and overcoming institutional inertia. These challenges may interact with innovation market failures in complex ways; for example, new knowledge is created in developing new financing models that allow credit-constrained consumers to adopt a new technology. Moreover, many of these additional policy priorities are particularly relevant for this middle stage of the innovation process but would not necessarily arise during early-stage R&D.

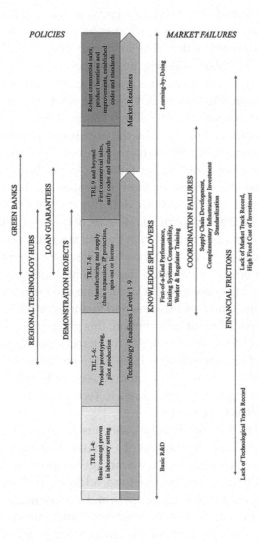

Fig. 1. Technology readiness levels, policy instruments, and innovation market failures. Color version available as an online enhancement.

Note: IP = intellectual property; R&D = research and development.

Source: Adapted from US Department of Energy, Office of Energy Efficiency and Renewable Energy (n.d.).

Table 1
Technology Readiness Levels

Technology Readiness Level	Description
TRL 1	Basic principles observed and reported
TRL 2	Technology concept and/or application formulated
TRL 3	Analytical and experimental critical function and/or characteristic proof of concept
TRL 4	Component and/or breadboard validation in laboratory environment
TRL 5	Component and/or breadboard validation in relevant environment
TRL 6	System/subsystem model or prototype demonstration in a relevant environment
TRL 7	System prototype demonstration in an operational environment
TRL 8	Actual system completed and qualified through test and demonstration
TRL 9	Actual system proven through successful mission operations

Source: US Government Accountability Office (2020).

In this paper, we seek to map the economics literature on innovation market failures to the stated goals of these newly scaled policy instruments within IIJA, CHIPS, and IRA. We also discuss the equity concerns of these policies in the context of the innovation process. An implicit theory of change behind policies such as demonstration projects or loan guarantees is that resources are not being allocated efficiently or equitably across the economy: there are unfunded projects that should be funded, for one reason or another. Understanding those potential reasons may help to focus discussions about where to allocate program resources and how to make these policies as effective as possible. After reviewing literature on innovation market failures and other policy priorities, we identify specific questions for program design and implementation that may help to inform these discussions.

Several key ideas emerge from this exercise. First, each of these newly scaled policy instruments has the potential to address multiple market failures and other policy concerns inherent in the technology innovation process, including knowledge spillovers, coordination failures, financial frictions, and distributional objectives. Program implementers may wish to apply the market failure framework when collecting input from stakeholders about which barriers are most inhibiting to early technology deployment. Developing hypotheses about which market failures matter most in a given context will allow for tailoring program design accordingly, which may increase the likelihood of successful program implementation. Furthermore, each of these newly scaled policies is providing funding that—in the absence of innovation market failures—would generally come from private capital markets. Thinking systematically about the ways that these policies are and are not filling similar roles as private capital fosters more effective program design. Where a program is "filling in" for the role played by private capital in other contexts, program implementers can mimic contract structures and other approaches that venture capitalists, commercial banks, and other investors have developed.[2] But to the extent a program is addressing objectives typically ignored by the private sector, such as increasing equity, it may be desirable to deviate intentionally from the practices of private funders, with the nature of those deviations informed by analysis of these distinct goals. Finally, the economics literature has consistently concluded that these are tricky market failures to rectify. And as significant as these new initiatives are, we are still in the early phase of what will be a long-term policy effort to address climate change. Building evaluation and learning into program design will generate new understanding of which of the relevant market failures most inhibit early deployment of climate technologies and which policy instruments address them most effectively.

The paper proceeds as follows. Section II describes the innovation market failures and other priorities that may be targeted with these policy instruments. The section also summarizes the relevant economic literature on these challenges and on policy interventions that have been used in other contexts. Section III describes the four policy instruments in question and their institutional history in US climate policy, linking their stated goals and approaches to the market failures and other priorities described in the previous section. Section IV discusses market failures that are not well addressed through these four policy instruments. Section V concludes and offers directions for future research.

II. Innovation Market Failures and Other Frictions

We begin by discussing the economics literature on three types of market failures of particular relevance to the middle stage of the innovation process—knowledge spillovers, financial frictions, and coordination failures—as well as literature related to the distributional implications of climate innovation. Readers may find it useful to refer to table 2, which provides definitions of key economic terms for a policy audience; these terms are *italicized* throughout the paper.

Table 2
Definition of Key Economics Terms

Concept	Key Terms
Market failures	A "**market failure**" refers to a situation in which the free market does not allocate goods or services efficiently; more technically, the term refers to conditions under which the First Welfare Theorem does not hold, and the equilibrium outcome is not Pareto efficient. In the presence of a market failure, reallocating goods and services could make all actors better off. A "**(Pigouvian) externality**" is one example of a market failure, in which private actors do not fully consider ("**internalize**") the costs or benefits that they impose on others in their decision-making, as those costs or benefits are not fully priced. Greenhouse gas emissions are a well-known example of a negative externality. The "**socially optimal**" level of some good or service is that which maximizes welfare, or total surplus, across all actors.
Knowledge spillovers	"**Appropriability**" refers to whether private actors can capture the value produced through their actions; for example, through increased profits. Value that is instead captured by other actors constitutes a "**positive spillover.**"
Financial frictions	"**Asymmetric information**" refers to a situation where one economic actor possesses information that another does not (e.g., about the quality of a new technology); this discrepancy is usually most relevant when the two actors are trying to transact (e.g., to agree on a financial contract). One potential consequence of asymmetric information is "**adverse selection**": project developers or entrepreneurs may have more information about the likelihood of success than investors and may only be willing to pay higher interest rates or post greater collateral for risky projects. Another potential consequence is "**moral hazard**": if investors cannot fully observe the behavior of project developers or entrepreneurs, the latter may have an incentive to engage in risky behavior or divert project funds to maximize their own surplus rather than that of the investor. The "**market for ideas**" refers to the buying and selling of innovations, often before they are developed into a final product. These transactions could take the form of technology licensing, acquisitions of technology companies, or strategic alliances, among other models.
Coordination failures	"**Transaction costs**" may include the costs of identifying counterparties, negotiating terms, enforcing contracts, and so forth. When transaction costs are high, economic actors face greater barriers to realizing economically beneficial transactions. "**Complete contracts**" refer to contracting arrangements in which all parties are able to enumerate their respective rights and responsibilities under any possible state of the world. Such contracts are thought to be impossible to write in practice, leading to incomplete contracts in which one party holds residual control rights. "**Pareto efficiency**" describes a situation in which no actor (e.g., consumer, firm) can be made better off without making another actor worse off. In a Pareto-dominated equilibrium, an alternative equilibrium exists that could make some actors better off without making any worse off.

A. Knowledge Spillovers

Perhaps the most well-established motivation for public support of the innovation process is the idea that innovation produces new knowledge, which has characteristics of a public good. Because information is not perfectly *appropriable*, private firms will not fully *internalize* (i.e., profit from) the *positive spillovers* from their innovative activities. Consequently, the private market will underprovide innovation relative to the social optimum (Nelson 1959; Arrow 1962). These knowledge spillovers have long been considered a defining feature of the early stages of the innovation process, especially in basic R&D. New knowledge generated in basic R&D is especially likely to be relevant for many different applications and thus nonappropriable by any individual firm. Ample empirical research, reviewed in Bloom, van Reenen, and Williams (2019), has suggested that the social return to R&D is higher than the private return, implying that firms underinvest in R&D relative to the *socially optimal* level, therefore creating a potential role for public sector support for R&D to correct this market failure.[3] This research has provided theoretical and empirical support for policies that strengthen firms' ability to internalize the full benefits of their R&D activities (such as intellectual property protections) and that increase overall R&D in the economy (such as R&D tax credits and public funding for research).

Economics research has also shown that spillovers can be generated through the development, adoption, and diffusion of new technologies. Learning-by-doing causes the marginal cost of the new technology to decrease with cumulative production as firms learn to produce more efficiently. If some of the knowledge gained through production experience benefits other firms, such positive spillovers could justify deployment subsidies, even in amounts above the externality directly avoided from fossil fuel generation (Gillingham and Stock 2018). Whether learning-by-doing spillovers justify generous deployment subsidies in practice appears to depend on the context. Covert and Sweeney (2022) find that interfirm spillovers have generated substantial cost reductions in the offshore wind industry, whereas Gillingham and Bollinger (2021) find evidence of very small learning spillovers in solar photovoltaic (PV) installations. Beyond learning-by-doing, other potentially relevant forms of knowledge spillovers during widespread technology deployment include learning-by-using, whereby new technology adopters generate information for others about the technology's existence or effectiveness (Jaffe et al. 2005; Gillingham and Bollinger 2021; Bollinger et al. 2022).

Industry observers have also suggested that knowledge spillovers may occur between early R&D and large-scale deployment. For one, the high up-front cost of many clean technologies means that innovative financing arrangements may be critical to deploying new technologies at scale. Likewise, many clean technologies must be integrated with existing systems, which requires training the local workforce to install and service the technology, working with regulators to understand the new technology, or adapting the technology developed at lab and pilot scale to operate with existing infrastructure. These financial, regulatory, and process innovations associated with initial deployment may be subject to the same knowledge spillovers of invention more generally. As an example, after SolarCity's success with offering leases for residential solar installations, which allowed a larger group of customers to avoid high up-front costs and to benefit from tax credits, many other installers adopted this innovative financing model. By 2014, 72% of the residential solar market used this model; SolarCity accounted for half of this total (Gross 2015; Trabish 2015). Of course, the efficient level of public support for these types of innovations depends on the magnitude of spillovers across firms, which in turn depends on the specific context.

B. Financial Frictions

In a world without financial frictions, all investment opportunities where revenues exceed costs (adjusted for risk and the timing of payments) would be able to secure funding. There is a long literature in economics studying deviations from this optimum, both theoretical and empirical. Explanations for frictions in financing positive net present value (NPV) projects are rooted in *asymmetric information* between demanders and suppliers of investment capital and the associated problems of *moral hazard* and *adverse selection*. Financial contracting has developed numerous methods to address these issues, but the solutions generally increase the cost of finance relative to a frictionless world, meaning that some positive NPV projects will not be undertaken.[4] In this section, we review the economic literature on financial frictions affecting innovation and entrepreneurship, focusing on the investment needed for the climate transition. We address three areas in particular: finance for innovation by start-ups, finance for innovation by incumbents, and finance for other forms of entrepreneurship.

Evidence suggests that R&D-intensive start-up firms face particular challenges in securing finance. The entrepreneur typically has more information about the technology than the investor, a situation that is

especially acute in funding new technologies because of how easily innovative ideas may spillover to competitors. This asymmetric information
makes it difficult for equity providers to assess the likelihood of a new
technology company's eventual success (Hall and Lerner 2010). Furthermore, early-stage technology companies have few assets that could be
pledged as collateral in loan contracts, and cash flows may not be sufficiently predictable to enable regular debt repayment (Hall and Lerner
2010). In both debt and equity contracts, it is difficult to contract directly
on inputs to the research process (Kerr and Nanda 2015).

Venture capital (VC) has emerged as an effective model for providing
equity financing to high-potential technology start-ups, developing certain contractual and governance strategies for overcoming the above-
mentioned frictions.[5] The VC model uses staged financing to treat funding rounds as a series of real options, where investment sizes increase
only as new information is revealed about the technology's probability
of success (Gompers 1995; Bergemann and Hege 1998, 2005). In addition, VC funds undertake robust monitoring and oversight of their portfolio companies to address moral-hazard issues in the R&D process
(Hellmann 1998; Cornelli and Yosha 2003; Chernenko, Lerner, and Zeng
2020). Although VC investment funds only a small share of new entrants
in the US economy—even a small share of patent-generating new entrants—it exerts a disproportionate influence on innovation, including
in the climate-technology sector.[6]

Yet in recent years, observers have debated the extent to which the
existing VC model is effective for addressing financial frictions facing
clean technology companies. Relying on data from 1980 to 2009, Nanda,
Younge, and Fleming (2015) argue that several structural factors had
limited the role of VC in funding clean technologies, ranging from capital intensity and long timelines, to limited exit opportunities and increased financing risk, to high commodity and policy risk (see also
Gaddy et al. 2017). More recently, industry observers have challenged
this view, pointing to the recent resurgence of VC interest in climate
technologies as well as the changing landscape of early technology
funders (Kahn and Naam 2021). The past decade has seen the emergence
of specialized climate-focused funds such as Breakthrough Energy Ven-
tures and Energy Impact Partners, new public funding from ARPA-E
and philanthropic capital from organizations such as Prime Coalition
and the Bezos Earth Fund, and the development of complementary in-
cubators and accelerators such as Activate and Greentown Labs (Prabhakar 2021).

Yet many industry observers continue to point to financial frictions in the middle of the innovation process, as climate technologies seek funding for demonstration plants or first-of-a-kind commercial facilities (Kahn and Jacobs 2022; Khatcherian 2022). Certain structural factors previously identified as barriers to VC funding for early-stage climate technologies may be relevant in understanding financial frictions at this stage.[7] New climate technologies continue to face technology risk (the "learning" phase, in the terminology of Nanda 2020) when implementing full-size demonstration projects, because technologies that succeeded as prototypes may not succeed at this size or when integrated with existing infrastructure. To manage this idiosyncratic risk, portfolio theory suggests that VC investors should fund a portfolio of start-up companies, but the high fixed costs of experimentation at the demonstration phase mean that many investors do not have sufficient resources (Kerr, Nanda, and Rhodes-Kropf 2014; Nanda et al. 2015; Nanda 2020; Jones 2022). The handful of VC firms able to deploy sufficiently large investments to fund these demonstration projects may have more attractive investment opportunities scaling up technologies that have already been derisked.[8] Moreover, the development of specialized climate portfolios or new contractual approaches to address these issues with technology demonstration would still face an undiversifiable risk that the market for these climate technologies will take a long time to develop, will never develop, or will not be very large. This undiversifiable risk makes climate-focused funds inherently riskier than other technology sectors. All these issues suggest that financial frictions may still persist in the middle phase of the technology development process, providing a potential theoretical justification for policy intervention.

Beyond the innovations funded in the VC ecosystem, less R&D-intensive start-ups may also face financial frictions. Economists have debated the extent to which other new entrants and small businesses face "credit rationing," whereby groups of potential borrowers are unable to obtain loans at any interest rate (i.e., any price).[9] The canonical model of Stiglitz and Weiss (1981) suggests that credit rationing may arise due to either adverse selection among borrowers (only the riskiest borrowers are willing to accept high interest rates) or moral hazard (borrowers facing higher interest rates undertake riskier projects to increase payoffs if successful; see also Leland and Pyle 1977). Economists have debated the extent to which financial markets have other tools to mitigate these issues (Bester 1985; Besanko and Thakor 1987; de Meza and Southey 1996) and whether credit rationing is observed in practice, with mixed evidence

(Berger and Udell 1992; Petersen and Rajan 1994, 2002; Beck and Demirguc-Kunt 2006; Kerr and Nanda 2010; Robb and Robinson 2012).

Nonetheless, entrepreneurs in newer sectors, such as those developing new climate-related business models, may be more likely to face challenges in securing funding for positive NPV projects. Several industry observers have commented on the reluctance of lenders to invest in the fixed cost of learning about a new industry and how to structure a new type of loan—say, energy-efficiency retrofits for small businesses—if they are uncertain how quickly that technology or business model will scale (Griffin 2014; Kahn and Shah 2022).

Finally, large incumbent firms are thought to face fewer financial frictions in general, given their longer history of operations, their larger share of "redeployable" assets that can be pledged as collateral, and their access to retained earnings for internal financing (Hall and Lerner 2010). However, incumbent firms' ability to finance innovative projects depends on their ability to access those projects in the first place. Economics research has documented a decline in internal corporate research since the 1980s (e.g., the Bell Labs model), with innovative activity increasingly shifting to universities and start-ups (Arora et al. 2020). Of course, incumbent firms are able to access external innovations through licensing, acquisitions, strategic alliances, or other models, but this *market for ideas* is notably less developed for climate technologies than for sectors such as biotechnology (Gans and Stern 2003; Kerr and Nanda 2015; Akcigit, Celik, and Greenwood 2016).[10] Climate technologies are more technologically differentiated than new pharmaceuticals or other biotechnology innovations, so the market is thinner for a given innovative idea (Nanda and Rothenberg 2011); for example, a new battery chemistry requires a fundamentally different set of skills and machinery to scale compared with methods of low-carbon steel production. Sectors such as biotechnology also benefit from well-defined innovation milestones based on clinical trials, which makes it easier to observe and contract on new ideas without compromising intellectual property (Kerr and Nanda 2015). Last, even if incumbents are able to source external climate innovations, the increasing separation between basic R&D by universities and start-ups and product development by incumbents means that this research may not be well suited for commercial applications at scale (see Arora et al. 2020 for general discussion and Siegmund et al. 2021 for an example from early electrolysis research).

Furthermore, incumbent firms may also face frictions in the type of finance they are able to secure for innovative projects, especially when trying to apply traditional project finance methods.[11] Firms may prefer to fund a project using off-balance-sheet financing for many reasons, such as the ability to divulge information only about the project rather than about the company as a whole, the ability to avoid contamination risk with the core business, and the ability to enter into horizontal agreements with competitors at the project level (Steffen 2018). Project finance has proved a popular approach to securing funding for renewable energy projects and now is often looked to as a potential solution for other types of climate infrastructure projects (Polzin et al. 2019). Because lenders only have recourse to project-level assets in the case of default, however, they are willing to accept far fewer risks in project financing arrangements (Yescombe 2014). This requisite risk transfer may not be possible for infrastructure projects using newer technologies. For example, given the long time horizons needed to recoup capital costs, lenders may require insurance to cover the risk that offtakers will exit the market, but such insurance products may not yet exist for offtake agreements in green commodity markets.

C.   Coordination Failures

A third market failure that might affect this middle phase of the innovation process is known as a "coordination failure," where uncertainty about how other economic actors will behave creates the possibility of multiple equilibria in outcomes (Cooper and John 1988; Cooper 1999). Under a coordination failure, firms or consumers may get stuck in a low-value equilibrium, because there is no mechanism or it is too costly for them to take the multiple coordinated actions that would be necessary to move them to a higher-value equilibrium.

A coordination failure may take several forms. In some cases, everyone could be better off from choosing a particular action, but they instead choose a different action because of their subjective beliefs about what others will do—leaving everyone worse off. To provide a stylized example, assume that car accident fatality rates are the same in a collision between two small cars and between two large cars, but that the fatality rate for a small car in an accident with a large car is higher. Further assume that drivers obtain no additional utility from large cars relative to small cars, but large cars produce more pollution externality. If drivers were able to coordinate on car size, the welfare-maximizing equilibrium would be achieved, where all drivers choose small cars. Yet such coordination may be difficult in practice, given the number of drivers on the road. Due to uncertainty about what others will do, many drivers will choose large cars to avoid the risk of a small car in an accident with a large car, resulting in a Pareto-dominated equilibrium (see table 3 for an illustration).

In other cases, coordination increases the overall level of surplus in the economy but will make some actors worse off unless transfers are made. In our stylized automobile safety example, imagine that different firms have the technology to produce large cars and small cars, respectively. Then coordinating driver adoption of small cars might increase overall welfare, by reducing the negative environmental externality, but the manufacturers of large cars would be worse off without additional transfers. In the discussion in this section, we focus on the first case—coordination failures with a Pareto-dominated equilibrium—to simplify ideas. Nonetheless, the second type of coordination failure with distributional consequences is also worth studying in the context of the climate transition, as certain firms and consumers will undoubtedly be made worse off by a coordinated effort to shift to low-carbon production.

In the diffusion of climate-mitigation technologies, coordination failures can arise because widespread adoption of a new technology may require near-simultaneous investments in the technology itself, supplier or customer capital, and shared infrastructure.[12] Many of the firms in these different sectors may believe that the necessary investments are only profitable if the needed investments in other sectors are made, and they may believe (correctly) that those investments will not be made because everyone is waiting to be convinced that the climate transition is going to occur.

Indeed, the challenge of coordinating on a low-carbon investment path has parallels to coordination failures in economic development. Beginning with the influential work of Rosenstein-Rodan (1943), economists

Table 3
Hypothetical Coordination Failures in Vehicle Choice

	Driver 1 in Small Car	Driver 1 in Large Car
Driver 2 in small car	Payoff to driver 1 = 5 Payoff to driver 2 = 5 Environmental externality = −1 Total surplus = 9	Payoff to driver 1 = 5 Payoff to driver 2 = 1 Environmental externality = −3 Total surplus = 3
Driver 2 in large car	Payoff to driver 1 = 1 Payoff to driver 2 = 5 Environmental externality = −3 Total surplus = 3	Payoff to driver 1 = 5 Payoff to driver 2 = 5 Environmental externality = −5 Total surplus = 5

have recognized that developing economies may confront a coordination failure whereby simultaneous investment in industrialization by many actors would be privately profitable, but unilateral investment in industrialization is not (see Murphy, Shleifer, and Vishny 1989 for a more recent formulation). This need for simultaneous investment arises because various inputs to production are complementary; the marginal product of one such input depends on the availability of other relevant inputs. For example, as an economy develops, the returns to investing in machinery to produce specialized inputs (e.g., specific grades of steel) will depend on other firms' investments in downstream manufacturing (e.g., automobile production). Likewise, the benefits to a worker from investing in specialized skills to operate this machinery depend on the availability of complementary skill sets among other workers (Rodrik 1996). In a world where *complete contracts* are possible and *transaction costs* are negligible, providers of various inputs to industrial production could collectively coordinate to produce the optimal level of specialized inputs. Yet in many real-world settings, such contracts would be impossible in practice: for example, because input providers are diffuse and transaction costs would be prohibitively high. This combination of increasing returns and imperfect contractability creates the possibility for coordination failures as new markets are developing.[13] Under such an outcome, the economy would be stuck in a low level of economic development due to failure to coordinate these disparate investments, even if doing so could increase the returns to both labor and capital (Collier 2007).

There are many analogous examples of imperfectly contractable complementary inputs in markets for new climate technologies.[14] As noted in the previous section, the migration of research to start-ups and universities, away from established firms with basic manufacturing capabilities and other complementary assets in place, means that there may be more opportunities for coordination failures to arise when climate technologies make the transition from labs to full-scale commercialization. Furthermore, many high-emitting sectors depend on extensive infrastructure and supply chains that must evolve alongside low-carbon technologies. Consider the decarbonization of maritime shipping: if maritime shipping makes the transition from diesel to a new type of fuel, say ammonia or methanol, this change will require not only scaling up the production of these new fuels but also contemporaneously redesigning ship engines and potentially ship layouts, building infrastructure to transport the new fuels to ports, building new refueling infrastructure at the ports themselves, training workers in handling the new fuels, developing new safety regulations for the use of these fuels, training workers in the maintenance of new engines and infrastructure, and so forth (Cameron and Turner 2021). Of course, these complementary inputs have developed for existing carbon-intensive methods of shipping, but this process has taken decades, even centuries in some cases. Given the urgency of climate change, this slow process of development may well be a Pareto-dominated equilibrium, where coordination to produce a faster transition could be welfare enhancing.

Yet it is often a formidable challenge to address coordination failures through policy. In economic development, suspected coordination failures led to policy prescriptions for a "big push" in public support for industrialization, to increase the profitability of each firm's individual investments. These policies, first influential in the 1950s, proved quite controversial (Matsuyama 1998).[15] Policies to address coordination failures are challenging to assess empirically because of the underlying discontinuities and increasing returns to scale, and there is a limited evidence base about which policy instruments have proved effective. Furthermore, it may even be difficult to identify specific interventions that have a reasonable chance of effectiveness, given the nature of the multiple equilibrium problem (Cooper 2005). Rodrik (2014) argues that missteps are inevitable, and policy makers should instead focus on "a set of mechanisms that recognizes errors and revises policies accordingly."

As a final point about coordination failures, it is worth commenting briefly on the distinction between coordination failures and Pigouvian externalities, as they are conceptually distinct but potentially easy to conflate in a climate context (de Mesquita 2016). With coordination failures, a short-term intervention may be sufficient to move to a new, self-sustaining equilibrium by changing agents' beliefs about others' behavior and thereby increasing the expected payoff from investing in complementary inputs. These beliefs may then prove self-reinforcing even after the policy has ended, especially if agents have made up-front investments in capacity (Rodrik 2004). By contrast, policies that cause agents to internalize the cost or benefits of Pigouvian externalities—most notably, by pricing the externalities directly—will induce efficient behavior only for as long as they are in force. From this perspective, the climate transition may more closely resemble a coordination problem in some sectors and a pure externality problem in others. For example, in the switch from gasoline-powered to electric light-duty vehicles, it is possible that only temporary policy interventions will be needed to help automakers descend the learning curve in electric vehicle production, accelerate the build-out of charging infrastructure, increase consumer confidence in the new products, and induce the entry of complementary services such as dealers and mechanics trained in electric drivetrains. On the other hand, industries that rely on carbon capture for decarbonization will likely always depend on externality-correcting policies even after technologies have reached maturity. Industrial production with the additional energy costs of carbon capture is likely to be more expensive than the equivalent process without carbon capture devices running, unless a significant market develops for captured CO_2.

D.   Distributional Concerns

In addition to these innovation market failures, key features of the newly scaled policy instruments are motivated by other policy priorities. Shifting to low-carbon methods of production will create winners and losers, and policy makers and other stakeholders are increasingly aware of and attentive to the distributional impacts of the energy transition.[16] Labor-market impacts have received particular focus, with policy makers drawing connections between job losses in "fossil fuel communities" and the historical loss of manufacturing employment due to globalization (Boushey 2021; Curtis and Marinescu 2022; Curtis, O'Kane, and Park 2024). Beyond the labor market, there are many ways in which emissions are correlated with demographic vulnerability (Metcalf 2023), and a long history of racism and other forms of discrimination means that some demographic groups have greater access to resources to manage the costs of climate transition. For these reasons, several of the newly scaled innovation policy instruments discussed in this paper—as well as many other recently implemented climate policies—explicitly promote redistribution as part of the climate transition.[17] These distributive goals interact in nuanced ways with the innovation market failures discussed in this paper.

  Several of these newly scaled policy instruments incorporate distributional considerations by targeting a subset of program budgets to places with certain characteristics. An important theme that emerges from the literature on place-based innovation policies is that location-specific benefits often differ across R&D, production, and consumption of new technologies. For example, if more jobs are created in the production (e.g., manufacturing) of new technologies as compared with earlier R&D (Glaeser and Hausman 2020), then place-based policies targeting production might more effectively address the risk of widespread job loss in locations where the employment base directly depends on fossil fuel–based energy or industrial production. Greenstone, Hornbeck, and Moretti (2010) document substantial gains in local productivity from the arrival of a "million dollar plant"; by contrast, efforts to stimulate economically distressed regions by providing incentives for new innovation clusters have met limited success (Lerner 2009; Glaeser and Hausman 2020; Kerr and Robert-Nicoud 2020). Nonetheless, the literature on place-based policies also poses a key question: rather than targeting places, why not develop policies to support the individuals affected by the climate transition directly? One reason why place-based policies may be important is the recent decline in US labor mobility, suggesting that affected individuals may not easily move to new employment; Ganong and Shoag (2017) document a corresponding plateau in income convergence at the state level. Evidence also suggests that the welfare benefits to a robust employment base exceed the monetary value of wages (Deaton and Case 2017; Autor, Dorn, and Hanson 2019).

How program implementers balance the dual objectives of maximizing aggregate emissions reductions and ensuring an equitable distribution of benefits and costs associated with the climate transition also depends on the characteristics of the technology in question. On the one hand, to the extent that R&D productivity depends on the training of the local workforce and the proximity to relevant labs and other institutions, the locations most conducive to productive innovation may not match economically distressed areas in greatest need of support (Glaeser and Hausman 2020). On the other hand, achieving widespread adoption of distributed climate technologies—which require large numbers of adopters to have a meaningful impact on emissions—may require developing business and financing models suited for local contexts. For example, business models for energy efficiency or building electrification may depend on the characteristics of local buildings, state and local regulations, and community access to credit.[18] Public support may be useful in ensuring that this place-based tailoring of climate innovation is inclusive of low-income and minority communities, given the considerable evidence that minority racial and ethnic groups are underrepresented in the innovation sector even relative to similar occupations (Gompers and Wang 2017; Cook, Gerson, and Kuan 2021; Ewens 2022). Other research has suggested that minority-owned small businesses face greater barriers to raising up-front and ongoing capital (Henderson et al. 2015; Fairlie, Robb, and Robinson 2022), so targeted support for entrepreneurship in minority communities may be particularly effective.

Similar considerations apply for the consumption of new climate technologies. In some cases, the benefits will be spatially diffuse regardless of where new technologies are developed, manufactured, or installed, given nationally and internationally integrated product markets and the global nature of climate change. In other cases, technologies may create cobenefits for adopters—such as improved indoor air quality from building electrification—so ensuring that consumption occurs in a wide variety of places is an important equity issue. Credit constraints are one example of a barrier that may prevent disadvantaged communities from realizing these benefits. Communities with greater access to credit will be more easily able to adopt low-carbon technologies with high up-front costs such as renewables, energy-efficient appliances, energy storage, building electrification, and so forth (Schleich 2019; Berkouwer and Dean 2022). Yet low-income and minority communities have lower access to credit in general and pay higher interest rates for access (Adams, Einav, and Levin 2009; Broady, McComas, and Ouazad 2021). Those who are not able to pay outright or to finance these up-front costs may be left with a disproportionate share of the burden of managing the wind-down of legacy infrastructure (Davis and Hausman 2022). Without deliberate efforts to increase access to credit for climate technologies—or other redistributive policies—the energy transition will be inherently unequal in its allocation of benefits and costs (see Borenstein and Davis 2016; for an exception, see Davis 2024).

III. Newly Scaled Policy Instruments

In this section, we discuss the institutional history of the newly scaled policy instruments and connect their stated goals to the literature on innovation market failures and distributional concerns (summarized in table 4 and fig. 1). We also offer questions for policy design and evaluation that may help disentangle which market failures matter most in a given context and which policy mechanisms are most effective (summarized in table 5).

A. Demonstration Projects

"Demonstration projects" typically refer to the first full-size manufacturing facilities, energy generating plants, or other capital-intensive infrastructure constructed to assess whether new technologies can operate successfully at scale and when integrated with existing systems.[19]

Table 4
Overview of How Policy Instruments May Address Goals

Market Failure or Policy Goal	Policy Instruments			
	Demonstration Projects	Loan Guarantees	Green Banks	Regional Technology Hubs
Knowledge spillovers	Share knowledge of systems integration and technology testing at scale	Share knowledge of financial innovation for new technologies and commercial track record	Share knowledge of financial innovation for new business models and commercial track record	Share knowledge of systems integration and supply chain
Coordination failures			Standardize contracts	Coordinate customers, suppliers, specialized infrastructure, other inputs
Financial frictions	Incur high fixed costs for technology derisking	Mitigate credit rationing; signals technical quality	Mitigate credit rationing	
Distributional concerns		Target uneven financial frictions	Can target uneven financial frictions; adapt distributed climate technologies for local markets	Create jobs; boost underserved locales

Select technology areas have previously received federal funding for demonstration projects, such as carbon capture and energy storage under the American Recovery and Reinvestment Act of 2009. Certain states, most notably New York and California, have also been active in funding a range of energy demonstration projects. Rozansky and Hart (2020) identify three waves of demonstration projects in the energy sector, precipitated by three crises: the energy crises in the 1970s and early 1980s and the Great Recession of 2008. Lester and Hart (2015) also note that the US Department of Defense has a successful track record of demonstration projects for advanced weapons systems.

Most recently, the IIJA appropriated $21.5 billion for energy demonstration projects and created a new Office of Clean Energy Demonstrations within the Department of Energy (DOE). Regional hydrogen hubs are the single largest investment area (discussed in a subsequent section).

Table 5
Key Questions for Program Design and Evaluation

Demonstration Projects	Loan Guarantees	Green Banks	Regional Technology Hubs
Would demonstration projects in this sector be underprovided if start-ups were well capitalized or incumbents were working in this area?	What are the largest fixed costs from underwriting a new technology? What information reduces this cost for future private lenders?	What are the largest fixed costs from underwriting a new business model? What information reduces this cost for future private lenders?	Would this industry be privately profitable to enter if complementary inputs and infrastructure were available, or would additional subsidies still be needed?
Which fixed costs of project development can be reduced through learning from demonstration projects?	Ignoring the fixed costs of underwriting, would commercial lenders be willing to finance this project at any interest rate?	Ignoring the fixed costs of underwriting, would commercial lenders be willing to finance this project at any interest rate?	Which fixed costs of industry development can be reduced through learning from regional demonstration projects?
What are the remaining uncertainties about whether a technology can be commercially successful at scale? What information from demonstration projects would reduce that uncertainty?	Do private lenders view support from LPO as a positive signal? What are the trade-offs between the quality of signal and the burden of the application process? How do private lenders view more years of operational data from one project (higher T) versus operational data from more projects (higher N)?	Does this business model require contract standardization to scale?	What are the remaining uncertainties about whether a supply chain can be commercially successful at scale? What information from regional demonstration projects would reduce that uncertainty?
How can program implementers share key information publicly without undermining the incentives of private developers to participate?	In what ways are public loan guarantees like commercial debt and in what ways not?	Is this distributed climate technology part of a least-cost portfolio of decarbonization solutions?	Are potential agglomeration economies specific to new technologies or cumulative with previous technologies?
In what ways is public funding for demonstration projects like venture capital and in what ways not?		How does the deployment of a distributed climate technology depend on local regulations, demographics, or infrastructure?	
		In what ways are green banks like commercial debt providers and in what ways not?	

Note: LPO = Loan Programs Office, US Department of Energy.

Other demonstration programs funded under the IIJA include $2.5 billion for advanced nuclear reactors, $2.5 billion for carbon capture, $6.3 billion for industrial emissions (which includes additional funding from IRA), $5 billion for power-grid modernization and resilience, and $500 million for long-duration energy storage. Demonstration project funding is also embedded in other parts of recent legislation; for example, CHIPS created a program for R&D, demonstration, and commercial applications of low-emissions steel manufacturing.

New knowledge creation—and by extension, the possibility for knowledge spillovers—plays an especially important role at the demonstration stage. To build a full-size facility that is integrated with existing infrastructure, firms must train workers to build and operate the equipment, work with regulators to permit the new facility and apply existing safety and environmental standards in a new context, resolve issues with the technology that were not apparent at the prototype stage, and so on (Hart 2018; Nemet, Zipperer, and Kraus 2018). Demonstration projects may also provide valuable information about whether a project is unlikely to be commercially successful (Kotchen and Costello 2018). Although some of this new knowledge will benefit the firm incurring these fixed costs, some will undoubtedly benefit competitors. The existence of a trained workforce or regulators familiar with new production methods should reduce barriers to entry for future competitors, as an example. Of course, there are certain types of uncertainty that would not be resolved through demonstration projects, such as uncertainty around commodity prices, customer demand, or the policy environment. Useful questions for program planning and evaluation are outlined in table 4: What types of uncertainty matter most to potential private lenders of early commercial projects? What information from demonstration project outcomes would reduce that uncertainty? How can program implementers share key information publicly without undermining the incentives of private developers to participate?

Demonstration projects have proved difficult to fund using traditional VC or project-finance approaches, leading many industry observers to suggest that financial frictions have also contributed to inadequate resources for this stage of the innovation process.[20] Although prototypes help to achieve certain technological milestones, they do not fully resolve the type of technology risk that occurs at full-size implementation. Certainly VC investors have made investments of comparable amounts to what would be needed for capital-intensive demonstration projects in recent years, as the supply of VC funding has grown considerably and as start-ups are raising more and larger funding rounds (Ewens and Farre-Mensa 2020). Yet as noted in our discussion of financial frictions above, many of the largest VC investments have gone to start-ups in the later "scale-up" phase, when technological risk and uncertainties about product-market fit have largely been resolved, rather than to capital-intensive start-ups in the earlier "learning" phase (Nanda 2020). Though hard to test empirically given the relatively small sample size of projects, it seems plausible that public support for demonstration projects will allow technologies with high fixed costs of experimentation to have an opportunity to be commercially successful. One implication might also be that publicly funded demonstration projects for technologies with lower costs of experimentation would be less impactful, all else equal.

A central challenge, then, is distinguishing between candidate projects that would struggle to obtain private funding because of market failures and those that cannot secure funding because they are simply bad projects. One path forward for program implementers might be to think systematically about the ways in which they are or are not similar to providers of private finance—venture capitalists being perhaps the closest fit in the case of demonstration projects. Then program implementers could strive to mimic the solutions that venture capitalists have adopted for overcoming asymmetric information problems to the extent that they are filling similar roles, and think critically about how to alter standard VC practices to the extent that they are not. For example, demonstration projects might still benefit from staged financing, as these projects are inherently risky and information is revealed over time about the likelihood of success.[21] On the other hand, new knowledge creation is an important part of undertaking demonstration projects, implying that the definition of success is not the level of private returns that a VC would expect but other metrics developed by program implementers that would include learning spillovers within these nascent industries.

B. Loan Guarantees

Originally authorized under the Energy Policy Act of 2005 and the Energy Independence and Security Act of 2007, the DOE's loan programs provide direct loans and loan guarantees to innovative energy projects, advanced vehicle manufacturing, and energy projects on tribal lands. These programs were first active under the Obama administration, funding their first 30 projects between 2009 and 2011, including funding for the Tesla Model S, the Nissan Leaf, and Solyndra.[22] Less well known

is that DOE's Loan Programs Office (LPO) supported the first five
utility-scale solar plants larger than 100 megawatts, after which private
financing for utility-scale solar projects increased significantly (McCall
2016). Studies have found loan guarantees to be effective in other contexts (Shi, Liu, and Yao 2016), though rigorous evidence on the impact
of DOE's loan programs is still limited (Bhandary, Gallagher, and Zhang
2021).

The IRA significantly increased total lending authority (by approximately $350 billion) and available credit subsidy (by $11.7 billion in ap-
propriations) for loan programs. Beyond increasing funding for existing
programs, the IRA and IIJA also created two new loan programs (for energy infrastructure upgrading and CO_2 transport, respectively).[23] Under
these new and newly scaled programs, the LPO guarantees repayment
of loan principal and interest—either from the US Treasury's Federal Financing Bank or from commercial lenders—for up to 80% of the costs of
approved projects. In contrast to demonstration projects, DOE's loan
programs fund projects where there is a reasonable expectation of repayment, which means they are not interested in funding projects that
still face residual technology risk. The LPO now describes its role as a
"bridge to bankability," focusing on projects that are "mature from a
technology standpoint but not mature from an access to capital standpoint" (DeHoratiis 2022).

Following the derisking of construction, engineering, and other technical implementation details at the demonstration stage, projects supported
by the LPO may generate additional knowledge spillovers from financial
innovation. Commercial lenders may be unwilling to incur the fixed costs
of learning how to underwrite new types of loans if the new knowledge
created has characteristics of a public good (Kahn and Shah 2022). Loan
programs may create two types of knowledge in this scenario. First, by
derisking projects and enabling them to proceed, they may help create
a track record for new types of projects in the marketplace, creating public knowledge that new business and financing models are commercially
viable.[24] Second, they may publicly share technical information about financial contracts employed in the early projects that they helped support, lowering the fixed costs for commercial lenders to enter the new
market in the future (St. John 2021).

DOE's loan programs may also overcome financial frictions, by enabling entrepreneurs or project developers to obtain financing for first-
of-a-kind or other early deployment projects. As noted above, banks may
choose not to lend to risky but positive expected NPV projects if the interest

rate required to compensate for risk induces sufficiently undesirable behavior or adverse selection among borrowers. By guaranteeing loan repayment, DOE may allow projects to be undertaken without a strong selection or behavioral response. Then, new knowledge created through these early projects may help reduce the fixed costs of underwriting future loan contracts or the riskiness of future lending in this area, enabling similar projects to secure private financing without a DOE guarantee later on. Beyond the track record of the first-of-a-kind project itself, successful vetting by DOE's scientific and engineering staff may also provide a positive signal for technological viability (Leland and Pyle 1977; Kahn and Shah 2022). Finally, even if subsequent deployments of a new climate technology might be eventually funded in the private market, once sufficient time has passed to gather years of data from the first-of-a-kind plant, additional support from the LPO for the second, third, or fourth project might accelerate this process (Kahn and Shah 2022). Given the ongoing atmospheric accumulation of greenhouse gas pollutants, compressing this process may be socially beneficial.[25]

Program implementers again may find it useful to think systematically about the ways in which DOE's loan programs are and are not acting like commercial lenders, to adopt practices that are common in the private lending market in the areas where they are similar, and to modify standard practices in the areas where they are not. For example, if program implementers are most focused on lowering the fixed costs of entering a new market, then they may wish to adopt standard commercial debt contracts once the hurdle of the underwriting process has been surmounted. By contrast, if program implementers are more focused on overcoming credit rationing in a new technology area, then they may instead wish to deviate from standard lending practices.

Of course, many of these potential channels of program impact are empirical questions that might be addressed through program evaluation or other information-gathering processes by program implementation staff. Relevant questions include: What are the greatest fixed costs of underwriting a new technology or business model, and what information can DOE provide from its loan programs that most substantially reduces this cost? If fixed costs of underwriting were accounted for, would commercial lenders be willing to finance these projects at any interest rate? Do commercial lenders view support from the LPO as a positive signal, and are they willing to adjust their behavior accordingly? Are there trade-offs between the quality of the signal and the fixed costs that applicants must incur to obtain support from the LPO? How would commercial lenders weight 1 or 2 years of operational data from several projects funded by the LPO relative to 5 or 6 years of operational data from a single project?

C. Green Banks

Contrary to its name, a "green bank" is not a deposit institution but rather a type of financial institution that uses public or quasi-public seed funding to provide debt capital to projects that align with its mandate.[26] In the United States, approximately 20 green banks have emerged at the state and local level; the New York and Connecticut green banks have been particularly significant.[27] These institutions have supported clean energy, energy efficiency, and other climate-related projects that the private sector would be otherwise unwilling to fund, using a variety of financial instruments. Funding amounts have typically ranged from $5 million to $50 million, though the scale of funding has also varied across different state and local green banks depending on their overall capitalization (Kehoe, Lee, and Radulovic 2021). In contrast to a direct subsidy program, green banks often seek to leverage public funding at the project level (by coinvesting with private funders, guaranteeing loans from private funders, or using other instruments to bring in private funding) or portfolio level (by receiving outside capital to increase the size of its balance sheet beyond the initial seed (Coalition for Green Capital 2019).[28] The president of the New York Green Bank has suggested that priority areas for green banks in coming years include vehicle-charging infrastructure, energy storage, and building decarbonization (Kessler 2022).

Discussions about establishing a national green bank in the United States have occurred for more than a decade, with the creation of a Clean Energy Deployment Administration included in the version of the Waxman-Markey Bill that passed in the House of Representatives in 2009.[29] Nonetheless, the IRA represents the first time that Congress has appropriated significant funding for this concept. As part of the General Assistance and Low-Income and Disadvantaged Communities Grant Program, the IRA appropriates $20 billion for projects that "reduce or avoid greenhouse gas emissions or other forms of air pollution in partnership with, and by leveraging investment from, the private sector; or assist communities in the efforts of those communities to reduce or avoid greenhouse gas emissions and other forms of pollution."[30] Of the $20 billion total, $8 billion is appropriated specifically for projects in "disadvantaged communities," and $12 billion is available for any community.[31]

The exact structure of funding for these projects is still unclear at the time of this writing; in its most recent announcement, the Environmental Protection Agency (EPA) noted that it anticipates making between 2 and 15 grants to eligible institutions, 1 of which may operate at a national scale.[32] Observers have suggested that EPA may fund existing green banks or help create new ones at the national, regional, state, or local level (Turner 2023).

Green banks in the United States have typically focused on supporting new business and financing models for already commercial climate technologies. For example, community solar projects are a well-known funding area for green banks over the past decade. Developed after the market for rooftop solar PV had emerged in the 2000s, community solar represented a new model of solar deployment in which renters, households with lower incomes or poorer credit scores, and others whose homes were not physically suited to rooftop solar panels could participate in distributed solar generation (Kessler 2022). Another example from the past decade is green-bank funding for energy efficiency retrofits in small businesses: dry cleaners, houses of worship, daycares, and retirement communities, among others.[33] New business and financing models were needed to enable energy efficiency retrofits with high up-front costs relative to the revenues of these small businesses and to develop financial contracts that were suitable for the small businesses' cash-flow patterns.

Just as commercial lenders may not initially understand how to structure loans for new types of large-scale climate infrastructure, they also may not initially understand how to structure loans for new methods of deploying distributed climate solutions. As in our above discussion about DOE's loan programs, insofar as new knowledge about how to structure these loans has characteristics of a public good, private lenders may underinvest in this learning. Green banks may help reduce fixed costs of issuing loans in new areas and create public knowledge about the viability of new business and financing models. With community solar projects, for example, representatives of the New York Green Bank have described their efforts to "flatten the learning curve for other lenders" by developing, successfully using, and publicly documenting scalable and replicable loan terms for community solar projects (Green Bank Network 2022).[34]

Furthermore, community-level climate projects may face additional financial frictions due to credit rationing. Motivated by this possibility, governments have long offered credit enhancements to small businesses, with a mixed record (Cowling 2010). Perhaps more compelling than general credit enhancements for small businesses is support for particularly risky phases of project development in nascent industries (Khatcherian 2022). As an example, the New York Green Bank has provided "interconnection bridge loans" to early community solar developers, allowing them to pay certain interconnection fees that were incurred before offtake agreements were signed and project finance became available (Green Bank Network 2018; New York Green Bank 2022). As an industry matures, these up-front fees may be instead paid out of retained earnings, avoiding costly external finance; alternatively, regulations may be updated to reflect the characteristics of new technologies and business models.

Beyond these initial investments in one-off projects, a coordinating force may also be needed to help distributed climate solutions reach widespread adoption. For small-scale deployments of climate technology, the transaction costs associated with customizing loan terms for each project are likely to be prohibitively high. One solution is converging on a standardized contract structure and terms, as financial markets have done successfully for residential mortgages or even rooftop solar installations. Standardization not only lowers transaction costs but also allows loans to be bundled together to attract much larger institutional capital providers (Griffin 2014; Kaufman 2018). For example, energy efficiency retrofits at a range of small and medium-sized businesses might be bundled together so that they no longer need to be treated as stand-alone projects despite differences in the underlying business. But standardization also requires agreeing on a standard, creating an opportunity for a green bank to help overcome coordinating frictions across disparate players in the market (Green Bank Network 2022). In many cases, the green bank might play that coordinating role directly; standardization would be an appropriate focus for a regional or national green bank (Green Bank Network 2022). Alternatively, the private sector may fill this coordinating role, with funding from a green bank to defray the up-front cost.[35]

Each of these potential market failures interacts with equity issues in the context of green banks. Many of the financial frictions identified above may be most acute in low-income or minority communities with more limited access to traditional forms of credit, providing stronger rationale for credit enhancements in low-income or minority communities (Miller and Soo 2020; Howell et al. 2021; Fairlie et al. 2022). Furthermore, place-based policies may be especially warranted to support business and financial innovation that enables climate technology to be deployed in communities that might not otherwise have access. Distributed climate solutions—which will only have a substantial impact on aggregate emissions if they are adopted by many different demographic groups—may unite the goals of achieving decarbonization at scale and ensuring equitable participation in the climate transition. A useful exercise for program implementers is distinguishing between distributed solutions that are part of a least-cost portfolio of decarbonization approaches and those that have higher abatement costs; although the former would not create equity-efficiency trade-offs, the latter are valuable primarily because they help to make the climate transition more inclusive.

D.   Regional Technology Hubs

Finally, recent federal legislation has appropriated funds for several large-scale regional technology hubs. IIJA provides $8 billion for 6 to 10 regional hydrogen hubs and $3.5 billion for 4 regional direct air capture (DAC) hubs.[36] The idea of bringing together diverse actors in a specific location to solve a particular technological challenge has an established history at the DOE. Under the Obama administration, the DOE funded several Energy Innovation Hubs, themselves inspired by bioenergy research centers from the George W. Bush administration, which sought to bring together basic and applied research to solve specific practical challenges (Cho 2021).[37] Beyond the DOE, other parts of the federal government have sought to combine local or regional economic development with a specific agency mission (reviewed in Chatterji, Glaeser, and Kerr 2014). As with the other policy instruments discussed in this paper, the regional technology hubs funded in IIJA develop an existing concept at much larger scale than hitherto attempted in the energy sector.

Both the regional hydrogen and DAC hubs are conceptually close to demonstration projects in terms of the knowledge spillovers that they may create. Indeed, the regional hydrogen hubs represent the largest single investment area overseen by DOE's Office of Clean Energy Demonstrations. Both the hydrogen and DAC programs prioritize funding a diversity of technologies (feedstocks for hydrogen production and methods of carbon capture, respectively), end uses (for hydrogen and captured CO_2), and geographic regions; demonstration of these technologies and end uses may generate knowledge about performance at scale and when integrated with existing infrastructure, as discussed above. Unlike stand-alone demonstration projects, however, the hubs are also explicitly focused on technology development in particular regions, which raises questions about potential knowledge spillovers in geographic space. The economics literature on knowledge spillovers suggests that such benefits are highly localized for individual firms (decaying within a few miles) but that overlapping interaction zones may create larger knowledge clusters at the city or county level (Kerr and Kominers 2015; Lychagin et al. 2016; Hausman 2022). Understanding these historical patterns may prove useful for program implementers when working with large multistate applicants (Bioret, Zhu, and Krupnick 2023).

The coordination failures that these regional technology hubs may address are even more likely to have an explicitly spatial dimension. Relative to demonstration projects, the hydrogen and DAC hubs face the same challenges of coordinating activities among producers, consumers, and a wide array of intermediate inputs, including enabling regulations, physical infrastructure, an appropriately trained workforce, upstream and downstream suppliers, and so forth. The magnitude of the positive externalities that these actors create for each other is likely to be larger when they are located closer together, thereby lowering transport costs from one to the other—a form of "agglomeration effects." Indeed, economists have suggested that agglomerative forces are likely to matter more for newer industries, as clusters of activity allow firms to share the fixed costs of common inputs (Carlino and Kerr 2015).[38] Given the specialized infrastructure needed for transporting CO_2 and H_2 and the increased risk of leakage the further they are transported, these industries may be particularly conducive to spatial concentration across the value chain, even relative to other nascent climate technologies (Nemet 2023). Finally, the highly regulated nature of these industries and the infrastructure that they require (e.g., pipelines) suggest another type of spatial externality: ease of coordinating the relevant permits and regulations, which are often promulgated at a state and local level.

Beyond the initial demonstration of a regional ecosystem for these new technologies, an additional goal is to seed self-sustaining industries. Economists have been largely pessimistic about the ability of policy makers to create new technology clusters at the local or regional level (Lerner 2009; Chatterji et al. 2014; Kerr and Robert-Nicoud 2020). There is, however, a conceptual distinction between proverbial efforts to "create the next Silicon Valley" and an effort to develop a specific new technology that focuses on building specialized infrastructure and production facilities in a specific location. Nonetheless, it is still useful to pay attention to the pitfalls that have befallen earlier attempts to create localized technology clusters.

One theme that emerges repeatedly in this literature is the importance of the right mix of firms for sustained innovation. On the one hand, large incumbent firms can serve as "anchor firms" that strengthen the innovation ecosystem and seed spin-off entrepreneurship (Agrawal and Cockburn 2003; Feldman 2005; Figueiredo, Guimarães, and Woodward 2009; Glaeser and Kerr 2009). On the other hand, too much support for large incumbent firms can crowd out new entrants and stifle more radical innovation (Agrawal, Cockburn, and Rosell 2010; Chatterji et al. 2014).[39] Therefore, diversity in firm size within a given industry location is important, combining anchor firms with a supportive environment for new entrants (Markusen 1996; Agrawal et al. 2014; Klepper 2010, 2016). How to achieve this balance in practice is tricky and not well understood, and likely depends on the characteristics of the technology in question. For example, electrolyzers for producing "green hydrogen" are modular technologies, whereas existing methods for producing "blue hydrogen" from fossil fuels with carbon capture are not; therefore, the efficient distribution of larger versus smaller firms may differ across different hydrogen hubs (see Carlino and Kerr 2015 for discussion of modularity and lab size).

Finally, we note that these regional technology hubs have an explicit focus on the distributional consequences of the climate transition. The enabling legislation instructs DOE to locate the DAC hubs "to the maximum extent practicable" in regions with existing or recently retired "carbon-intensive fuel production or industrial capacity," prioritizing projects that are "likely to create opportunities for skilled training and long-term employment to the greatest number of residents of the region." In addition, the legislation instructs DOE to locate two of the four DAC hubs in "economically distressed communities" with "high levels of coal, oil, or natural gas resources." For hydrogen hubs, DOE is also instructed to prioritize applications that are likely to provide skilled training and long-term employment to residents.

The opportunity for agglomeration effects in the development of the nascent hydrogen and DAC industries—leading to more and faster development in a specific location—creates a potential policy synergy between innovation and equity goals. If agglomeration economies are specific to the new technologies, rather than cumulative with previous technologies, then at this early stage of technology deployment, it might be possible to create agglomeration benefits in many different places. By launching these nascent industries in disadvantaged places, or places that will be disadvantaged by the transition away from fossil fuels, policy makers may mitigate regional inequities and take advantage of agglomeration benefits going forward. That said, concerns about equity are multidimensional, and providing employment or other economic benefits does not address the concerns of environmental justice groups about air pollution or hazardous waste associated with these industries.

IV.   Unaddressed Market Failures

An explicit goal of many of these policies is to support clean technologies temporarily, as they find a foothold in the market, but then to allow the private sector to realize large-scale deployment. Even if these policy instruments are necessary to enable widespread commercialization, they may not be sufficient. As we have emphasized in this paper, there may be innovation market failures—especially in this middle part of the innovation process, during initial technology deployment—that are effectively targeted through these policy instruments. In some cases, these policy instruments may help to shift an industry to a new equilibrium, as financial innovations are developed and diffused, standards are adopted, and dispersed market actors shift their subjective beliefs about each other's actions. Technologies developed in the United States may also create international spillovers, especially in developing economies.[40] However, these policy instruments may not address all of the innovation market failures that slow the initial deployment of climate technology. For example, none of these policy instruments directly addresses the underdeveloped "market for ideas" in many climate-technology areas, although these policies may ameliorate this issue indirectly by helping incumbents secure external financing for demonstration or first-of-a-kind projects, thereby making acquisitions or alliances more attractive. These policy instruments also do not address broader organizational and institutional reasons why it may be difficult to develop and commercialize technology aimed at solving very long-term problems, such as managerial myopia (Stein 1989) and other forms of short-termism (Budish, Roin, and Williams 2015).

Most crucially, none of the policy instruments discussed in this paper addresses the carbon externality directly. It is important not to confuse a lack of demand for clean technologies due to unpriced externalities with, for example, a lack of financing (van den Heuvel and Popp 2022). In many cases, the recent injection of federal funding into these policy instruments creates greater urgency to address underlying demand for clean technologies.

Indeed, an implicit assumption in the theory of change underlying these newly scaled policy instruments is that climate change is such a significant problem that this underlying demand for carbon reduction will emerge in the medium term, one way or another. Certainly some firms (and ultimately consumers) have signaled a willingness to pay a "green premium" for low-carbon inputs in the near term, which may prove critical during this period of early deployment. Yet voluntary adoption is inherently small relative to the magnitude of the overall externality and cannot provide the necessary scale in the medium term. In other cases, the federal government will provide direct subsidies that overlap with these innovation-focused policies, helping to unlock additional sources of demand. For example, federal tax credits for carbon removal ("45Q" tax credits, funded in IRA) should help bolster the market for DAC in tandem with funding for regional DAC hubs.[41] Yet these tax credits will eventually expire, and the market for carbon capture will ultimately depend on a stable price signal reflecting the negative externalities from emitting CO_2. Some noncarbon technologies will eventually become sufficiently cost-effective that they can compete with carbon-intensive technologies even without any price on carbon or green premium. But most climate-mitigation technologies will not be cost-effective without further policies such as a carbon price to induce demand for carbon reduction in the medium to long term. If those direct mitigation-inducing policies do not develop, the newly scaled technology policy instruments will fail as both technology and climate policies, as they will have built bridges to nowhere.

V. Conclusion

This paper maps the economics literature about innovation market failures to the stated goals of policy instruments newly scaled under recent climate-related legislation. Understanding the range of potential underlying market failures may help to focus discussions about how to implement these policies as effectively as possible. Because each of these newly scaled policy instruments has the potential to address several different innovation market failures, applying the market-failures framework to stakeholder input about the most important barriers may help program implementers to tailor program design accordingly. For example, green banks may prioritize different projects or contract structures if trying to

reduce the fixed costs of underwriting new business models versus trying to avoid credit rationing due to high perceived risk. More generally,
the market-failure framework can help program implementers think systematically about the ways they can learn from and appropriately imitate
the tools and practices of private funders, and the ways they should deviate from private capital providers to address policy concerns that private funders do not share.

Of course, although the existence of market failures or redistributive
goals is necessary for effective policy intervention, they are by no means
sufficient to ensure that policy is able to achieve its goals. In some cases,
government is well suited to easing frictions that the private sector is unable to address. In other cases, the market failures in question are extremely tricky to eliminate. Much of the economics literature reviewed
in this paper provides a sobering reminder that these innovation market
failures often fall into the latter category. Given this challenge, experimentation and continuous evaluation are key components of program
implementation. Climate change is simultaneously very urgent and very
long term as a policy priority. The "shocks" of recent climate legislation create opportunities to learn systematically about which market failures are most inhibiting and which instruments address them most effectively (Aldy 2022). This learning does not happen automatically but
requires evaluation to be built into program design at every stage of
the process.

Endnotes

Author email addresses: Armitage (armitage@bu.edu), Jaffe (adam.jaffe@motu.org
.nz), Bakhtian (nmb@alumni.stanford.edu). The authors would like to thank Michael
Kearney, Josh Lerner, Ramana Nanda, and Tom Kalil for helpful conversations and the
editors Matthew Kotchen and Catherine Wolfram for valuable feedback. For acknowledgments, sources of research support, and disclosure of the authors' material financial relationships, if any, please see https://www.nber.org/books-and-chapters/environmental
-and-energy-policy-and-economy-volume-5/innovation-market-failures-and-design
-new-climate-policy-instruments.

1. Under the American Recovery and Reinvestment Act of 2009, the Department of
Energy's Loan Programs Office provided $16.1 billion in loans for innovative energy pro-
jects, as well as $8.4 billion in loans for advanced vehicle manufacturing under the Energy
Independence and Security Act of 2007; IRA has scaled these programs even further. Also
note that some sources refer to $21.5 billion in appropriations for demonstration projects
under IIJA; this amount combines the $13.5 billion for demonstration projects listed above
and $8 billion for regional hydrogen hubs, which we have instead categorized under re-
gional technology hubs.

2. Note that government capital "filling in" for private capital is not the same as the
concern about government capital "crowding out" private capital. Crowding out refers
to a situation where private actors reduce their investment as a result of the government

investment, so that total investment is not increased by the full amount of government spending. This could happen if policy makers misjudge the extent of market failures and support projects where private incentives are in fact adequate. But if policy makers judge market failures appropriately, they will be supporting projects in which private actors are not investing, so there would not be crowding out.

3. For one, empirical research using patent citations has traced spillovers across patenting firms, mediated by factors such as geographic or technological distance (Jaffe 1986; Trajtenberg 1990; Jaffe, Trajtenberg, and Henderson 1993; Griffith, Lee, and van Reenen 2011). This research has consistently concluded that individual firms do not fully recoup the benefits of their R&D.

4. It is not necessarily the case that these costs are higher for climate-mitigation technologies than for other investments (though some have argued that they are, as discussed in the main text). Instead, government might choose to intervene to overcome these barriers for climate-mitigation technologies but not for other technologies because of the interactions with unpriced carbon externalities.

5. So influential has the VC model been in unlocking funding for innovation that Kenneth Arrow famously claimed, "Venture capital has done much more, I think, to improve efficiency than anything" (Arrow 1995).

6. In reviewing utility patents granted by the US Patent and Trademark Office between 2000 and 2020, Dalla Fontana and Nanda (2023) find that VC-backed patents are a small share of overall "Net Zero" patents, but that the potentially more innovative subset of "Deep Tech" patents constitute a larger share of VC-backed firms' overall patenting, compared with the share of Deep Tech patents within the patenting of other young firms or mature firms. This finding is consistent with other work on VC-backed patenting across multiple sectors, which also finds that VC-backed patents are higher quality and more economically important than the average patent (Howell et al. 2020).

7. Without implicating him in any errors, the authors are grateful to Ramana Nanda for a helpful conversation about these issues.

8. On the one hand, Ewens and Farre-Mensa (2020) document a substantial increase in funding for VC-backed start-ups, due to investment from pension funds, mutual funds, hedge funds, and other nontraditional investors. This increase in funding has enabled start-ups to raise larger funding rounds and to stay private for longer. Nonetheless, the associated increases in VC funding have been highly concentrated in a small number of VC firms. Lerner and Nanda (2020) document that about 5% of VC firms investing in US start-ups raised half of the total VC funding over 2014–18. Furthermore, direct investments in start-ups from nontraditional investors have prioritized liquidity, investing in later funding rounds and in larger companies, obtaining stronger rights related to share redemption and initial public offerings, and ceding more traditional control rights (Chernenko et al. 2020).

9. Stiglitz and Weiss (1981) also include under the definition of credit rationing circumstances where some observationally identical potential borrowers are able to obtain loans and others are not, and those who are denied are unable to obtain loans even at higher interest rates.

10. Nanda et al. (2015) also note the critical role of incumbents such as Cisco, Lucent, HP, and Juniper Networks in acquiring start-ups in the information technology and networking industry.

11. Project finance is an external financing arrangement that relies on project-level assets and projected cash flows rather than the balance sheets of the project developer.

12. In the climate-economics literature, coordination failures have largely been considered in the context of international agreements. That is, if countries collectively agreed to curb their emissions, global surplus would increase; yet countries fail to coordinate because they cannot credibly contract with each other on emissions reductions (e.g., Barrett and Dannenberg 2012). One exception is Mielke and Steudle (2018), which examines coordination failures in decisions about whether to invest in low-carbon production. More broadly, coordination failures are a useful lens through which to study new technology markets in the early stages of commercial deployment.

13. Many papers have considered the existence of coordination failures in national and regional economic development. A nonexhaustive list includes Azariadis and Drazen

(1990), Krugman (1991), Matsuyama (1991), and Adserà and Ray (1998). For a helpful review, see de Mesquita 2016.

14. The build-out of electric vehicle (EV) charging infrastructure is one example that has received significant attention in the economics literature. Yet there are two distinct challenges here that are often conflated. First is the network externality associated with the charging infrastructure itself; even if charging stations were owned by a vertically integrated monopolist automaker, the industry would still face increasing returns to scale associated with charging-station investment in specific geographies. The second challenge is one of complementary investments, sometimes referred to as the "chicken and egg" problem, as it may be difficult for diverse automakers to coordinate with diverse charging-station providers on investments in new EVs and new charging stations, respectively. Many nascent climate technologies encounter this latter problem, even where there is not an explicit spatial network. For discussion of coordination problems in electric vehicle deployment and in the climate transition more broadly, see Boushey (2023).

15. In a US context, Kline and Moretti (2013) document the Tennessee Valley Authority's effectiveness in inducing long-run manufacturing productivity through a "big push" of investment. By contrast, Carlino and Kerr (2015) reflect on the "very questionable record of targeted government interventions to create ecosystems for innovation" (see also Kerr and Robert-Nicoud 2020).

16. We note that there are other dimensions of a just and equitable transition besides distributional issues, but we focus on distributive justice here because it is particularly suited to the tools of economics.

17. More broadly, the Biden administration's Justice40 initiative sets a goal that 40% of benefits from certain federal investments, including climate-related investments, flow to disadvantaged communities. Many provisions of recent legislation are consistent with this goal. See https://www.whitehouse.gov/environmentaljustice/justice40.

18. The local share of homeowners versus renters is another relevant characteristic. See Davis (2012) for evidence on lower adoption rates of efficient appliances among renters, even controlling for energy prices, weather, income, and other demographic characteristics.

19. Khatcherian (2022) provides a useful distinction between "demonstration projects," which are unlikely to be profitable, and "first-of-a-kind" projects, which are intended to be profitable, noting that definitions sometimes vary within the industry.

20. In this regard, climate technologies are not necessarily different from other capital-intensive technology areas that require significant time and resources to derisk. For example, in the early years of semiconductor manufacturing, the federal government funded "pilot transistor production lines"; early semiconductor manufacturing was also helped by defense procurement contracts awarded to new entrants with little track record (Fabrizio and Mowery 2007).

21. This idea echoes Rodrik (2014), who notes that one opposition argument to industrial policy is that government does not have the necessary information to "pick winners." Rodrik counters that this argument is largely irrelevant, as industrial policy should not be viewed as a one-time decision but rather a continuous process of recognizing errors and updating as the market develops.

22. The Recovery Act made it easier to fund projects, hence why the first projects were funded during these years.

23. See https://www.energy.gov/lpo/inflation-reduction-act-2022 and https://www.energy.gov/lpo/carbon-dioxide-transportation-infrastructure. Beyond increases in lending authority and credit subsidy, recent legislation has also changed other details of DOE's loan programs. In 2020, Congress allowed DOE to issue loan guarantees for up to 6 projects using a particular innovative energy technology, if regional variation significantly affects technology deployment; previously, DOE was limited to only 2 loan guarantees for a given innovative technology. IIJA also expanded the scope of the advanced vehicle manufacturing loan program to include medium- and heavy-duty vehicles, maritime vessels, aviation, and other transportation, in addition to light-duty vehicles; the innovative clean-energy loan guarantees program also expanded to include projects related to critical minerals. Other changes have streamlined the application process and reduced the up-front payments required for applications to be considered.

24. Beyond new knowledge created among commercial lenders and other market participants, the process of negotiating and contracting on loan terms will also likely result in new knowledge for entrepreneurs or other project developers who have not previously raised debt for this specific technology. If lenders are not unbounded in the rates (i.e., prices) that they are able to charge, due to concerns about adverse selection or moral hazard, then they may not be able to extract this additional surplus from borrowers.

25. An analogy might be the development of COVID-19 vaccines under the federal government's Operation Warp Speed. Given the urgency of the public health crisis, government intervention was able to collapse various stages of the innovation process to happen simultaneously rather than sequentially, as well as simultaneously scale up the supply chain for complementary products to reduce bottlenecks in production. For additional discussion, see https://www.npr.org/transcripts/1053003777 and https://crsreports.congress.gov/product/pdf/IN/IN11560.

26. This section focuses on community-level projects supported by green banks in the United States to date, in contrast to the large-scale climate infrastructure and manufacturing facilities supported by the LPO. However, the distinction between these types of programs may be increasingly blurred under recent legislation, with the opportunity to establish a green bank–like entity at the national level and with the LPO beginning to focus on distributed energy technologies.

27. EPA identified 21 green banks at the state and local level as of 2021; see https://www.epa.gov/statelocalenergy/green-banks.

28. The increasing focus on portfolio-level leverage represents an evolution of the green-bank concept in the United States. Early efforts focused largely on achieving maximum project-level leverage. For further discussion, see Coalition for Green Capital (2018).

29. For additional legislative history, see https://bipartisanpolicy.org/download/?file=/wp-content/uploads/2020/06/Looking-Forward-with-a-Clean-Energy-Deployment-Administration.pdf.

30. Note that the text of the IRA—or EPA's recent notice of initial program design—does not actually use the phrase "green bank." However, the definition of an eligible funding recipient in the legislation closely adheres to accepted definitions of a green bank, and commentators have typically referred to this provision of the IRA as funding for green banks.

31. Closely related is the IRA funding for the Zero Emissions Technologies Grant Program, which allocates $7 billion for projects that "enable low-income and disadvantaged communities to deploy or benefit from zero-emission technologies."

32. For EPA's announcement of initial program design, see https://www.epa.gov/newsreleases/epa-announces-initial-program-design-greenhouse-gas-reduction-fund. An eligible recipient is defined in the IRA as "a nonprofit organization that (A) is designed to provide capital, leverage private capital and provide other forms of financial assistance for the rapid deployment of low- and zero-emission products, technologies, and services; (B) does not take deposits other than deposits from repayments and other revenue received from financial assistance using the grant funds; (C) is funded by public or charitable contributions; and (D) invests in or finances projects alone or in conjunction with other investors."

33. For these examples of commercial energy-efficiency retrofits supported by state and local green banks, see Green Bank Network (2022).

34. It is also worth noting that one reason commercial lenders were unwilling to participate in early community solar projects in New York, according to a representative of the New York Green Bank, was the confusion around complex regulations for how distributed energy resources would be compensated in the state. The New York Green Bank was able to work with their state regulatory colleagues to develop loan terms that were compatible with the new rules. A far more efficient approach might have been for the state to develop simpler rules in the first place.

35. One start-up founder described how funding from the New York Green Bank allowed his company to develop a proof-of-concept credit pool for standardized energy-efficiency retrofits; subsequently, the company was able to fund an even larger credit pool using commercial debt (Green Bank Network 2022).

36. Beyond these large programs in IIJA, CHIPS authorized $10 billion for the Regional Technology and Innovation Hubs Program, administered by the Department of Commerce. These Tech Hubs cover several different technology areas, some of which are relevant for climate technologies, including advanced energy technology, storage, and energy efficiency. The program seeks to strengthen regional technological capabilities in these priority areas, with the goal of improving US global competitiveness and expanding access to jobs in the innovation sector.

37. The Energy Innovation Hubs were funded at $25 million over 5 years, with the possibility of renewal. They were recently wound down, having achieved mixed success (Cho 2021).

38. "Agglomeration effects" refer to the benefits of clustering economic actors together in geographic space by reducing the transportation costs of ideas (knowledge spillovers), people (workforce), and goods (customer-supplier linkages). Existing research also supports the idea that agglomerative forces between customers and suppliers decay less quickly with distance than do knowledge spillovers (Kerr and Kominers 2015).

39. In some contexts, larger firms may be less likely to alter their behavior in response to government policy. Criscuolo et al. (2019) study the causal effects of an industrial policy supporting distressed regions in the United Kingdom. They find that investment subsidies have a positive impact on employment only for smaller firms, which they suggest may result from larger firms' better ability to "game the system."

40. Of course, recent climate-related legislation may also result in negative international spillovers, as domestic content requirements may redirect activity away from established supply chains outside the United States.

41. 45Q and 45V tax credits also play a similar role with regional hydrogen hubs.

References

Adams, W., L. Einav, and J. Levin. 2009. "Liquidity Constraints and Imperfect Information in Subprime Lending." *American Economic Review* 99 (1): 49–84.

Adserà, A., and D. Ray. 1998. "History and Coordination Failure." *Journal of Economic Growth* 3 (3): 267–76.

Agrawal, A., and I. Cockburn. 2003. "The Anchor Tenant Hypothesis: Exploring the Role of Large, Local, R&D Intensive Firms in Regional Innovation Systems." *International Journal of Industrial Organization* 21 (9): 1227–53.

Agrawal, A., I. Cockburn, A. Galasso, and A. Oettl. 2014. "Why Are Some Regions More Innovative Than Others? The Role of Small Firms in the Presence of Large Labs." *Journal of Urban Economics* 81 (5): 149–65.

Agrawal, A., I. Cockburn, and C. Rosell. 2010. "Not Invented Here? Innovation in Company Towns." *Journal of Urban Economics* 67 (1): 78–89.

Akcigit, U., M. A. Celik, and J. Greenwood. 2016. "Buy, Keep, or Sell: Economic Growth and the Market for Ideas." *Econometrica* 84 (3): 943–84.

Aldy, J. 2022. "Learning How to Build Back Better through Clean Energy Policy Evaluation." Working Paper no. RWP22-010 (August), Resources for the Future, Washington, DC.

Arora, A., S. Belenzon, A. Patacconi, and J. Suh. 2020. "The Changing Structure of American Innovation: Some Cautionary Remarks for Economic Growth." *Innovation Policy and the Economy* 20:39–93.

Arrow, K. 1962. "Economic Welfare and the Allocation of Resources for Invention." In *The Rate and Direction of Inventive Activity*, ed. R. Nelson, 609–26. Princeton, NJ: Princeton University Press.

Arrow, K. 1995. Interview with Kenneth Arrow. Federal Reserve Bank of Minneapolis, December 1, 1995. https://www.minneapolisfed.org/article/1995/interview-with-kenneth-arrow.

Autor, D., D. Dorn, and G. Hanson. 2019. "When Work Disappears: Manufacturing Decline and the Falling Marriage Market Value of Young Men." *American Economic Review: Insights* 1 (2): 161–78.

Azariadis, C., and A. Drazen. 1990. "Threshold Externalities in Economic Development." *Quarterly Journal of Economics* 105 (2): 501–26.

Barrett, S., and A. Dannenberg. 2012. "Climate Negotiations under Scientific Uncertainty." *Proceedings of the National Academy of Sciences of the United States of America* 109 (43): 17372–76.

Beck, T., and A. Demirguc-Kunt. 2006. "Small and Medium-Size Enterprises: Access to Finance as a Growth Constraint." *Journal of Banking and Finance* 30 (11): 2931–43.

Bergemann, D., and U. Hege. 1998. "Venture Capital Financing, Moral Hazard, and Learning." *Journal of Banking and Finance* 22 (6): 703–35.

———. 2005. "The Financing of Innovation: Learning and Stopping." *RAND Journal of Economics* 36 (4): 719–52.

Berger, A. N., and G. F. Udell. 1992. "Some Evidence on the Empirical Significance of Credit Rationing." *Journal of Political Economy* 100 (5): 1047–77.

Berkouwer, S. B., and J. T. Dean. 2022. "Credit, Attention, and Externalities in the Adoption of Energy Efficient Technologies by Low-Income Households." *American Economic Review* 112 (10): 3291–330.

Besanko, D., and A. V. Thakor. 1987. "Collateral and Rationing: Sorting Equilibria in Monopolistic and Competitive Credit Markets." *International Economic Review* 28 (3): 671–89.

Bester, H. 1985. "Screening vs. Rationing in Credit Markets with Imperfect Information." *American Economic Review* 75 (4): 850–55.

Bhandary, R. R., K. S. Gallagher, and F. Zhang. 2021. "Climate Finance Policy in Practice: A Review of the Evidence." *Climate Policy* 21 (4): 529–45.

Bioret, L., Y. Zhu, and A. Krupnick. 2023. "Hydrogen Hubs: Get to Know the Encouraged Applicants." *Resources*, February 7. https://www.resources.org/common-resources/hydrogen-hubs-get-to-know-the-encouraged-applicants.

Bloom, N., J. van Reenen, and H. Williams. 2019. "A Toolkit of Policies to Promote Innovation." *Journal of Economic Perspectives* 33 (3): 163–84.

Bollinger, B., K. Gillingham, A. J. Kirkpatrick, and S. Sexton. 2022. "Visibility and Peer Influence in Durable Good Adoption." *Marketing Science* 41 (3): 453–76.

Borenstein, S., and L. W. Davis. 2016. "The Distributional Effects of US Clean Energy Tax Credits." *Tax Policy and the Economy* 30 (1): 191–234.

Boushey, H. 2021. Speech delivered to NBER Environmental and Energy Policy and the Economy Conference, Washington, DC, May 20. https://www.whitehouse.gov/wp-content/uploads/2021/05/Heather-Boushey-NBER-Climate-remarks-May-20-2021.pdf.

Boushey, H. 2023. "The Modern American Industrial Strategy: Building a Clean Energy Economy from the Bottom Up and Middle Out." Speech delivered at the University of California Berkeley, March 22, 2023. https://news.berkeley.edu/2023/06/16/berkeley-talks-transcript-heather-boushey.

Broady, K., M. McComas, and A. Ouazad. 2021. "An Analysis of Financial Institutions in Black-Majority Communities: Black Borrowers and Depositors Face Considerable Challenges in Accessing Banking Services." Report (November), Brookings Institution, Washington, DC.

Budish, E., B. N. Roin, and H. Williams. 2015. "Do Firms Underinvest in Long-Term Research? Evidence from Cancer Clinical Trials." *American Economic Review* 105 (7): 2044–85.

Cameron, A., and A. Turner. 2021. "Lord Adair Turner Talks about What Has to Happen in the 2020s for Net Zero to Be Achievable." Decarb Connect, December. https://share.transistor.fm/s/dd87fa6f.

Carlino, G., and W. R. Kerr. 2015. "Agglomeration and Innovation." In *Handbook of Regional and Urban Economics*, Vol. 5, ed. G. Duranton, J. V. Henderson, and W. C. Strange, 349–404. Amsterdam: Elsevier.

Chatterji, A., E. Glaeser, and W. Kerr. 2014. "Clusters of Entrepreneurship and Innovation." *Innovation Policy and the Economy* 14:129–66.

Chernenko, S., J. Lerner, and Y. Zeng. 2020. "Mutual Funds as Venture Capitalists? Evidence from Unicorns." *Review of Financial Studies* 34 (5): 2362–410.

Cho, A. 2021. "Department of Energy's 'Mini–Manhattan Projects' for Key Energy Problems Wind Down." *Science*, August 11. https://www.science.org /content/article/department-energy-s-mini-manhattan-projects-key-energy -problems-wind-down.

Coalition for Green Capital. 2018. "Green Banks in the United States: 2018 Annual Industry Report." Report (May), Coalition for Green Capital and American Green Bank Consortium. https://greenbanknetwork.org/wp-content /uploads/2019/07/GreenBanksintheUS-2018AnnualIndustryReport.pdf.

Coalition for Green Capital. 2019. "Mobilizing $1 Trillion towards Climate Action: An Analysis of the National Climate Bank." Report (September). https:// greenbanknetwork.org/wp-content/uploads/2019/09/US-National-Climate -Bank-1T-investment-white-paper.pdf.

Collier, P. 2007. *The Bottom Billion: Why Are the Poorest Countries Failing and What Can Be Done about It*. Oxford: Oxford University Press.

Cook, L. D., J. Gerson, and J. Kuan. 2021. "Closing the Innovation Gap in Pink and Black." Working Paper no. 29354, NBER, Cambridge, MA.

Cooper, R. 1999. *Coordination Games*. Cambridge: Cambridge University Press.

———. 2005. "Economic Policy in the Presence of Coordination Problems." *Revue d'Économie Politique* 115 (4): 379–90.

Cooper, R., and A. John. 1988. "Coordinating Coordination Failures in Keynesian Models." *Quarterly Journal of Economics* 103 (3): 441–63.

Cornelli, F., and O. Yosha. 2003. "Stage Financing and the Role of Convertible Securities." *Review of Economic Studies* 70 (1): 1–32.

Covert, T., and R. Sweeney. 2022. "Winds of Change: Estimating Learning by Doing without Cost or Input Data." Working paper (March). https://api .semanticscholar.org/CorpusID:247974350.

Cowling, M. 2010. "The Role of Loan Guarantee Schemes in Alleviating Credit Rationing in the UK." *Journal of Financial Stability* 6 (1): 36–44.

Criscuolo, C., R. Martin, H. G. Overman, and J. van Reenen. 2019. "Some Causal Effects of an Industrial Policy." *American Economic Review* 109 (1): 48–85.

Curtis, E. M., and I. Marinescu. 2022. "Green Energy Jobs in the US: What Are They and Where Are They?" Working Paper no. 30332, NBER, Cambridge, MA.

Curtis, E. M., L. O'Kane, and R. J. Park. 2024. "Workers and the Green-Energy Transition: Evidence from 300 Million Job Transitions." *Environmental and Energy Policy and the Economy* 5:127–161.

Dalla Fontana, S., and R. Nanda. 2023. "Innovating to Net Zero: Can Venture Capital and Start-Ups Play a Meaningful Role?" *Entrepreneurship and Innovation Policy and the Economy* 2:79–105.

Davis, L. W. 2024. "The Economic Determinants of Heat Pump Adoption." *Environmental and Energy Policy and the Economy* 5:162–199.

Davis, L. W. 2012. "Evaluating the Slow Adoption of Energy Efficient Investments: Are Renters Less Likely to Have Energy Efficient Appliances?" In

The Design and Implementation of US Climate Policy, ed. Don Fullerton and Catherine D. Wolfram, 301–32. Chicago: University of Chicago Press.

Davis, L. W., and C. Hausman. 2022. "Who Will Pay for Legacy Utility Costs?" *Journal of the Association of Environmental and Resource Economists* 9 (6): 1047–85.

Deaton, A., and A. Case. 2017. "Mortality and Morbidity in the 21st Century." *Brookings Papers on Economic Activity* Spring:397–476.

DeHoratiis, G. 2022. "Building a Bridge to Bankability for CCUS." Presentation, US Department of Energy, Loan Programs Office, August. https://netl.doe .gov/sites/default/files/netl-file/22CM_GS_DeHoratiis.pdf.

de Mesquita, E. B. 2016. "Coordination Problems." In *Political Economy for Public Policy*, ed. E. B. de Mesquita. Princeton, NJ: Princeton University Press.

de Meza, D., and C. Southey. 1996. "The Borrower's Curse: Optimism, Finance and Entrepreneurship." *Economic Journal* 106 (435): 375–86.

Ewens, M. 2022. "Race and Gender in Entrepreneurial Finance." Working Paper no. 30444, NBER, Cambridge, MA.

Ewens, M., and J. Farre-Mensa. 2020. "The Deregulation of the Private Equity Markets and the Decline in IPOs." *Review of Financial Studies* 33 (12): 5463–509.

Fabrizio, K. R., and D. C. Mowery. 2007. "The Federal Role in Financing Major Innovations: Information Technology during the Postwar Period." In *Financing Innovation in the United States, 1870 to the Present*, ed. N. R. Lamoureaux and K. L. Sokoloff. Cambridge, MA: MIT Press.

Fairlie, R., A. Robb, and D. T. Robinson. 2022. "Black and White: Access to Capital among Minority-Owned Start-Ups." *Management Science* 68 (4): 2377–400.

Feldman, M. 2005. *The Locational Dynamics of the U.S. Biotech Industry: Knowledge Externalities and the Anchor Hypothesis*. Heidelberg: Physica.

Figueiredo, O., P. Guimarães, and D. Woodward. 2009. "Localization Economies and Establishment Size: Was Marshall Right after All?" *Journal of Economic Geography* 9 (6): 853–68.

Gaddy, B. E., V. Sivaram, T. B. Jones, and L. Wayman. 2017. "Venture Capital and Cleantech: The Wrong Model for Energy Innovation." *Energy Policy* 102:385–95.

Ganong, P., and D. Shoag. 2017. "Why Has Regional Income Convergence in the U.S. Declined?" *Journal of Urban Economics* 102:76–90.

Gans, J. S., and S. Stern. 2003. "The Product Market and the Market for 'Ideas': Commercialization Strategies for Technology Entrepreneurs." *Research Policy* 32 (2): 333–50.

Gillingham, K., and B. Bollinger. 2021. "Social Learning and Solar Photovoltaic Adoption." *Management Science* 67 (11): 7091–112.

Gillingham, K., and J. H. Stock. 2018. "The Cost of Reducing Greenhouse Gas Emissions." *Journal of Economic Perspectives* 32 (4): 53–72.

Glaeser, E. L., and N. Hausman. 2020. "The Spatial Mismatch between Innovation and Joblessness." *Innovation Policy and the Economy* 20:233–99.

Glaeser, E. L., and W. R. Kerr. 2009. "Local Industrial Conditions and Entrepreneurship: How Much of the Spatial Distribution Can We Explain?" *Journal of Economics and Management Strategy* 18 (3): 623–63.

Gompers, P. A. 1995. "Optimal Investment, Monitoring, and the Staging of Venture Capital." *Journal of Finance* 50 (5): 1461–89.

Gompers, P. A., and S. Q. Wang. 2017. "Diversity in Innovation." Working Paper no. 17-067 (January), Harvard Business School, Cambridge, MA.

Green Bank Network. 2018. "Community Solar in New York State." Remarks by Jason Moore and Max Heering, New York Green Bank, and Max Joel,

NY-SUN Program Manager, NYSERDA, April 25. https://greenbanknetwork
.org/portfolio/community_solar_ny_green_bank.

Green Bank Network. 2022. "Green Banking at Scale: Green Banks at the City,
State, and National Level." Remarks by Gregory Randolf, Managing Director
at New York Green Bank; Marcelo Rouco, Founder, Chairman, and Chief Ex-
ecutive Officer at Ecosave, Inc.; Sarah Davidson, Director at New York Green
Bank; Jeffrey Diehl, Executive Director and Chief Executive Officer at Rhode
Island Infrastructure Bank; Eli Hopson, CEO at DC Green Bank; and Bert
Hunter, Executive Vice President and Chief Investment Officer at Connecticut
Green Bank, September 20. https://greenbanknetwork.org/portfolio/green
-banking-at-scale.

Greenstone, M., R. Hornbeck, and E. Moretti. 2010. "Identifying Agglomeration
Spillovers: Evidence from Winners and Losers of Large Plant Openings." *Journal of Political Economy* 118 (3): 536–98.

Griffin, A. 2014. "Future of Environmental Finance." Remarks by Alfred Griffin,
President of the New York Green Bank, at the Future of Environmental Finance Forum, Environmental Finance Center, University of North Carolina
Chapel Hill, May. https://greenbanknetwork.org/portfolio/ny-green-bank
-president-on-the-future-of-environmental-finance.

Griffith, R., S. Lee, and J. van Reenen. 2011. "Is Distance Dying at Last? Falling
Home Bias in Fixed-Effects Models of Patent Citations." *Quantitative Economics* 2 (2): 211–49.

Gross, D. 2015. "The Miracle of SolarCity." *Slate*, July 31, 2015. https://slate.com
/business/2015/07/solarcity-the-company-didnt-invent-the-solar-panel-but
-it-invented-something-even-more-important.html.

Hall, B. H., and J. Lerner. 2010. "The Financing of R&D and Innovation." In
Handbook of The Economics of Innovation, Vol. 1, ed. B. H. Hall and N. Rosen-
berg, 609–39. Amsterdam: North-Holland.

Hart, D. 2018. "Beyond the Technology Pork Barrel? An Assessment of the Obama
Administration's Energy Demonstration Projects." *Energy Policy* 119:367–76.

Hausman, N. 2022. "University Innovation and Local Economic Growth." *Review of Economics and Statistics* 104 (4): 718–35.

Hellmann, T. 1998. "The Allocation of Control Rights in Venture Capital Contracts." *RAND Journal of Economics* 29 (1): 57–76.

Henderson, L., C. Herring, H. D. Horton, and M. Thomas. 2015. "Credit Where
Credit Is Due? Race, Gender, and Discrimination in the Credit Scores of Business Startups." *Review of Black Political Economy* 42 (4): 459–79.

Howell, S. T., T. Kuchler, D. Snitkof, J. Stroebel, and J. Wong. 2021. "Lender Au-
tomation and Racial Disparities in Credit Access." Working Paper no. 29364,
NBER, Cambridge, MA.

Howell, S. T., J. Lerner, R. Nanda, and R. R. Townsend. 2020. "How Resilient Is
Venture-Backed Innovation? Evidence from Four Decades of U.S. Patenting."
NBER Working Paper Series. Working Paper no. 27150 (May), NBER, Cam-
bridge, MA.

Jaffe, A. B. 1986. "Technological Opportunity and Spillovers of R&D: Evidence
from Firms' Patents, Profits, and Market Value." *American Economic Review*
76 (5): 984–1001.

Jaffe, A. B., R. G. Newell, and R. N. Stavins. 2005. "A Tale of Two Market Failures:
Technology and Environmental Policy." *Ecological Economics* 54 (2–3): 164–74.

Jaffe, A. B., M. Trajtenberg, and R. Henderson. 1993. "Geographic Localization
of Knowledge Spillovers as Evidenced by Patent Citations." *Quarterly Journal
of Economics* 108 (3): 577–98.

Jones, B. F. 2022. "Where Innovation Happens, and Where It Does Not." In *The Role of Innovation and Entrepreneurship in Economic Growth*, ed. Michael J. Andrews, Aaron K. Chatterji, Josh Lerner, and Scott Stern, 577–602. Chicago: University of Chicago Press.

Kahn, S., and S. Jacobs. 2022. "Helping Early-Stage Climatetech Startups Survive the Valley of Death." *Catalyst*, July 14. https://www.canarymedia.com/podcasts/catalyst-with-shayle-kann/crossing-the-valley-of-death.

Kahn, S., and R. Naam. 2021. "Can Deeptech Venture Capital Solve Climate Change?" *Catalyst*, November 11. https://www.canarymedia.com/podcasts/catalyst-with-shayle-kann/deep-tech-venture-climate-capital-catalyst-shayle-kann-podcast.

Kahn, S., and J. Shah. 2022. "Inside the Department of Energy's Loan Deal to Back Hydrogen." *Catalyst*, January 10. https://www.canarymedia.com/podcasts/catalyst-with-shayle-kann/inside-the-department-of-energys-loan-deal-to-back-hydrogen.

Kaufman, R. 2018. "Can Green Banks Scale Clean Energy?" Yale Insights: Management in Practice, November. https://insights.som.yale.edu/insights/can-green-banks-scale-clean-energy.

Kehoe, J., M. Lee, and V. Radulovic. 2021. "Catalyzing Investment with a National Climate Bank: Lessons from Subnational Green Banks." C2ES Report (June), Center for Climate and Energy Solutions, Arlington, VA. https://www.c2es.org/wp-content/uploads/2021/06/catalyzing-investment-with-a-national-climate-bank.pdf.

Kerr, W. R., and S. D. Kominers. 2015. "Agglomerative Forces and Cluster Shapes." *Review of Economics and Statistics* 97 (4): 877–99.

Kerr, W. R., and R. Nanda. 2010. "Banking Deregulations, Financing Constraints, and Firm Entry Size." *Journal of the European Economic Association* 8 (2/3): 582–93.

———. 2015. "Financing Innovation." *Annual Review of Financial Economics* 7 (1): 445–62.

Kerr, W. R., R. Nanda, and M. Rhodes-Kropf. 2014. "Entrepreneurship as Experimentation." *Journal of Economic Perspectives* 28 (3): 25–48.

Kerr, W. R., and F. Robert-Nicoud. 2020. "Tech Clusters." *Journal of Economic Perspectives* 34 (3): 50–76. https://www.aeaweb.org/articles?id=10.1257/jep.34.3.50.

Kessler, A. 2022. "Green Banks and Financing the Energy Transition." Pivotal 180 in Conversation, October. https://pivotal180.com/green-banks-and-financing-the-energy-transition.

Khatcherian, K. 2022. "Barriers to the Timely Deployment of Climate Infrastructure." Technical report (April), Prime Coalition, Cambridge, MA. https://static1.squarespace.com/static/60903dcf05bc23197b2b993b/t/6269c7a70847634d26c0d81b/1651099594061/2022+Climate+Infrastructure+Full+Report_final.

Klepper, S. 2010. "The Origin and Growth of Industry Clusters: The Making of Silicon Valley and Detroit." *Journal of Urban Economics* 67 (1): 15–32.

———. 2016. *Experimental Capitalism: The Nanoeconomics of American High-Tech Industries*. Princeton, NJ: Princeton University Press.

Kline, P., and E. Moretti. 2013. "Local Economic Development, Agglomeration Economies, and the Big Push: 100 Years of Evidence from the Tennessee Valley Authority." *Quarterly Journal of Economics* 129 (1): 275–331.

Kotchen, M. J., and C. Costello. 2018. "Maximizing the Impact of Climate Finance: Funding Projects or Pilot Projects?" *Journal of Environmental Economics and Management* 92:270–81.

Krugman, P. 1991. "History versus Expectations." *Quarterly Journal of Economics* 106 (2): 651–67.

Leland, H. E., and D. H. Pyle. 1977. "Informational Asymmetries, Financial Structure, and Financial Intermediation." *Journal of Finance* 32 (2): 371–87.

Lerner, J. 2009. *Boulevard of Broken Dreams: Why Public Efforts to Boost Entrepreneurship and Venture Capital Have Failed—and What to Do about It*. Princeton, NJ: Princeton University Press.

Lerner, J., and R. Nanda. 2020. "Venture Capital's Role in Financing Innovation: What We Know and How Much We Still Need to Learn." *Journal of Economic Perspectives* 34 (3): 237–61.

Lester, R. K., and D. M. Hart. 2015. "Closing the Energy-Demonstration Gap." *Issues in Science and Technology* 31 (2): 48–54.

Lychagin, S., J. Pinkse, M. E. Slade, and J. van Reenen. 2016. "Spillovers in Space: Does Geography Matter?" *Journal Of Industrial Economics* 64 (2): 295–335.

Markusen, A. 1996. "Sticky Places in Slippery Space: A Typology of Industrial Districts." *Economic Geography* 72 (3): 293–313.

Matsuyama, K. 1991. "Increasing Returns, Industrialization, and Indeterminacy of Equilibrium." *Quarterly Journal of Economics* 106 (2): 617–50.

———. 1998. "Economic Development as Coordination Problems." In *The Role of Government in East Asian Economic Development: Comparative Institutional Analysis*, ed. M. Aoki, H.-K. Kim, and M. Okuno-Fujiwara. Oxford: Oxford University Press.

McCall, M. 2016. "Update: How DOE Loan Guarantees Helped Launch the Utility-Scale PV Solar Market." US DOE, Loan Programs Office, February 11, 2016. https://www.energy.gov/lpo/articles/update-how-doe-loan-guarantees-helped-launch-utility-scale-pv-solar-market.

Metcalf, G. E. 2023. "The Distributional Impacts of a VMT-Gas Tax Swap." *Environmental and Energy Policy and the Economy* 4:4–42.

Mielke, J., and G. A. Steudle. 2018. "Green Investment and Coordination Failure: An Investors' Perspective." *Ecological Economics* 150:88–95.

Miller, S., and C. K. Soo. 2020. "Do Neighborhoods Affect the Credit Market Decisions of Low-Income Borrowers? Evidence from the Moving to Opportunity Experiment." *Review of Financial Studies* 34 (2): 827–63.

Murphy, K. M., A. Shleifer, and R. W. Vishny. 1989. "Industrialization and the Big Push." *Journal of Political Economy* 97 (5): 1003–26.

Nanda, R. 2020. "Financing 'Tough Tech' Innovation." In *Global Innovation Index 2020: Who Will Finance Innovation?* ed. S. Dutta, B. Lanvin, and S. Wunsch-Vincent, 113–19. Ithaca, NY: Cornell University Press.

Nanda, R., and J. Rothenberg. 2011. "A Quiet Revolution in Clean Energy Finance." *Harvard Business Review*, October 26. https://hbr.org/2011/10/quiet-revolution-clean-energy-finance.

Nanda, R., K. Younge, and L. Fleming. 2015. "Innovation and Entrepreneurship in Renewable Energy." In *The Changing Frontier: Rethinking Science and Innovation Policy*, ed. A. B. Jaffe and B. F. Jones, 199–232. Chicago: University of Chicago Press.

Nelson, R. R. 1959. "The Simple Economics of Basic Scientific Research." *Journal of Political Economy* 49:297–306.

Nemet, G. 2023. "Opportunities and Risks of Scaling Up Carbon Dioxide Removal." *Resources Radio*, February 28. https://www.resources.org/resources-radio/opportunities-and-risks-of-scaling-up-carbon-dioxide-removal-with-gregory-nemet.

Nemet, G. F., V. Zipperer, and M. Kraus. 2018. "The Valley of Death, the Technology Pork Barrel, and Public Support for Large Demonstration Projects." *Energy Policy* 119:154–67.

New York Green Bank. 2022. "Annual Plan 2022–23." Report. https://greenbank .ny.gov/-/media/Project/Greenbank/Files/AnnualPlan_2022-FINAL.pdf.

Petersen, M. A., and R. G. Rajan. 1994. "The Benefits of Lending Relationships: Evidence from Small Business Data." *Journal of Finance* 49 (1): 3–37.

———. 2002. "Does Distance Still Matter? The Information Revolution in Small Business Lending." *Journal of Finance* 57 (6): 2533–70.

Polzin, F., F. Egli, B. Steffen, and T. S. Schmidt. 2019. "How Do Policies Mobilize Private Finance for Renewable Energy? A Systematic Review with an Investor Perspective." *Applied Energy* 236:1249–68.

Prabhakar, A. 2021. "Philanthropy's Role in Addressing Climate Change." Columbia Energy Exchange, December 30. https://www.energypolicy.colum bia.edu/philanthropys-role-addressing-climate-change.

Robb, A. M., and D. T. Robinson. 2012. "The Capital Structure Decisions of New Firms." *Review of Financial Studies* 27 (1): 153–79.

Rodrik, D. 1996. "Coordination Failures and Government Policy: A Model with Applications to East Asia and Eastern Europe." *Journal of International Economics* 40 (1): 1–22.

Rodrik, D. 2004. "Industrial Policy for the Twenty-First Century." Working paper, Harvard Kennedy School, Cambridge, MA.

———. 2014. "Green Industrial Policy." *Oxford Review of Economic Policy* 30 (3): 469–91.

Rosenstein-Rodan, P. N. 1943. "Problems of Industrialisation of Eastern and South-Eastern Europe." *Economic Journal* 53 (210/211): 202–11.

Rozansky, R., and D. M. Hart. 2020. "More and Better: Building and Managing a Federal Energy Demonstration Project Portfolio." Report (May), Information Technology and Innovation Foundation, Washington, DC. https://itif.org /publications/2020/05/18/more-and-better-building-and-managing-feder al-energy-demonstration-project.

Schleich, J. 2019. "Energy Efficient Technology Adoption in Low-Income Households in the European Union—What Is the Evidence?" *Energy Policy* 125:196–206.

Shi, X., X. Liu, and L. Yao. 2016. "Assessment of Instruments in Facilitating Investment in Off-Grid Renewable Energy Projects." *Energy Policy* 95:437–46.

Siegmund, D., S. Metz, V. Peinecke, T. E. Warner, C. Cremers, A. Grevé, T. Smolinka, D. Segets, and U.-P. Apfel. 2021. "Crossing the Valley of Death: From Fundamental to Applied Research in Electrolysis." *Journal of the American Chemical Society Au* 1 (5): 527–35.

Steffen, B. 2018. "The Importance of Project Finance for Renewable Energy Projects." *Energy Economics* 69:280–94.

Stein, J. C. 1989. "Efficient Capital Markets, Inefficient Firms: A Model of Myopic Corporate Behavior." *Quarterly Journal of Economics* 104 (4): 655–69.

Stiglitz, J. E., and A. Weiss. 1981. "Credit Rationing in Markets with Imperfect Information." *American Economic Review* 71 (3): 393–410.

St. John, J. 2021. "Jigar Shah's Big Idea for Getting Rooftop Solar and Smart Appliances to Low-Income Americans." Canary Media, November 23. https:// www.canarymedia.com/articles/policy-regulation/jigar-shahs-big-idea -for-getting-rooftop-solar-and-smart-appliances-to-low-income-americans.

Trabish, H. K. 2015. "Why Solar Financing Is Moving from Leases to Loans."
Utility Dive, August 17. https://www.utilitydive.com/news/why-solar-fi
nancing-is-moving-from-leases-to-loans/403678.
Trajtenberg, M. 1990. "A Penny for Your Quotes: Patent Citations and the Value
of Innovations." *RAND Journal of Economics* 21 (1): 172–87.
Turner, A. 2023. "New Details about the Inflation Reduction Act's Greenhouse
Gas Reduction Fund and Takeaways for Cities." Climate Law: A Sabin Center
Blog, February 16. https://blogs.law.columbia.edu/climatechange/2023
/02/16/new-details-about-the-inflation-reduction-acts-greenhouse-gas-re
duction-fund-takeaways-for-cities.
US Department of Energy, Office of Energy Efficiency and Renewable Energy.
n.d. "Technology-to-Market." https://www.energy.gov/eere/buildings
/technology-market.
US Government Accountability Office. 2020. "Technology Readiness Assessment Guide: Best Practices for Evaluating the Readiness of Technology for
Use in Acquisition Programs and Projects." Report no. GAO-20-48G (January). https://www.gao.gov/assets/gao-20-48g.pdf.
van den Heuvel, M., and D. Popp. 2022. "The Role of Venture Capital and Governments in Clean Energy: Lessons from the First Cleantech Bubble." Working Paper no. 29919, NBER, Cambridge, MA.
Yescombe, Y. R. 2014. *Principles of Project Finance.* 2nd ed. Oxford: Elsevier.

The Shadow Price of Capital: Accounting for Capital Displacement in Benefit-Cost Analysis

Richard G. Newell, *Resources for the Future,* United States of America
William A. Pizer, *Resources for the Future and NBER,* United States of America
Brian C. Prest, *Resources for the Future,* United States of America

Executive Summary

Government analysts have long used discount rates based on investment rates of return to approximate the effect of capital displacement. However, we show how this approach is not well grounded in economic theory and produces highly biased results, particularly in the context of decisions involving long-lived impacts such as climate change. We demonstrate how analysts can use the conceptually correct shadow price of capital (SPC) approach in a straightforward manner to account for concerns about capital displacement in federal regulatory analysis. We derive a formula for the SPC as a function of four key parameters and propose a central SPC value of 1.1, with a reasonable range of 1.1–1.2. We then illustrate how the SPC approach could be easily implemented in practice using the example of the 2015 Clean Power Plan Regulatory Impact Analysis, showing that estimated net benefits are far less sensitive to capital-displacement concerns under the analytically correct SPC approach as compared with the inappropriate approach of using a 7% investment rate of return. Our work is particularly important given the ongoing efforts to revise federal guidance for benefit-cost analysis and discounting.

JEL Codes: D61, E21, E22, H43

Keywords: discounting, shadow price of capital, benefit-cost analysis

I. Introduction

A long-standing 1993 executive order, EO 12866, requires any economically significant federal regulation to be accompanied by a benefit-cost

Environmental and Energy Policy and the Economy, volume 5, 2024.

analysis (BCA). BCAs require a choice of discount rates to compare costs and benefits that accrue at different periods of time, and for impacts with long-lived consequences, the result of a BCA can be highly sensitive to the choice of the discount rate. For 20 years, federal guidelines for BCAs, including appropriate approaches to discounting, have been set by a guidance document known as Circular A-4 (White House 2003), which the federal government is now proposing to update.[1] In 2003, Circular A-4 recommended two discount rates to adjust estimated future costs and benefits to present-day equivalents: 3% and 7%. The 3% consumption discount rate is meant to reflect the discount rate applicable to impacts on individual households (as measured by their consumption), with individuals being the ultimate concern of economic welfare analysis. In contrast, the 7% investment rate of return—which is sometimes called the opportunity cost of capital—is meant to reflect the possibility that costs may displace capital investment, which has a higher rate of return than the consumption rate due to economic distortions such as taxes and transaction costs (Boardman et al. 2017), as well as a risk premium. Importantly, both the consumption and investment rates for the purposes of this discussion should reflect risk-free returns. If not, additional work must be done to adjust for the potential difference in risk between the source of discount rate data and the proposed policy benefits. As we discuss later, there is reason to believe that the estimated 7% investment rate of return is not truly risk free, but we set that point aside for the moment for the purposes of discussion.

Circular A-4 notes, however, that the economic literature has shown that the "analytically preferred" method to account for the higher investment rate of return is instead to use the "shadow price of capital" (SPC) approach, in which impacts affecting capital investments are converted to consumption-equivalent values. Once all impacts are measured consistently in terms of consumption, all costs and benefits are appropriately discounted at the consumption discount rate. "Analytically preferred" is another way of saying "welfare-grounded," meaning based in the concepts of welfare economics, which takes as its starting point the well-being of households as measured by their consumption over time.

Nonetheless, the analytically preferred SPC approach is rarely used in practice. Instead, federal BCAs typically include a sensitivity case that discounts all costs and benefits at the investment rate of return, set at 7% in 2003 by Circular A-4. The use of the investment rate was intended to serve as a simplified way to account for capital displacement, perhaps because the SPC rate was seen as too complex for use by agency analysts. However, in this paper we show that the SPC approach is actually both simpler and much better grounded in welfare economics than the current 7% approach and can be implemented with currently available information.

Using an investment rate of return as one of the discount rate sensitivity cases is common practice in federal regulatory impact analyses (RIAs), but economists have demonstrated that it is only conceptually consistent with the analytically preferred SPC method under very restrictive and unrealistic conditions that are almost never satisfied (Li and Pizer 2021). Simply discounting benefits at an investment rate of return ignores the differences between the time pattern of the benefits and that of the capital returns being displaced. That is, discounting future benefits at the investment rate of return to account for immediate cost impacts on capital investment mismeasures the value to households if those time patterns differ. This reflects well-known problems with using investment rates of return to compare policy options, rather than an appropriate consumption discount rate.

To see why the use of an investment rate yields incorrect conclusions, consider a simple example of a policy that costs $1 in capital today and creates a benefit of $100 delivered 100 years into the future. Households would value that benefit at $5.20 in present value based on a 3% discount rate (= $100/1.03^{100}$). The cost of the policy as felt by consumers is not the $1 in capital itself, but rather the lost stream of returns that capital would have earned, which for the moment we will assume is 7% annually in perpetuity. The costs to consumers therefore take the form of a perpetuity of $0.07 annually, the present value of which, discounted at the consumer's discount rate of 3%, is $0.07/3 % = $2.33. Hence, the net benefits of this policy are positive: $5.20 − $2.33 = $2.87. By contrast, if one were to instead try to account for capital displacement by discounting benefits at a 7% rate as Circular A-4 suggests, one would instead mistakenly calculate negative net benefits because the present value of benefits would be merely $0.12(= $100/1.07^{100}$). This is just one example of how using an investment discount rate in a BCA can yield wrong conclusions when costs and benefits have different time patterns.

Recent work not only confirms that the long-standing approach of using a 7% discount rate is inconsistent with the welfare-grounded SPC approach but also shows that the degree of embedded inaccuracy tends to compound the longer the time frame of the policy being evaluated (Li and Pizer 2021). It is therefore particularly inaccurate for actions with long-term consequences, such as actions that reduce greenhouse gas emissions. This paper explains why the discounting sensitivity case using a 7% investment rate of return is not theoretically grounded and can yield extremely misleading estimates of the costs and benefits of policies with long-lived impacts, such as climate change.

Moreover, this paper explains how to move beyond the inconsistent but common practice of applying a 7% discount rate to address concerns about capital displacement. Instead, we show how the welfare-grounded SPC approach is simple to implement in practice, would not involve major changes in analytical procedures, and would simplify federal BCAs by dispensing with multiple internally inconsistent discount rates within a given BCA. We demonstrate how one would implement this by reevaluating the final RIA for the 2015 Clean Power Plan using the SPC framework and Circular A-4's 2003 recommended 3% consumption discount rate. This demonstrates that the SPC approach would be simple to implement, account for concerns about capital displacement without resorting to the inconsistent 7% discount rate approach, and yield results similar to those reached by recently conducted RIAs in cases where the time horizon is not particularly long. We also explore scenarios that use a 2% consumption discount rate, which evidence suggests is now a more appropriate estimate than 3% going forward. For example, the federal government's recent revisions to Circular A-4 proposed a value of 1.7%, as discussed in more detail below.

These results have clear policy implications given the Biden administration's ongoing efforts to update Circular A-4 to "reflect new developments in scientific and economic understanding" and the Office of Management and Budget's (OMB) recently proposed revisions.[2] Although the concept of the SPC is not a new idea (e.g., Bradford 1975; Lind 1990; Lyon 1990; Moore et al. 2004), it was not widely understood in 2003, when Circular A-4 was drafted, just how large the bias would be from the use of an investment rate of return for discounting in the case of policies with long-lived impacts, such as regulations addressing greenhouse gas emissions.

In April 2023, OMB proposed a comprehensive revision of Circular A-4, which includes changes to discounting as well as other issues such as distributional effects. OMB has proposed two specific changes relating to discounting. First, OMB has proposed updating the estimate of the consumption rate of interest to 1.7%, which reflects average real returns to 10-year US Treasury notes from 1993 to 2022.[3] This 30-year average approach is conceptually analogous to the calculation underlying the 3% estimate developed in the 2003 version of Circular A-4.

Second, OMB has eliminated the recommendation to discount using a 7% discount rate to account for capital displacement and instead suggests using the SPC. In particular, OMB suggests using two values of the shadow price—1.0 (reflecting an open economy with perfect capital mobility) and 1.2 (reflecting a closed economy with limited international capital flows). These SPC values would then be applied to the estimated share of benefits and costs accruing to capital if the analyst has such an estimate. If no estimate is available, OMB has recommended two "outer-bound" cases: one assuming all benefits and no costs accrue to capital, and another assuming the reverse. These proposed revisions are broadly consistent with our recommendations in this paper, which we would note was drafted before OMB's proposed revisions were published. The main difference is that our central SPC value is 1.1, rather than OMB's proposed value of 1.2, which we discuss below.

The paper proceeds as follows. First, we explain the conceptual basis that motivated the use of an investment rate for discounting recommended in Circular A-4, when it is and is not equivalent to the welfare-grounded SPC approach, and how much the two approaches can differ. Second, we derive a formula for the SPC as a function of four parameters: the consumption discount rate, the investment rate of return, the depreciation rate of capital, and the savings rate. Third, we use reasonable estimates of those parameters to propose SPC values for use in regulatory analysis and other decision contexts. Finally, we demonstrate how the SPC could be implemented in practice, using the Clean Power Plan RIA as an example. In this example, we are balanced in applying the SPC to both costs and benefits—that is, including the possibility that benefits may augment capital, alongside the traditional concern that costs may displace capital investment.

II. Rationale for Discounting at the Investment Rate to Account for Capital Displacement Is Simplistic and Theoretically Unsupported

This section describes the mathematical logic underlying Circular A-4's approach of incorporating capital displacement concerns by simply discounting benefits at a rate of 7%. This section also illustrates why it does not accurately reflect the fundamental concern except in very limited situations. Circular A-4 notes that the SPC approach is analytically preferred, but for simplicity, A-4 nonetheless recommends two rates for sensitivity analysis: a consumption discount rate (estimated historically at 3%) and an investment rate of return (estimated historically at 7%), notionally as a bound on how capital displacement might affect BCAs. The latter rate is sometimes referred to as the "opportunity cost of capital." The use of the consumption rate is appropriate when all costs and benefits fall on consumption and no costs or benefits displace capital.

However, the 7% investment rate of return is only an appropriate opposing bound under very specific assumptions. In particular, discounting benefits at the investment rate is only appropriate if (1) the capital is displaced immediately and permanently and both the displaced returns and benefits to be discounted are paid out as perpetuities, or (2) more generally, if the pattern of benefits and investment returns are the same, and (3) only costs (and not benefits) affect investment.[4] A matching time pattern is a necessary condition to the validity of using the investment rate, implying that the use of the investment rate to reflect capital displacement is only appropriate in very limited circumstances, such as those summarized above. By contrast, the costs of regulations or other policies tend to play out over time (say, due to changes in regulated entities' variable costs), but these changes do not typically precisely parallel the time profile of benefits (say, due to reduced long-term damages from climate change).

To illustrate when the use of an investment rate is and is not appropriate, we walk through the special case in (1) above and compare using the investment rate of return as a substitute for the welfare-grounded SPC approach. For permanent capital displacement, each $1 of immediate costs leads to a permanent $1 loss in capital. This has no immediate impact on consumers, but suppose that dollar of capital would have returned the investment rate of return, denoted r_i, to consumers every year in perpetuity. That is, the return is assumed to go entirely to consumers and does not further affect capital through savings. Therefore, a dollar of permanently displaced capital implies consumers face a cost equal to r_i every year into the future. The present value of this stream of consumer costs equals

$$\text{PV(Consumer Costs)} = \frac{r_i}{1 + r_c} + \frac{r_i}{(1 + r_c)^2} + \frac{r_i}{(1 + r_c)^3} + \cdots = \frac{r_i}{r_c},$$

where r_c is the consumption discount rate and the final equality, r_i/r_c, derives from the equation for the present value of a perpetuity. Thus, a dollar of permanently displaced capital is equivalent to r_i/r_c dollars of lost consumption today, and the hypothetical shadow price is r_i/r_c. For $r_i = 7\%$ and $r_c = 3\%$, this ratio would be $0.07/0.03 = 2.33$. (Note, however, that we will show later in the paper that an SPC = 1.1 is a more generally appropriate value once one properly accounts for savings and depreciation, which we assume away for the purposes of this thought experiment.)

This shadow price can easily be used to calculate net benefits within this extreme scenario. Assume a regulation that generates $B of consumer benefits annually for each $1 of permanently displaced capital costs. Then, under the SPC approach in this stylized example, the net present value is given by

$$\text{PV(Net Benefits}_{\text{SPC}}) = \text{PV(Consumer Benefits)}$$
$$- \text{PV(Consumer Costs)} = \frac{\$B}{r_c} - \$1\frac{r_i}{r_c}. \quad (1)$$

Using the shadow price equal to r_i/r_c, this project passes a benefit-cost test if the right-hand side of equation (1) is greater than zero, or $\$B > r_i$.

However, government analyses do not currently account for capital displacement using the SPC approach. The alternative approach to account for capital displacement commonly used by government analysts, per Circular A-4, is to discount the flow of benefits ($B) at the investment rate of return, r_i. Despite there being little conceptual reason to change the benefit calculation to reflect the nature of costs, the intuition given is that the benefits from a project or policy should deliver the same or greater return than if the costs were invested, essentially comparing the internal rate of return. In this simple extreme case of permanent capital displacement and a perpetuity benefit, using the investment rate of return yields the same result as the SPC approach regarding whether a project passes the benefit-cost test. To see why, note that the net benefits would be equal to the perpetuity value of the benefit flows, $B, discounted to the present at the investment rate of return r_i, minus the immediate $1 of costs:[5]

$$\text{PV(Net Benefits}_{r_i}) = \frac{\$B}{r_i} - \$1. \quad (2)$$

Comparing the expressions for net benefits under the two approaches—equation (1) for the SPC approach and (2) for the investment rate of return—they both reach the same directional conclusion that the project passes a benefit-cost test if, and only if, $\$B > r_i$. This is the implicit logic underlying Circular A-4's recommendation to discount all costs and benefits at the 7% rate; that is, it can mimic the result of the SPC approach under certain conditions, such as when costs permanently displace capital and benefits are paid out as a perpetuity.

Discounting both costs and benefits at the investment rate yields an equivalent result as the SPC approach in this specific case—but not more generally. The equivalency breaks down as soon as the time pattern of regulatory benefits and ordinary capital investment returns differs. It is particularly problematic when regulatory benefits are much longer lived than ordinary capital investment returns. In the above special case, they are both assumed to be perpetuities.

To illustrate how the investment rate of return approach goes wrong as a proxy for the correct SPC approach, suppose the benefits of this $1 in regulatory cost do not pay out as a perpetuity with $B paid every year, but rather as a fixed payment of $B = $10 received at $T = 40$ years. For this example, we will again use $r_c = 3\%$ and $r_i = 7\%$ as our consumption and investment discount rates, respectively. Therefore, the present value of those benefits would be $\$10/1.03^{40} = \$3.07$. As previously shown, using the SPC approach in this example, the $1 in immediate investment-displacing cost is valued at $\$1 \times (r_i/r_c) = \$1 \times 7\% /3\% = \$2.33$. Hence, this investment yields positive net benefits of $0.73 (equaling $3.07 in benefits minus $2.33 in costs), thereby passing the benefit-cost criteria. Had we instead discounted benefits at the investment rate of return of 7% as in the OMB guidance (in lieu of the SPC approach), we would have computed a present value of benefits of only $\$10/1.07^{40} = \$0.67$, yielding the opposite conclusion of negative net benefits of –$0.33 (equal to $0.67 in benefits minus $1 in costs), erroneously concluding that the policy failed on benefit-cost grounds. This illustrates how discounting at the investment rate goes particularly wrong analytically for situations with near-term costs and long-term benefits.

A subtle point is that in addition to the difference in sign, the 7% investment discounting approach is implicitly calculating net benefits in terms of "capital equivalents." In terms of consumption equivalents, the result of using the 7% approach to which one should compare the $0.73 in net benefits from the SPC would be – $0.78 (i.e., – $0.33 × 2.33)—even further from the correct answer than initially apparent.

Another way to illustrate how using 7% goes awry is to convert the net benefit result from the SPC approach to capital equivalents, which would be $0.31 (i.e., $0.73/2.33). If one were to solve for the single discount rate that yields the analytically correct conclusion in terms of capital—positive net benefits of $0.31—the resulting rate would be about 5.2%, which has moved toward the 3% consumption rate.[6] For longer time horizons, such as those relevant to climate change, the rate will move even closer to the consumption discount rate (3% in this example).

In general, the discount rate ρ^* that should be used to discount benefits in year T to correctly replicate the results of the SPC approach is the solution to the following equation:

$$\frac{\$B}{(1+r_c)^T} - \text{SPC} = \left(\frac{\$B}{(1+\rho^*)^T} - \$1 \right) \text{SPC}.$$

The left-hand side of this equation is net benefits in consumption terms under the SPC approach. The term in parentheses on the right-hand side is net benefits in capital terms, which is then converted to consumption equivalents by multiplying by the SPC. Simple algebraic manipulation yields a value for ρ^* given by

$$\rho^* = (1+r_c)(\text{SPC})^{\frac{1}{T}} - 1. \tag{3}$$

This replicates equation (16) in Li and Pizer (2021) and demonstrates that ρ^* converges to r_c as the time horizon grows larger. For the case of $T = 100$, SPC $= 7/3$, we find $\rho^* = 3.9\%$.

This exercise demonstrates another important point: the SPC is a simpler way to correctly account for capital displacement than discounting at a higher investment rate of return. Namely, if one wishes to account for investment displacement in the initial period by applying a higher discount rate (i.e., above the consumption rate) to future costs and benefits, then one must first determine the appropriate rate ρ^*. As we have shown, the appropriate rate in this circumstance is generally lower than the investment rate of return for sufficiently long time horizons, and both depend on the time pattern of both benefits and costs and on the SPC—even in this very simple example. Furthermore, determining the rate ρ^* requires conducting a full SPC analysis in any event.

One might imagine that a shortcut would be to use a bounding value for ρ^*—but this would be incorrect. For example, over a single year, $\rho^* = \text{SPC} - 1 + r_c(\text{SPC})$, which will be considerably larger than r_i for any typical SPC ≥ 1.1. Hence, the only straightforward and correct approach is to simply conduct the SPC analysis from the start. We turn next to showing how the SPC approach can be used straightforwardly in practice.

III.   Derivation of the SPC Formula

The welfare-grounded approach is to employ the SPC and use a consumption discount rate, so the natural question is what numeric value should be used for the SPC in BCAs. The SPC, which reflects the welfare value lost from displaced capital investment, depends on how long it remains displaced in the economy. The degree of the displacement's persistence is determined by broad economic equilibrium dynamics, including depreciation and savings, suggesting that the SPC should be guided by macro-derived models of savings and investment. Li and Pizer (2021) present such a model reflecting the degree of permanence of capital displacement, demonstrating that the SPC depends on four parameters:

1. μ, the depreciation rate of capital, which determines how quickly capital would have decayed over time had it not been displaced;

2. s, the savings rate (gross of depreciation), which replenishes capital over time;

3. r_i, the investment rate of return (net of depreciation), which determines the annual income (savings and consumption) lost per dollar of displaced capital; and

4. r_c, the consumption discount rate, which converts future consumption into equivalent present values.

Li and Pizer (2021) and Pizer (2021) derive an analytical expression for the SPC as a function of these parameters, generalizing methods developed by Marglin, Bradford, and others in the 1960s and 1970s (e.g., Marglin 1963a, 1963b; Bradford 1975). We repeat a version of that derivation for reference.

Here, we pause to highlight an important conceptual linkage between the consumption and investment rates as we have described them. As previously noted, for the purposes of calculating the SPC, both the consumption and investment rates must represent risk-free rates. Working with r_c and r_i as risk-free rates, in the absence of economic distortions such as taxes, arbitrage would ensure that r_i and r_c are equal (Boardman et al. 2017).[7] Taxes introduce a wedge between the pretax capital return r_i and the rate of return received by consumers. That is, given a tax rate τ, there is a direct relationship between the two rates: $r_i = r_c/(1 - \tau)$. Although in principle the following derivation could replace all values of r_i with $r_c/(1 - \tau)$, we nonetheless retain the r_i notation in the following derivation for simplicity and intuition.

Moving on to the derivation, we start by noting that the SPC is defined as the change in immediate consumption equivalent to the present value of the stream of consumption losses associated with the immediate displacement of $1 of capital, discounted at the consumption discount rate. Computing this requires considering the effect that such an immediate displacement of capital would have on consumption over time, given savings rates, investment returns, and depreciation.

We denote an immediate exogenous change in capital in period t as ΔK_t. Given a net (after depreciation) investment return r_i and a depreciation rate μ, K_t produces a change in gross returns (before depreciation) in the next period of $(r_i + \mu)\Delta K_t$. Of that amount, a fraction s is saved, leading to an augmentation of the change in capital formation of $s(r_i + \mu)$. The resulting change in the capital stock in the next period, denoted ΔK_{t+1}, will thus be the direct change in capital stock less depreciation, plus the indirect change in savings induced by the change in capital $s(r_i + \mu)\Delta K_t$:

$$\Delta K_{t+1} = (1 - \mu)\Delta K_t + s(r_i + \mu)\Delta K_t = [s(r_i + \mu) + (1 - \mu)]\Delta K_t.$$

Similarly, in period $t + 2$, ΔK_{t+1} will in turn produce gross returns of

$$\Delta K_{t+2} = [s(r_i + \mu) + (1 - \mu)]\Delta K_{t+1} = [s(r_i + \mu) + (1 - \mu)]^2\Delta K_t.$$

And more generally,

$$\Delta K_{t+h} = [s(r_i + \mu) + (1 - \mu)]^h\Delta K_t.$$

The portion of the increased returns that are not saved yields consumption benefits of $(1 - s)(r_i + \mu)\Delta K_t$. This change in consumption in period $t + 1$ is given by

$$\Delta C_{t+1} = (1 - s)(r_i + \mu)\Delta K_t.$$

An analogous equation holds for period $t + 2$, into which we substitute the above expression for ΔK_{t+1}, yielding

$$\Delta C_{t+2} = (1 - s)(r_i + \mu)\Delta K_{t+1} = (1 - s)(r_i + \mu)[s(r_i + \mu) + (1 - \mu)]\Delta K_t,$$

and more generally, by recursive substitution we find an expression for the change in consumption for each time period into the future:

$$\Delta C_{t+h} = (1 - s)(r_i + \mu)[s(r_i + \mu) + (1 - \mu)]^{h-1}\Delta K_t.$$

The SPC is the present value of these consumption losses, discounted at the consumption discount rate, per unit of displaced capital, ΔK_t:

$$SPC = \sum_{h=1}^{\infty}\frac{1}{(1 + r_c)^h}\frac{\Delta C_{t+h}}{\Delta K_t} = \sum_{h=1}^{\infty}\frac{(1 - s)(r_i + \mu)[s(r_i + \mu) + (1 - \mu)]^{h-1}}{(1 + r_c)^h}$$

$$SPC = \sum_{h=1}^{\infty}\frac{(1 - s)(r_i + \mu)}{1 + r_c}\left(\frac{s(r_i + \mu) + 1 - \mu}{1 + r_c}\right)^{h-1}$$

$$SPC = \frac{(1 - s)(r_i + \mu)}{r_c + \mu - s(r_i + \mu)}. \tag{4}$$

IV.   Estimation of a Numerical Value for the SPC

Equation (4) demonstrates that the SPC is a function of four parameters: the consumption discount rate r_c, the investment rate of return r_i, the savings rate s, and the depreciation rate μ. We draw on recent work to obtain estimates of these parameters. As in Li and Pizer (2021), Pizer (2021), and Moore et al. (2004), we use a depreciation rate of 10%. We use the 50-year average US savings rate of about 22% as measured by the gross fixed capital formation as a percentage of gross domestic product from the World Bank.[8] We vary estimates of the consumption discount rate and the investment rate of return, as estimates of these have varied in recent years. We focus on a value of 2% for the consumption discount rate, which reflects a growing consensus that such a value is a more appropriate estimate of the consumption discount rate than Circular A-4's 3% value (CEA 2017; Rennert et al. 2021, 2022; Carleton and Greenstone 2022; EPA 2022; Newell, Pizer, and Prest 2022). This is also roughly in line with OMB's consumption rate estimate of 1.7% in its recently proposed update to Circular A-4. We also include Circular A-4's existing benchmark of 3% for the consumption discount rate for comparison. There is less evidence that the investment rate of return has changed materially from the 2003 Circular A-4's 7% estimate (CEA 2017). Updated data based on the approach of Gomme, Ravikumar, and Rupert (2011) also suggests the pretax return on capital remains about 7% without any adjustment for risk.[9]

As previously noted, the assumed wedge between the risk-free consumption and investment rates of return owes to the economic distortion introduced by taxes. However, the implied tax wedges that would rationalize a 7% investment rate with a 2% or 3% consumption rate are 71% and 57% respectively, which is implausibly high compared with the average historical capital tax rates of around 35% in the Gomme data (i.e., $[7\% - 2\%]/7\% = 71\%$ and $[7\% - 3\%]/7\% = 57\%$).[10] In any numerical estimation of the SPC, one should therefore assess whether the tax rate implied by the spread between r_c and r_i is reasonable, and these implied rates are clearly not. This suggests an inconsistency in the triplet values of $r_c = 2\%$, $r_i = 7\%$, and $\tau \approx 35\%$.

The somewhat obvious source of this inconsistency is that the estimated historical capital return of 7% is not risk free, and because of this embedded risk premium, it would not be appropriate to use 7% as the relevant investment return for the purposes of estimating the SPC. Best practice in BCAs warrants separating discounting from risk and discounting using

relatively risk-free rates (Lind et al. 2011). Indeed, estimates of the equity
risk premium are substantial; the data set maintained by Damodaran
(2022) suggests that the risk premium has averaged about 4% historically.[11]
Subtracting this 4% risk premium from the unadjusted 7% investment
rate of return yields a risk-adjusted pretax investment return of about
3% (not to be confused with Circular A4's current 3% consumption discount rate). Subtracting taxes from this risk-adjusted 3% investment rate
using the above 35% average capital tax rate yields 1.95%, which closely
aligns with the 2% consumption discount rate favored above and vali-
dates the internal consistency of these values. For this reason, we focus
on a central triplet of r_c = 2%, r_i = 3.1%, and τ = 35% in calculating the
SPC (where all discount rates are in real terms). We also show alternative
sets of SPC calculations using variations in the key parameters, where
we vary the tax rate and infer the investment rate accordingly as r_i =
$r_c/(1 - \tau)$.

Table 1 shows the results. Panel A shows the results under Circular A-
4's 3% consumption rate. We start in row 1 using both of Circular A-4's
recommended rates, 3% and 7%, which yields an SPC value of 1.43. As
previously noted, however, the implied tax wedge between the two
rates is implausibly high at 57%. Rows 2–4 retain the 3% consumption
rate but instead calculate the investment return consistent with reasonable estimates of the capital tax rate (30%, 35%, and 40%), yielding SPC
values of 1.13, 1.16, and 1.20, respectively.

Panel B updates the consumption rate to 2% to correspond with the
aforementioned consensus that risk-free interest rates have trended
downward since Circular A-4 was written in 2003. If we use this lower
consumption rate but retain Circular A-4's 7% investment rate, we
would find an SPC of 1.6, but again with an implausibly high implied
tax wedge of 71%. Calculating the investment rate by grossing up the
2% rate according to our three capital tax rates yields SPC values of
1.09, 1.12, and 1.15. We take as our central estimate the SPC value of
1.1, corresponding to a 2% consumption discount rate, a 35% tax rate,
and a 3.1% pretax risk-adjusted investment rate of return (all in real
terms). Using OMB's proposed 1.7% discount rate and our three tax
rates would yield very similar SPC values of 1.08, 1.10, and 1.13 (not
shown in table 1), all of which similarly round to our central value of
1.1.

In panel C, we compare these values to the SPC estimates from Moore
et al. (2004), which presents estimates under two approaches to calibrat-
ing the parameter that corresponds to consumption rate of interest in

equation (4).[12] Moore et al. use slightly different rates of return from our central case, and they use a lower savings rate of 17%, although the SPC estimates are not very sensitive to the savings rate. They find two SPC values: 1.33 and 1.09, with 1.09 representing their preferred estimate. The parameters underlying their 1.33 estimate once again imply an implausibly high implied tax wedge of 67%.

Overall, table 1 suggests a range of SPC estimates tied to the chosen consumption and investment rates with SPC values of between 1.09 and 1.60, with a central value of about 1.1. If we limit ourselves to scenarios with plausible tax wedges of 30%–40%, the range of reasonable SPC values narrows to between 1.1 and 1.2. In summary, we propose an SPC value of 1.1 based on the parameter values in row 7 of table 1. This value is the same as the recommendation in Moore et al. (2004) and is very close to the value proposed in Pizer (2021).[13]

Table 1
Estimates of the SPC under Different Parameters

Description (%)	Consumption Rate of Interest (r_c) (%)	Investment Rate of Return (r_i) (%)	Savings Rate (s) (%)	SPC	Tax Wedge (%)	Is the Tax Wedge Plausible?
Panel A: Using a 3% Consumption Rate						
(1) $r_c = 3$ and $r_i = 7$	3	7	22	1.43	57	X
(2) $\tau = 30$	3	4.3	22	1.13	30	✓
(3) $\tau = 35$	3	4.6	22	1.16	35	✓
(4) $\tau = 40$	3	5.0	22	1.20	40	✓
Panel B: Using a 2% Consumption Rate						
(5) $r_c = 2$ and $r_i = 7$	2	7	22	1.60	71	X
(6) $\tau = 30$	2	2.9	22	1.09	30	✓
(7) $\tau = 35$	2	3.1	22	1.12	35	✓
(8) $\tau = 40$	2	3.3	22	1.15	40	✓
Panel C: Comparison with Moore et al. (2004)						
(9) Moore et al. (2004) CRI-SPC	1.5	4.5	17	1.33	67	X
(10) Moore et al. (2004) OGR-SPC	3.5	4.5	17	1.09	22	✓

Note: All calculations use a depreciation rate of 10%, as in Li and Pizer (2021), Pizer (2021), and Moore et al. (2004). Rows 1, 5, 9, and 10 assume the investment return and compute the implied tax wedge, whereas rows 2–4 and 6–8 assume the tax wedge and compute the implied investment rate of return. SPC = shadow price of capital; CRI = consumption rate of interest; OGR = optimal growth rate model.

V. A Simple Approach to the SPC, with an Illustrative Example

With a value for the SPC in hand, its application is straightforward: simply adjust any capital-displacing costs (or benefits) in any year upward by multiplying by the SPC. Formally, assuming that a share α of costs displaces capital, and share $(1 - \alpha)$ of costs displaces consumption, then adjusted costs would be calculated as

$$\text{Adjusted Costs} = \alpha \text{SPC(Unadjusted Costs)}$$
$$+ (1 - \alpha)(\text{Unadjusted Costs}).$$

Although historically the focus has been on adjusting costs for capital displacement, we take a more balanced approach in what follows, also accounting for the possibility that benefits may augment investment, rather than consumption. Given this, the approach for adjusting benefits is the same as adjusting costs. These calculations convert costs and benefits into consumption equivalents, so all such adjusted costs and benefits can then be directly compared and discounted at the consumption discount rate. This allows analysts to dispense with the common but inappropriate approach of using the investment rate of return and avoid the inconsistency of different discount rates in a single analysis.

The use of an investment rate further assumes all costs displace capital and no benefits accrue to capital, which may or may not be a reasonable assumption. By contrast, the SPC approach allows for a more nuanced assessment of capital impacts by applying the SPC only to the estimated share of costs and benefits that fall on capital. In some applications, the appropriate shares may be clear. As an alternative, we propose three general cases. The first is a default, central case that assumes that the share of all costs and benefits affecting investment is equal to the savings rate, which we have set to 22% in the preceding analysis based on historical averages. Savings augment investment, and therefore assuming as a central benchmark that 22% of costs and benefits affect investment (rather than consumption directly) is consistent with overall economic conditions.

For the other two cases, we propose the inclusion of two extreme cases that assume either that all costs displace capital or that all benefits augment capital. These two extremes would bound the central case that assumes that 22% of costs and benefits fall on investment. All cases use the consumption discount rate, bringing clarity and consistency to the appropriate discount rate.

This SPC sensitivity approach is both simpler and much better grounded in welfare economics than the current 7% approach and can be implemented with currently available information. Moreover, it is much less biased in its assumptions with regard to whether costs displace investment or benefits augment investment—the latter possibility being underappreciated (Li and Pizer 2021). For example, reduced damages from climate change may prevent destruction of long-lived assets, such as coastal infrastructure, and reduced mortality avoids the destruction of human capital as well as leading to more savings and investment.

This approach also addresses an important set of recommendations of a formative report by the National Academies on the social cost of greenhouse gas (NASEM 2017) that discounting approaches in BCAs having climate impacts should apply a consumption discount rate to consumption-equivalent impacts and be internally consistent across various categories of benefits and costs (Prest, Pizer, and Newell 2021; Rennert et al. 2021).

To demonstrate the simplicity of the SPC sensitivity approach, we show how analysts could have implemented the SPC in the RIA for the 2015 Clean Power Plan. That RIA compared costs and benefits calculated using different discount rates, raising concerns about analytical consistency. The SPC approach would avoid such concerns but still account for the important issue of capital displacement.

For reference, figure 1 shows the main panel of the original table from the Clean Power Plan RIA, illustrating the problematic mixing of different discount rates. Table 2 shows a recreation of the 2015 Clean Power

Table ES-9.   Monetized Benefits, Compliance Costs, and Net Benefits Under the Rate-based Illustrative Plan Approach (billions of 2011$) [a]

	Rate-Based Approach					
	2020		2025		2030	
Climate Benefits [b]						
5% discount rate	$0.80		$3.1		$6.4	
3% discount rate	$2.8		$10		$20	
2.5% discount rate	$4.1		$15		$29	
95th percentile at 3% discount rate	$8.2		$31		$61	
	Air Quality Co-benefits Discount Rate					
	3%	7%	3%	7%	3%	7%
Air Quality Health Co-benefits [c]	$0.70 to $1.8	$0.64 to $1.7	$7.4 to $18	$6.7 to $16	$14 to $34	$13 to $31
Compliance Costs [d]	$2.5		$1.0		$8.4	
Net Benefits [e]	$1.0 to $2.1	$1.0 to $2.0	$17 to $27	$16 to $25	$26 to $45	$25 to $43

Fig. 1.   Original clean power plan regulatory impact analysis table

Table 2

Monetized Benefits, Compliance Costs, and Net Benefits of the 2015 Clean Power Plan, under 2015 RIA and Updated SPC Approach, 3% Consumption Discount Rate

		Value (Billions of 2011$)			
		2020	2025	2030	Source
	Benefits				
(1)	Climate benefits (3% rate)	2.8	10	20	Table ES-9
(2)	Air quality health cobenefits	.7–1.8	7.4–18	14–34	Table ES-9
(3)	Total benefits (no SPC adjustment)	3.5–4.6	17.4–28	34–54	(1) + (2)
(3a)	Adjusted benefits, assuming 22% capital augmentation	3.6–4.7	17.8–28.6	34.7–55.2	(3) × 22% × SPC + (3) × (1 − 22%)
(3b)	Adjusted benefits, assuming 100% capital augmentation	3.9–5.1	19.19–30.8	37.4–59.4	(3) × SPC
	Compliance costs				
(4)	Costs (no SPC adjustment)	2.5	1.0	8.4	Table ES-9
(4a)	Adjusted costs, assuming 22% capital displacement	2.6	1.0	8.6	(4) × 22% × SPC + (4) × (1 − 22%)
(4b)	Adjusted costs, assuming 100% capital displacement	2.8	1.1	9.2	(4) × SPC
	Net benefits				
(5)	No SPC adjustment	1.0–2.1	16.4–27.0	25.6–45.6	(3)–(4) and Table ES-9
(6)	22% of costs and benefits impact capital	1.0–2.1	16.8–27.6	26.2–46.6	(3a)–(4a)
(7)	100% of costs displace capital	.8–1.9	16.3–26.9	24.8–44.8	(3)–(4b)
(8)	100% of benefits augment capital	1.4–2.6	18.1–29.8	29.0–51.0	(3b)–(4)

Note: We use shadow price of capital (SPC) = 1.1 in all cases. Some values differ slightly from those in fig. 1 due to rounding. EPA Clean Power Plan RIA (Regulatory Impact Analysis) available at https://www3.epa.gov/ttnecas1/docs/ria/utilities_ria_final-clean-power-plan-existing-units_2015-08.pdf.

Plan BCA using the SPC approach. We show the net benefits calculation using the "snapshot" approach for three specific years—2020, 2025, and 2030—as was done in the original RIA. The original RIA mixed 3% and 7% discount rates, but we dispense with the need for the 7% discount rate by accounting for the potential for capital displacement using the SPC. This greatly simplifies the net benefits table.

If the 10% premium is only applied to 22% of the costs or benefits (as per the above central recommendation), the adjustment to costs is smaller. For costs, this yields $2.55, $1.02, and $8.58 billion (row 4a). The adjustment to benefits is similarly modest, changing benefits in 2030 from $34–$54 billion to $34.7–$55.2 billion (row 3a).

Putting these together, the estimated net benefits are similarly little changed when we apply the SPC on both sides of the ledger, increasing net benefits in 2030 from \$25.6–\$45.6 billion to \$26.2–\$46.6 billion (row 6). That is, net benefits in 2030 change by 2.2%, as the 10% premium is applied to the 22% of both costs and benefits affecting capital.

Our bounding cases are shown in rows 7 and 8. In the first extreme case of applying the SPC to 100% of costs (but not to benefits), net benefits in 2030 change from \$25.6–\$45.6 billion (row 5) to \$24.8–\$44.8 billion (row 7). In the other extreme sensitivity case, we apply the SPC to 100% of benefits to account for the potential capital impacts of environmental improvements, such as reduced mortality bolstering the value of human capital, or individual savings. This increases estimated net benefits in 2030 from \$25.6–\$45.6 billion (row 5) to \$29–\$51 billion (row 8).

Stepping back, it is notable that even with a wide range of assumptions about capital displacement, the estimated annual benefits across rows 5 through 8 are generally within relatively narrow ranges of each other. Focusing on 2030, across all scenarios the maximum difference between estimates is 15%—the two extreme estimates of \$24.8 billion in row 7, assuming all costs displace capital, versus \$29.0 billion in net benefits in row 8, assuming all benefits augment capital. This contrasts with the major sensitivity exhibited when using a 7% discount rate for climate benefits instead of 3%, which can change gross benefits by about a factor of 9 (see appendix fig. A1 in Li and Pizer 2021).

Note that even if we were to use an SPC on the upper end of the plausible range—1.4 in row 1 of table 1, consistent with a 3% consumption rate and a 7% investment rate—the net benefits would be similarly much less sensitive under the SPC approach than under the approach of simply discounting at those two rates. For example, using a 7% discount rate for benefits would reduce net benefits in 2030 by approximately \$19–\$21 billion: \$20 billion versus approximately \$20/9 = \$2 billion in climate benefits, plus \$1–\$3 billion in reduced health benefits (see fig. 1). By contrast, applying an SPC of 1.4 to 100% of the \$8.4 billion in costs in 2030 would reduce net benefits by a much smaller \$3.4 billion. This again demonstrates the inappropriate nature of relying on a 7% investment discount rate instead of using the welfare-grounded SPC approach, particularly when a BCA includes long-lived impacts like climate benefits that are sensitive to the discount rate.

Indeed, most of that disparity between the two approaches (changing net benefits by \$18–\$20 billion when using a 7% discount rate versus \$3.4 billion under the SPC approach) is attributable to changes in long-lived climate benefits as measured by the social cost of carbon. For shorter-lived, nonclimate benefits, the effects of the two approaches are much closer to each other. As previously noted, the SPC approach applied to all costs using an SPC of 1.4 reduces net benefits by $3.4 billion in 2030, whereas the use of a 7% discount rate reduces health benefits, which are near-term impacts, by the similar amount of $1–$3 billion (see fig. 1). This reinforces the earlier analytical result that the use of the SPC is especially important when impacts to be discounted are long-lived.

VI.   Conclusion

Government analysts have long used discount rates based on investment rates of return to approximate the effect of capital displacement. However, as we discuss, this approach is very inappropriate and produces highly biased results, in particular in the context of decisions involving long-lived impacts like climate change. We demonstrate how analysts can use the welfare-grounded SPC approach in a straightforward manner to account for concerns about capital displacement in federal regulatory analysis. We propose a central SPC value of 1.1, with a reasonable range of 1.1–1.2. This estimate could easily be implemented in regulatory analysis by multiplying any costs or benefits that fall on capital by the SPC. If the share of costs or benefits is not known, then analysts can conduct sensitivity analyses to bound the effect of capital by alternatively assuming all costs and no benefits fall on capital, and vice versa. We illustrate how it could be easily implemented in practice using the example of the 2015 Clean Power Plan RIA. This shows that estimated net benefits results are far less sensitive to capital displacement concerns under the welfare-grounded SPC approach as compared with the inappropriate approach of using an unadjusted 7% investment rate of return. Our work is particularly important given the ongoing efforts to revise the federal guidance document for best practices in BCA and discounting, Circular A-4, to "reflect new developments in scientific and economic understanding."

Endnotes

Author email addresses: Pizer (pizer@rff.org), Prest (prest@rff.org). For acknowledgments, sources of research support, and disclosure of the authors' material financial relationships, if any, please see https://www.nber.org/books-and-chapters/environmental-and-energy-policy-and-economy-volume-5/shadow-price-capital-accounting-capital-displacement-benefit-cost-analysis.

1. See https://www.federalregister.gov/documents/2023/04/07/2023-07364/re
quest-for-comments-on-proposed-omb-circular-no-a-4-regulatory-analysis.

2. See https://www.federalregister.gov/documents/2021/01/26/2021-01866/mod
ernizing-regulatory-review.

3. The 30-year average spanning the years 1991–2020 yields a value very close to 2%.

4. We later show that in addition to accounting for capital displacement by compliance costs, a more balanced approach to applying the SPC would allow for the possibility that benefits may also augment capital.

5. In this special case, the $1 of costs is assumed to accrue immediately, so it need not be discounted.

6. Specifically, $10/1.052^{40} - \$1 = \$0.31$.

7. Boardman et al. (2017) note that transaction costs could also play a role, but in the modern liquid financial system it is difficult to believe these would be large. As in the literature, we focus on taxes as the main driver.

8. Data from https://data.worldbank.org/indicator/NE.GDI.FTOT.ZS?locations=US. 22% (more specifically, 21.6%) represent the average from 1972 to 2021, which is the longest period available. The 30-year average (1992–2021) is 21.0%.

9. Data are available at https://paulgomme.github.io/#data. Over the longest time period available (Q2 1947–Q4 2021), the pretax return to capital averaged 7.4%. The 30-year average (Q1 1992–Q4 2021) was 6.7%.

10. According to the Gomme data, the tax rate on capital has averaged 35% over the longest available time span (Q1 1947–Q1 2020). The 30-year average (Q2 1990–Q1 2020) is 30%.

11. The average over the longest available period (1960–2022) of Damodaran's central risk premium estimate is 4.2% (using the "Implied ERP [FCFE]" column of his "histimpl .xls" data set, available at https://pages.stern.nyu.edu/adamodar). The 30-year average (1993–2022) is 4.4%.

12. These two cases both use the SPC but vary in the parameter used in place of the consumption rate of interest. The first approach is the approach described in this paper: the consumption rate of interest combined with the SPC, or CRI-SPC. The second replaces the consumption rate of with the equilibrium condition of a Ramsey-style optimal growth rate model, or OGR-SPC.

13. Pizer (2021) recommends an SPC value of 1.2, which is based on a 40% tax rate, as in rows 4 and 8, and a slightly different savings rate, which together yielded an estimate of 1.2.

References

Boardman, Anthony E., David H. Greenberg, Aidan R. Vining, and David L. Weimer. 2017. *Cost-Benefit Analysis: Concepts and Practice*. Cambridge: Cambridge University Press.

Bradford, David F. 1975. "Constraints on Government Investment Opportunities and the Choice of Discount Rate." *American Economic Review* 65 (5): 887–99.

Carleton, Tamma, and Michael Greenstone. 2022. "A Guide to Updating the US Government's Social Cost of Carbon." *Review of Environmental Economics and Policy* 16 (2): 196–218.

CEA (Council of Economic Advisers). 2017. "Discounting for Public Policy: Theory and Recent Evidence on the Merits of Updating the Discount Rate." Issue Brief. https://obamawhitehouse.archives.gov/sites/default/files/page/files/201701_cea_discounting_issue_brief.pdf.

Damodaran, Aswath. 2022. "Equity Risk Premiums (ERP): Determinants, Estimation, and Implications—The 2022 Edition." March 23. https://ssrn.com/abstract=4066060.

EPA (Environmental Protection Agency). 2022. "Report on the Social Cost of Greenhouse Gases: Estimates Incorporating Recent Scientific Advances." External Review Draft. https://www.epa.gov/system/files/documents/2022-11/epa_scghg_report_draft_0.pdf.

Gomme, Paul, B. Ravikumar, and Peter Rupert. 2011. "The Return to Capital and the Business Cycle." *Review of Economic Dynamics* 14 (2): 262–78.

Li, Qingran, and William A. Pizer. 2021. "Use of the Consumption Discount Rate for Public Policy over the Distant Future." *Journal of Environmental Economics and Management* 107 (May): 102428. https://doi.org/10.1016/j.jeem.2021.102428.

Lind, Robert C. 1990. "Reassessing the Government's Discount Rate Policy in Light of New Theory and Data in a World Economy with a High Degree of Capital Mobility." *Journal of Environmental Economics and Management* 18 (2): S8–S28.

Lind, Robert C., Kenneth J. Arrow, Gordon R. Corey, Partha Dasgupta, Amartya K. Sen, Thomas Stauffer, Joseph E. Stiglitz, and Jacob A. Stockfisch. 2011. *Discounting for Time and Risk in Energy Policy*. Washington, DC: RFF. https://doi.org/10.4324/9781315064048.

Lyon, Randolph M. 1990. "Federal Discount Rate Policy, the Shadow Price of Capital, and Challenges for Reforms." *Journal of Environmental Economics and Management* 18 (2): S29–S50.

Marglin, Stephen A. 1963a. "The Opportunity Costs of Public Investment." *Quarterly Journal of Economics* 77 (2): 274–89. https://doi.org/10.2307/1884403.

———. 1963b. "The Social Rate of Discount and the Optimal Rate of Investment." *Quarterly Journal of Economics* 77 (1): 95–111. https://doi.org/10.2307/1879374.

Moore, Mark A., Anthony E. Boardman, Aidan R. Vining, David L. Weimer, and David H. Greenberg. 2004. "'Just Give Me a Number!' Practical Values for the Social Discount Rate." *Journal of Policy Analysis and Management* 23 (4): 789–812.

NASEM (National Academies of Sciences, Engineering, and Medicine). 2017. *Valuing Climate Damages: Updating Estimation of the Social Cost of Carbon Dioxide*. Washington, DC: National Academies Press.

Newell, Richard G., William A. Pizer, and Brian C. Prest. 2022. "A Discounting Rule for the Social Cost of Carbon." *Journal of the Association of Environmental and Resource Economists* 9 (5): 1017–46.

Pizer, William A. 2021. "A Shadow-Price-of-Capital Approach to Harmonize Discounting for Greenhouse Gases in Broader Benefit-Cost Analyses." Comments on regulations, Resources for the Future, Washington, DC. https://media.rff.org/documents/OMB-2021-0006-0059_attachment_1.pdf.

Prest, Brian C., William A. Pizer, and Richard G. Newell. 2021. "Improving Discounting in the Social Cost of Carbon." *Resources*, October 21. https://www.resources.org/archives/improving-discounting-in-the-social-cost-of-carbon.

Rennert, Kevin, Frank Errickson, Brian C. Prest, Lisa Rennels, Richard G. Newell, William Pizer, Cora Kingdon, et al. 2022. "Comprehensive Evidence Implies a Higher Social Cost of CO_2." *Nature* 610 (7933): 687–92.

Rennert, Kevin, Brian C. Prest, William Pizer, Richard G. Newell, David Anthoff, Cora Kingdon, Lisa Rennels, et al. 2021. "The Social Cost of Carbon: Advances in Long-Term Probabilistic Projections of Population, GDP, Emissions, and Discount Rates." *Brookings Papers on Economic Activity* Fall:223–75.

White House. 2003. "Circular A-4." Office of Management and Budget, Washington, DC. https://obamawhitehouse.archives.gov/omb/circulars_a004_a-4.

Environmental Justice and the Clean Water Act: Implications for Economic Analyses of Clean Water Regulations

Tihitina Andarge, *University of Massachusetts Amherst,* United States of America
Yongjie Ji, *Iowa State University,* United States of America
Bonnie L. Keeler, *University of Minnesota,* United States of America
David A. Keiser, *University of Massachusetts Amherst,* United States of America
Conor McKenzie, *University of Minnesota,* United States of America

Executive Summary

Since President Clinton's Executive Order 12898, federal agencies have been required to conduct environmental justice analyses of federal rules and regulations. More recently, the Biden administration instituted several efforts to reform regulatory review and promote a more equitable distribution of environmental benefits and burdens. This paper seeks to understand how prior guidelines have been implemented in federal regulatory reviews related to the Clean Water Act and provide a baseline for future studies of the distributional effects of clean water regulations. We reviewed 18 regulatory impact assessments relating to the Clean Water Act conducted since 1992. Only five of these studies conducted a quantitative analysis of distributional impacts, and none of the 18 assessments found disproportionately adverse effects on low-income or minority communities. Anticipating that future regulatory review will require more comprehensive distributional analyses, we combine national data on the location of regulated point sources with demographic characteristics to determine the baseline distribution of water pollution facilities. Overall, we find that discharge locations tend to be located in areas with higher poverty rates, higher White population shares, and less education. We find that rurality partly explains this pattern. We conclude with a discussion of the policy implications of these analyses.

JEL Codes: Q50, Q52, Q53, Q56, Q58

Keywords: environmental justice, Clean Water Act, surface water pollution

Environmental and Energy Policy and the Economy, volume 5, 2024.

I. Introduction

Environmental justice (EJ) has featured prominently in the Biden administration's policy initiatives. Two major efforts, the Justice40 Initiative and the White House's memo on Modernizing Regulatory Review, seek to greatly expand the federal government's role in promoting equity as it relates to environmental improvements and regulations (White House 2021; USEPA 2022a).[1] The Justice40 Initiative seeks to direct 40% of the overall benefits of certain environmental federal initiatives to disadvantaged communities. The Modernizing Regulatory Review memo directs federal agencies to provide concrete suggestions for improving how regulatory review is performed with an eye to advancing social and racial equity while promoting regulations that promote traditional goals of economic growth and safeguarding public health and safety. Both initiatives were announced on President Biden's first day in office.

A large EJ literature discusses the goal of providing more equitable environmental policies and programs (Lee 2002; Mohai et al. 2009). Numerous studies have documented how low-income populations and communities of color in the United States are more likely to face greater exposure to air pollution (Colmer et al. 2020; Tessum et al. 2021; Wang, Apte, and Marshall 2022), extreme heat (Benz and Burney 2021), flood risks (Tate et al. 2021), and hazardous waste facilities (Bullard et al. 2008). In the water sector, researchers have found disparities in the affordability and quality of drinking water (Balazs and Ray 2014; Mueller and Gasteyer 2021), access to safe and reliable water distribution services (Deitz and Meehan 2019), and the enforcement of and compliance with clean water regulations (Konisky, Reenock, and Conley 2021; Mueller and Gasteyer 2021).

Only a handful of studies have investigated the distribution of facilities that discharge surface water pollution in the United States across social and demographic characteristics, and these have been at the state or regional scale (Wilson et al. 2002; Liévanos 2017; Son et al. 2021). As a result, there is limited information on how the benefits of federal regulations that target major sources of water pollution are distributed. Since 1970, the United States has spent more on surface water pollution control programs than on any other environmental initiative (Keiser and Shapiro 2019). The economic impacts of these investments remain poorly quantified (Keiser, Kling, and Shapiro 2019), raising questions about both equity and efficiency implications of federal water quality policies.

This paper combines a qualitative assessment of how agencies have attempted to assess ex ante the distributional impacts of proposed Clean

Water Act (CWA) rules and regulations with a quantitative analysis of the distribution of polluting facilities in federal data sets. We conduct the first analysis to better understand prior EJ efforts as they relate to federal surface water quality regulations, which often vary by industry. We conduct the second analysis for two reasons. First, our analysis highlights particular industries where EJ concerns may be most prevalent and thus may require more detailed focus in future industry-specific rules. Second, prior EJ analyses performed by the US Environmental Protection Agency (EPA) focus on the distributional consequences of proposed rules, not necessarily distributional differences in surface water pollution sources. Thus, our analysis complements these prior efforts to provide a more comprehensive picture related to surface water pollution.

We proceed by first characterizing how the EPA has implemented federal guidance under Executive Order (EO) 12898—Federal Actions to Address Environmental Justice in Minority Populations and Low-Income Populations (1994)—to assess the EJ impacts of surface water pollution regulations. We searched government databases and reports from the Office of Internal and Regulatory Affairs for economic analyses associated with the CWA, compiling a data set of 18 economic analyses of major water quality rules going back to 1992. For each economic analysis in our data set, we reviewed how the agency evaluated any potential justice or distributional impacts. Agencies are required to assess equity and distributional considerations as mandated in EO 12898, even if rules will have only positive or uniform effects on water quality. In our review, only five studies attempted to quantify distributional impacts, and no rule was determined to have disproportionately high or adverse effects on low-income or minority communities. Those rules which did not perform quantitative analysis made their determinations based on the rule's scope and effect. For example, a determination of no distributional effects was justified by including a statement that the rule was likely to have a limited effect on water quality or lead to general improvements in water quality that would not disproportionately burden certain communities.

The second step in our analysis assesses the distribution of industrial and municipal point source polluters across a range of demographic characteristics. Effluent standards for point source polluters are a cornerstone of the CWA, and thus a large fraction of economic analyses of the act has focused on these emitters. To explore how the potential distribution of water quality benefits varies with point sources, we compile three main categories of data: (1) the location and operation status of nearly 700,000 point source polluters from 1990 to 2022, (2) demographic and socioeconomic information of residents living within close proximity to these polluters, and (3) information on the type and amount of pollution from these sources. We capture the relationship between the number of pollution discharge locations and demographic data using pseudo-Lorenz curves, calculate related Gini coefficients, and employ cross-sectional models to assess relationships between point source variables and demographic characteristics. Although data limitations prevent us from examining the economic damages associated with this pollution, our analysis provides one of the first national pictures of how surface water pollution sources vary with demographics and socioeconomic characteristics.

Our results show that facility outfall locations, or discharge points, tend to be located in areas where a greater fraction of the population is White, living below the poverty threshold, and without a college degree. We also find that most outfalls are located in rural areas; the top 40% of US Census block groups in terms of rural population share contain nearly all outfalls. When we examine the distribution of outfalls within rural areas, we find less unevenness in the distribution of outfalls, suggesting that rurality may partly explain the overall pattern that we observe across all facilities.

We find that the presence of outfalls varies across industrial sectors. Pollution outfalls from industrial sectors such as mining, manufacturing, and wholesale trade are more likely to be located in areas with higher poverty and lower levels of education. We observe a similar pattern when we focus on industries within manufacturing that have more toxic discharges. When conditioning on rurality, we observe similar patterns across industries for poverty and education, though the distributions are more even. For some industries, we find different results for race. For example, in rural areas, we find that outfalls from manufacturing and transportation and communications tend to be concentrated in areas where a greater share of the population is non-White. In rural areas, we also find that outfalls from facilities with more toxic discharges are located disproportionately in Census block groups with higher non-White population shares. These findings suggest that when we look across the United States as a whole, water pollution outfalls tend to be located not only in areas with higher poverty and lower levels of education but also in areas with a greater share of the population that is White. When we focus more narrowly on the rural areas of the country where most outfalls are located, the relationships with poverty and education remain qualitatively similar, but there are some important differences with respect to the share of the population that is non-White.

Overall, our findings demonstrate the importance of considering distributional consequences of water pollution regulations and highlight particular industries where additional attention may be warranted. We conclude the study with recommendations to guide future assessments.

II.   EJ Benefits in EPA Analyses and Context within EJ Literature

A.   Literature

Federal Actions to Address Environmental Justice in Minority Populations and Low-Income Populations (EO 12898) was signed by President Clinton on February 11, 1994, with the following stated purpose: "To the greatest extent practicable and permitted by law . . . each Federal agency shall make achieving environmental justice part of its mission by identifying and addressing, as appropriate, disproportionately high and adverse human health or environmental effects of its programs, policies, and activities on minority populations and low-income populations in the United States and its territories."

In addition to EO 12898, federal guidance on benefit-cost analysis also permits consideration of distributional impacts. The Office of Management and Budget's (OMB) guidance to federal agencies on the development of regulatory analysis known as Circular A-4 (White House 2003) includes the following guidance for agencies in assessing distributional effects of proposed rules or regulations: "Where distributive effects are thought to be important, the effects of various regulatory alternatives should be described quantitatively to the extent possible, including the magnitude, likelihood, and severity of impacts on particular groups . . . Your analysis should also present information on the streams of benefits and costs over time to provide a basis for assessing intertemporal distributional consequences, particularly where intergenerational effects are concerned."

Together, EO 12898 and Circular A-4 affirm the importance of assessing distributional impacts of regulatory policies. Circular A-4 provides slightly greater methodological detail, noting that a quantitative analysis should be used where possible and that assessments should include information on the magnitude, likelihood, and severity of impacts over time. Both guidance documents stop short of prescribing specific methodologies, leaving agencies to make their own determination of affected populations, appropriate comparison groups, and whether any observed disparities count as "disproportionately high and adverse."

Previous scholars have reviewed the implementation of federal guidelines for EJ analysis across multiple federal agencies. Vajjhala, Szambelan, and van Epps (2008) found large gaps in the information required for effective analysis of potentially differential impacts on minority and low-income populations. A 2002 report by the National Environmental Justice Advisory Council found that implementation of EO 12898 varied greatly, with no consistent framework applied across agencies or regulations (NEJAC 2020). An EPA inspector general report released 10 years after the signing of EO 12898 found that the agency had yet to consistently integrate EJ into its day-to-day operations, had failed to take the critical initial steps to define the populations covered by the order, and had not developed criteria for determining disproportionate impacts (USEPA 2004b).

Clearly there is a perceived disconnect between the mandate to consider EJ impacts in federal regulatory analysis and the implementation of this guidance in practice. Earlier reviews looked broadly across multiple agencies, focusing on identifying the frequency of key terms such as "disproportionately high," "distributional consequences," and "achieving environmental justice" but not the actual methodologies or substance of any distributional analysis, and did not include more recent regulatory impact assessments in their reviews. Here, we build on these past studies with an explicit focus on regulations under the CWA.

B. Methods

We compiled all major rules and regulations related to the CWA by searching public reports, including the Reports to Congress on the Costs and Benefits of Federal Regulations (1995–2009), Costs of Federal Regulations and Unfunded Mandates on State, Local, and Tribal Entities (2010–14), and the Annual Reports to Congress on the Benefits and Costs of Federal Regulations and Agency Compliance with the Unfunded Mandates Reform Act (2015–20). These reports summarize significant regulatory activities for Congress and therefore should identify and report on any new or modified rules or regulations. We further supplemented this review through conversations with EPA staff economists. The development of regulations is governed by a rulemaking process, including a notice of proposed rulemaking and a public comment period. Agencies may produce analyses at each stage of the rulemaking process. Here we focused only on final rules (table A1), but we included each rule's supporting technical, economic, and environmental analysis documents.

For each of the 18 Clean Water rules in our database, we document the approach that EPA took to assess any potential distributional impacts of the rule or regulation. As noted above, to comply with EO 12898, EPA is required to assess whether programs, policies, and activities will have "disproportionately high and adverse human health or environmental effects" on minority populations and low-income populations. We reviewed each regulatory assessment for text related to EO 12898 as well as supporting materials or other analyses conducted as part of EPA assessments of the benefits and costs of water quality regulations.

Table A1 lists the 18 rules related to the CWA. For each rule, we examine the demographic characteristics used by EPA to assess disproportionate impacts, the spatial scale of the analysis including the selection of affected population and reference populations, the specific types of water-quality benefits assessed, and the final determination of any EJ impacts. In many cases, the text of the rule contained little information on the actual analytical procedures used to determine distributional impacts, which required us to look through supporting documentation in search of methodological details.

C.   Results

Of the 18 rules in our data set, no rule was deemed by EPA analysts to have disproportionately high or adverse human health or environmental effects on minority or low-income populations. In the majority of assessments, this determination was made because the proposed rule or regulation would be uniformly applied to all facilities or because regulations would improve environmental quality for all residents.

For example, the Effluent Limitations Guidelines and New Source Performance Standards for the Meat and Poultry Products Point Source Category (USEPA 2004a) includes the following brief text regarding environmental justice impacts under EO 12898: "EPA has determined that this rulemaking will not have a disproportionate effect on minority or low-income communities because the technology-based effluent limitations guidelines are uniformly applied nationally irrespective of geographic location. The final regulation will reduce the negative effects of meat and poultry products industry waste in our nation's waters to benefit all of society, including minority and low-income communities. The cost impacts of the rule should likewise not disproportionately affect low-income communities given the relatively low economic impacts of the rule."

Only five of the rules included a quantitative analysis of distributional impacts (table 1). In the 2015 Effluent Limitations Guidelines and Standards for Steam Electric Power rule (RIN 2040–AF77), the EPA evaluated the demographic characteristics of individuals living in proximity to steam electric facilities, individuals served by public water systems downstream, and populations exposed to steam electric power facility wastewater through consumption of recreationally caught fish. EPA found disparities between the affected population and state or national averages and determined that regulatory options that increase pollutant exposure compared with the baseline may disproportionately affect minority and low-income communities. However, the estimated changes in exposure between the baseline and regulatory options were small and EPA determined that these changes did not meet the criteria of disproportionately high and adverse effects.

The majority of rules (13 out of 18) included some mention of race and income as the demographic variables of interest. A few studies also considered indigeneity, national origin, effects on children, and impacts on subsistence anglers. However, the choice of demographics, as well as affected and comparison populations, was not consistent across analyses, and the justifications regarding which variables and populations to include were not entirely transparent. In the 2004 Final Regulations to Establish Requirements for Cooling Water Intake Structures at Phase II Existing Facilities, EPA calculated the poverty rate and the percentage of the population classified as non-White for populations living within a 50-mile radius of each of the 543 in-scope facilities and compared these rates with national averages. A 2014 rule on cooling water intake structures also used a 50-mile radius from a regulated facility to assess affected individuals and included any anglers who live outside of the 50-mile facility buffer but within a 50-mile radius of the river segments, or river reaches, nearest to the facilities.

For the rules that did assess potential benefits of regulation (or forgone benefits), the most commonly assessed benefits were impacts on subsistence fishing, cancer risks from exposure to toxic chemicals, and general health impacts. Beyond subsistence fishing for tribal communities, we found no mention of potential impacts on cultural values or other nonmaterial benefits of clean water.

In summary, in our review of the implementation of EO 12898 in rules and regulations related to surface water pollution under the CWA, we observed inconsistency in the scale and scope of analysis of distributional impacts. A majority of rules did not conduct a quantitative analysis of impacts, and no rules were determined to have "disproportionately high and adverse impacts." These findings are consistent with other recent

Table 1
Summary of Quantitative CWA Environmental Justice Assessments (1992–2019)

Rule	Demographic Characteristics Evaluated	Spatial Scale of Analysis	Benefits Assessed	Determination
National Emission Standards for Hazardous Air Pollutants for Source Category: Pulp and Paper Production; Effluent Limitations Guidelines, Pretreatment Standards, and New Source Performance Standards: Pulp, Paper, and Paperboard Category (1998)	Race, income, indigeneity	EPA analyzed subsistence anglers fishing in the vicinity of bleached kraft mills from the consumption of dioxin-contaminated fish. EPA also examined county-level race and income data to assess whether bleached kraft mills have a disproportionate effect on minority and low-income populations.	Subsistence fishing, cancer risks. Price increases due to increased compliance costs	EPA expects the final rule to reduce substantially the cancer risks to tribal populations.
Effluent Limitations Guidelines and New Source Performance Standards for the Metal Products and Machinery Point Source Category (2003)	Race, national origin, income level, indigeneity	EPA assessed counties traversed by water receiving discharges from 32 sample MP&M facilities and compared them with state averages.	Subsistence fishing, cancer risks, systemic health risk	EPA expects that the rule will neither promote nor discourage environmental justice.
National Pollutant Discharge Elimination System—Final Regulations to Establish Requirements for Cooling Water Intake Structures at Phase II Existing Facilities (2004)	Race, income	EPA analyzed demographics of communities within a 50-mile radius of affected facilities compared with national averages.	Subsistence fishing	All populations, including minority and low-income populations, would benefit from improved environmental conditions as a result of this rule.

Rule	EJ dimensions	Benefit population	Exposure pathways	Findings
National Pollutant Discharge Elimination System—Final Regulations to Establish Requirements for Cooling Water Intake Structures at Existing Facilities and Amend Requirements at Phase I Facilities (2014)	Race, income	EPA defined the benefit population as (1) all individuals who live within a 50-mile radius of the facilities and (2) any additional anglers who live outside of the 50-mile facility buffer but within a 50-mile radius of the river segments, or river reaches, nearest to the facilities. EPA compared this with the general state population.	Subsistence fishing	EPA expects that this final rule will help to preserve the health of aquatic ecosystems near regulated facilities and that all populations, including minority and low-income populations, will benefit from improved environmental conditions.
Effluent Limitations Guidelines and Standards for the Steam Electric Power Generating Point Source Category (2015)	Race, income	EPA assessed affected communities within 50 miles of steam electric power plants and compared them with state averages.	Subsistence fishing, cancer risks, IQ decrements, systemic health risks	EPA's analysis finds very small changes in exposure between the baseline and regulatory options, amounting to very small changes in risk for this population.

Note: This table provides a summary of the five quantitative environmental justice (EJ) analyses of the water pollution rules in our data set (1992–2019). It does not include the 13 water pollution rules that did not contain quantitative EJ analyses. CWA = Clean Water Act.

publications investigating the consideration of distributional and equity considerations in federal regulatory review across a broad range of agencies and policy domains (Robinson, Hammitt, and Zeckhauser 2016; Cecot and Hahn 2022; Revesz and Yi 2022).

III.   EJ Analysis of Point Source Polluters: Methods and Data

As noted above, President Biden has made EJ a priority of his administration. Indeed, proposed updates to the guidance documentation for analyzing the costs and benefits of regulations known as Circular A-4 were recently released by the OMB (White House 2023). The revised guidance includes an expanded section on proper procedures for conducting distributional analyses, including the importance of placing any proposed rules or regulations in context based on an assessment of baseline distributions of environmental benefits or burdens. The OMB guidance also states that it is "not sufficient for your analysis to merely state that the chosen alternative does not make relevant groups worse off; it is important to analyze and describe the benefits and costs of different regulatory alternatives for different groups." Given the limited nature of EJ analyses in prior regulatory reviews under the CWA, we present a baseline assessment of the distribution of regulated water pollution facilities that could inform future applications of distributional analyses of clean water rules or regulations.

A.   Methods

Our EJ analysis is descriptive in nature. We do not intend to describe causal relationships between socioeconomic characteristics and pollution. Rather, as an important first step, we seek to describe how the location of pollution outfalls varies with socioeconomic characteristics and demographics; we leave important questions of causality to future studies.[2]

Our analysis implements two empirical approaches. First, we construct pseudo-Lorenz curves that provide a visual representation of the relationship between water pollution sources and several measures of demographics and socioeconomic characteristics.[3] We call these pseudo-Lorenz curves because Lorenz curves traditionally focus on income distributions.[4] This representation enables an easy means to visualize how water-pollution sources are distributed within society. Our primary analyses focus on the number of water pollution outfalls, or discharge points, from regulated water pollution dischargers. We focus on facilities and their outfalls given that this information is more consistently reported over space and time than other measures. In supplementary analyses, we examine how outfalls may (imperfectly) reflect the quantity and toxicity of pollution. We link each outfall to its Census block group, given that this is the finest spatial unit for which we have available demographic information.

To construct our pseudo-Lorenz curves, we first rank the communities (2010 Census block groups) according to a particular socioeconomic variable (i.e., a measure of race, income, education, etc.). If there is more than one Census block group with the same value, we rank those Census block groups with the lowest number of outfalls (or other measure of pollution) first. This ranking forms the variable for our x-axis. We normalize the x-axis ranking from 0 to 1. Once we have ranked Census block groups, we calculate the cumulative distribution value of outfalls (or other measure of pollution) from 0 to 1. To form our pseudo-Lorenz curves, we plot the pair of calculated x and y values for each Census block group. In addition, for each pseudo-Lorenz curve, we compute the Gini coefficient, which is two times the area between the 45-degree line and the pseudo-Lorenz curve.[5] The Gini coefficient is a relative inequality index; an equiproportional increase in the amount of outfalls would leave the Gini coefficient unchanged even though the outfall gap would double.

In addition to these curves, we estimate complementary cross-sectional models that quantify the magnitude of the relationship between the presence of outfalls and these demographic and socioeconomic characteristics by estimating the following equation:

$$y_i = \alpha + \beta D_i + \varepsilon_i, \tag{1}$$

where y_i is an indicator for whether an outfall is present in Census block group t, D_i is one of the demographic or socioeconomic characteristics we consider, and ε_i is the error term. In supplementary analyses, we replace y_i with other measures of water pollution that we discuss below. To account for potential correlation in our error term within geographic areas, we cluster standard errors at the county level.

B.   Data

Our analysis uses three primary sources of data. Two of these sources provide information on the location and discharge of pollution from point sources in the United States. The third source provides information on residents within close proximity to these sources.

Point Source Location and Operating Status

We combine several data sets from EPA's Enforcement and Compliance History Online database and the Integrated Compliance Information System–National Pollution Discharge Elimination System (ICIS-NPDES) to construct a data set of outfalls active during the 1990–2022 period. We use the permit issue dates to pinpoint when a facility first becomes active.[6] If a permit is missing an issue date, we drop that observation. To determine when a facility becomes inactive, we use the permit termination date if the permit's status is "terminated" and the maximum of the termination, retirement, and expiration dates if the permit's status is "not needed." If a permit should have an end date but has missing values for the termination, retirement, and expiration dates, then we drop that observation. This provides us with information on 761,905 of 814,130 facilities in the United States.

We obtain the geographic coordinates for a facility's outfall(s) from ICIS-NPDES Discharge Points. We use the coordinates to geolocate each outfall inside a Census block group using the 2010 Tiger/Line Block Group shapefile. If an observation is missing outfall coordinates, we instead use the facility coordinates, which we supplement from ICIS-NPDES Facilities and the Facility Registry Service, and assume it has a single outfall at those coordinates. If a permit is missing both the outfall and facility coordinates, then we drop that observation. In addition, we drop facilities outside of the conterminous United States and offshore facilities because we are not able to locate them inside Census block groups. After this process, we are left with information on 687,788 facilities (863,511 outfalls).[7]

To determine which industrial division a facility belongs to, we use information on the industrial codes reported with the permits. We place facilities into 11 broad industrial categories based on their two-digit Standard Industrial Classification (SIC) codes: (1) Agriculture, Forestry, and Fishing; (2) Mining; (3) Construction; (4) Manufacturing; (5) Transportation and Communications Services; (6) Electric, Gas, and Sanitary Services; (7) Wholesale Trade; (8) Retail Trade; (9) Finance, Insurance, and Real Estate; (10) Services; and (11) Public Administration (see table A2 for descriptions of each industrial division). We place a facility in one of these categories if any one of its two-digit SIC codes belongs to that category.[8] Of the 687,788 facilities (863,511 outfalls), we are able to identify the industrial category for 385,613 facilities (551,072 outfalls). Because a sizable portion of facilities in our sample is missing industrial codes, focusing only on facilities with information on their SIC codes may lead to sample selection bias if missing values are nonrandom. Therefore, we conduct analyses on both the full sample and the subsample containing facilities with SIC information. In addition, we identify publicly owned treatment works (POTWs) using a facility type indicator associated with each permit, and we remove these facilities from the 11 industrial categories. We examine these facilities separately given their major point of emphasis within the CWA. There are 18,168 POTWs with 29,289 outfalls in our sample. Last, we identify Major dischargers in the pooled sample and in each industry.[9]

Effluent Data

In addition to the location, operating status, and industrial division of facilities, we obtain estimates of flow from ICIS-NPDES Discharge Monitoring Reports (DMRs). DMRs must be regularly submitted by facilities with permits that require sampling and monitoring, which tend to be large point sources, standard industrial dischargers, and POTWs.[10] The DMRs contain outfall-level information on flow and the quantity and concentration of the discharged pollutants. We restrict the data to observations for which the monitoring location code corresponds to gross effluent. We use these data to determine the amount of flow, in millions of gallons per day (MGD), discharged from an outfall as an imperfect proxy for the quantity of pollution, recognizing that higher flow does not necessarily correspond to higher pollution levels. There are several types of measures, called statistical base codes in ICIS-NPDES, for flow (e.g., 1-day geometric mean, 12-day average, 12-month average, etc.). We focus on monthly averages because this is one of the most frequently reported types of flow measures. Facilities calculate monthly averages by taking the average of all flow measurements at each outfall during a calendar month and including it in their DMRs.[11] Of 687,788 facilities, monthly average flow measurements are available for 68,608. We take the mean of monthly average flow at the Census block group level. As a separate check on this measure of flow, we use the volume and percentile of wastewater discharge estimated by the Climate and Economic Justice Screening Tool.[12]

Socioeconomic Data

Our socioeconomic and demographic data are from the 1990, 2000, 2010, and 2020 Censuses and 5-year American Community Survey (ACS) estimates for 2013 and 2019. Because the Census block group–level demographic information from ACS is based on the 2010 Census boundary, we normalize all demographics to 2010 Census block groups using the Integrated Public Use Microdata Series National Historical Geographic Information System project (IPUMS NHGIS).[13] In cases where there are no harmonized data series for our variables of interest, we use crosswalk matrices between 1990, 2000, 2010, and 2020 Census boundaries to construct our own harmonized series. The socioeconomic variables we use are the share of the population that identify as non-White, the share of the population that identify as Black or African American, the share of the population that identify as non-White Hispanic, the share of individuals with income lower than the federal poverty line, the share of the population ages 25 and above without a college degree or higher, and the share of population that is in a rural area. Given the number of possible variables, we limit our main analysis of pseudo-Lorenz curves to the share of the population that is non-White, the share of the population below the poverty line, the share of the population without a college degree or higher, and the share of the population living in a rural area.[14] This enables us to focus on measures that reflect some racial differences, income differences, education differences, and urban/rural differences. In the regression analyses, we further explore differences across additional measures of race and ethnicity (share Black or African American, share non-White Hispanic).

Matching Point Sources to Demographic and Socioeconomic Data

The availability of demographic and socioeconomic data at the Census block group level is somewhat limited temporally, which prevents us from constructing an annual panel data set of matched outfalls and demographics. For this reason, we match outfalls to demographic and socioeconomic data as follows: (1) outfalls active during 1990–99 are matched to 1990 Census data, (2) outfalls active during 2000–12 are matched to 2000 Census data, (3) outfalls active during 2013–18 are matched to 2013 ACS data, and (4) outfalls active during 2019–22 are matched to 2019 ACS data.[15]

Additional Sources of Data

The Toxic Release Inventory (TRI) database contains facilities that emit toxic chemicals with highly adverse health and environmental impacts. To account for potential toxicity-related differences in the distribution of outfalls along socioeconomic characteristics, we separately examine water pollution facilities that also appear on the TRI. In addition, as the presence of an outfall need not necessarily result in poor water quality, we perform additional analyses using measures that capture some ambient water quality conditions. Section 303(d) of the CWA requires states to construct a list of impaired waters that do not meet state-established water-quality standards. We obtain information on the total impaired stream length (km) with any listed CWA 303(d) impairment from the EPA's EnviroAtlas database.[16] As this information is provided at the subwatershed level, we aggregate the Census block group–level socioeconomic variables to the subwatershed level.[17] Then, we construct the pseudo-Lorenz curves by ranking subwatersheds rather than Census block groups.

Data Summary

Figure 1 displays the location of all outfalls used in our analysis. Our data provide broad coverage of water pollution facilities across the United States. Table 2 provides summary statistics from our most recent time period. In this period, there are more than 600,000 outfalls at active facilities in approximately half of all Census block groups. We have data on the industrial code for approximately 60% of these outfalls. Of these records, construction, manufacturing, mining, and electric, gas, and sanitary services have the most outfalls. In these summary statistics, we see that Census block groups with facilities across all industries tend to have a

Fig. 1.   Map of outfalls from active facilities (1990–2022). Color version available as an online enhancement.

Notes: This map depicts outfalls from facilities active at any point during the 1990–22 period.

Table 2

Number of Outfalls by Industrial Classifications and Corresponding Demographics (2019–2022)

Industry	No. of Outfalls	No. of CBGs	Non-White (%)	Non-College (%)	Poverty (%)	Rural Population (%)
Agriculture, Forestry, Fishing	9,403	3,963	11	78	12	83
Construction	91,375	20,490	20	71	14	34
Electric, Gas, Sanitary Services	45,654	17,126	17	75	14	57
Finance, Insurance, Real Estate	12,799	5,304	17	72	12	49
Manufacturing	90,311	26,377	22	77	15	43
Mining	64,841	9,747	15	79	14	73
Public Administration	12,949	6,059	19	72	14	38
Retail Trade	3,891	2,602	22	76	15	44
Wholesale Trade	20,902	8,906	24	79	17	39
Services	13,232	7,814	17	72	13	54
Transportation and Communications	31,012	11,155	25	75	16	30
POTWs	26,417	16,370	15	77	14	63
All industries w/ SIC code	374,295	65,580	20	74	14	41
All industries	632,609	97,643	21	72	14	37
All CBGs (CONUS average)	632,609	216,330	27	70	15	23

Note: This table provides summary statistics of the total number of outfalls and the distribution of outfalls by industrial classification for the 2019–22 period. The table also shows corresponding Census block group demographic information for all Census block groups and by industrial classification. A given facility may belong to multiple industries. "All industries w/ SIC code" summarizes these statistics for outfalls that correspond to facilities with at least one Standard Industrial Classification code. "All industries" summarizes these statistics for all outfalls, regardless of the availability of the industrial code. "All CBGs" summarizes these statistics for all Census block groups in the conterminous United States (CONUS) for comparison purposes. POTWs = publicly owned treatment works (i.e., public wastewater treatment).

lower non-White population share than Census block groups without permitted facilities. Compared with Census block groups without permitted facilities, the share without a college degree in Census block groups with permitted facilities is slightly higher for about half of the industries and substantially higher for the other half. The share below the poverty line is higher in some industries and lower in others compared with the average for the conterminous United States (CONUS). The biggest difference we see in these summary statistics is the share of the population living in a rural area. In our data, Census block groups with facilities are more likely to be classified as "rural" relative to CONUS averages.

IV. EJ Analysis of Point Source Polluters: Results

A. Pseudo-Lorenz Curves and Gini Coefficients

We begin by reporting the pseudo-Lorenz curves for the count of outfalls. Figures 2 and 3 display these results. We present results with the share of the population that is non-White, the share of the population below the federal poverty line, the share of the population without a college degree, and the share of the population living in rural areas. Each figure displays the distribution of outfalls in each time period. Gini coefficients are reported in parentheses in the legend, next to the line for the respective time period. The 45-degree line is a reference point for an equal distribution of outfalls. The way in which we define our indicator variables is such that any curve to the right of this 45-degree line suggests that these outfalls are located disproportionately in areas that are historically underserved or potentially disadvantaged. Similarly, a positive Gini coefficient indicates that outfalls are located disproportionately in such areas; a larger Gini coefficient suggests a greater concentration of outfalls in those areas.

In figure 2, we summarize these curves across all industrial sectors for each indicator. As described in Subsection III.A, we first rank Census block groups according to the particular demographic variable of interest. A normalized ranking from 0 to 1 serves as our x-variable. We then graph the cumulative distribution value of outfalls on the vertical axis. For example, figure 2B shows that in the 1990–99 time period, the first 40% of Census block groups ranked in terms of poverty (i.e., the richest 40% of Census block groups) contain approximately 20% of the total number of outfalls. The figure also shows that the poorest 20% of Census block groups (moving from 0.8 to 1.0 on the x-axis) contain approximately 30% of the total number of outfalls. We find that Census block groups with greater numbers of outfalls tend to be located disproportionately in areas with a higher share of the population that is White, in areas with a greater share of the population that is below the poverty line, and in areas with a greater share of the population that does not have at least a college education. However, the variation in outfalls has smoothed out over time for race, poverty, and education. It is important to note the means of the distributions may also be changing over time. Thus, although the distribution has become more equal over time, it is not necessarily the case

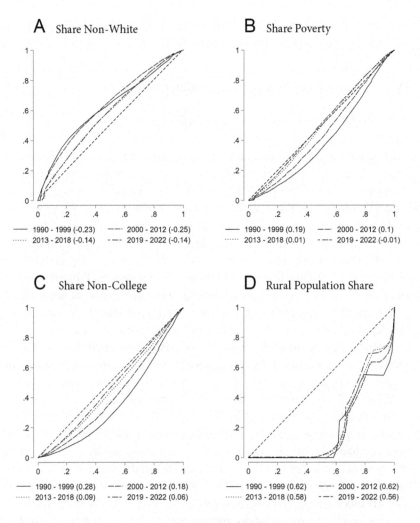

Fig. 2. Pseudo-Lorenz curves for the count of all outfalls by race, poverty, education, and rurality. (*A*) Share non-White. (*B*) Share poverty. (*C*) Share non-college. (*D*) Rural population share. Color version available as an online enhancement.

Notes: This figure displays pseudo-Lorenz curves for the count of all outfalls across all industrial sectors by the share of the population non-White (fig. 2*A*), the share of the population below the poverty line (fig. 2*B*), the share of the population without a college education or higher (fig. 2*C*), and the share of the population living in rural areas (fig. 2*D*). The 45-degree line represents equal distribution. Each figure shows pseudo-Lorenz curves for the 1990–99 period (solid line), 2000–12 period (even-dashed line), 2013–18 period (dotted line), and 2019–22 period (uneven dashed line). Gini coefficients for each period are in parentheses in the legend.

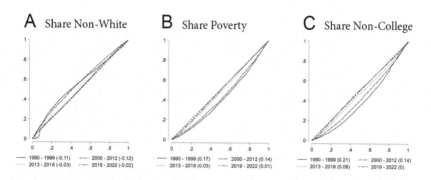

Fig. 3. Pseudo-Lorenz curves for the count of all outfalls by race, poverty, and education for the top 40% of Census block groups in terms of rural population share. (*A*) Share non-White. (*B*) Share poverty. (*C*) Share non-College. Color version available as an online enhancement.

Notes: This figure displays pseudo-Lorenz curves for the count of all outfalls across all industrial sectors by the share of the population non-White (fig. 3*A*), the share of the population below the poverty line (fig. 3*B*), and the share of the population without a college education or higher (fig. 3*C*). The 45-degree line represents equal distribution. Each figure shows pseudo-Lorenz curves for the 1990–99 period (solid line), 2000–12 period (even-dashed line), 2013–18 period (dotted line), and 2019–22 period (uneven dashed line). Gini coefficients for each period are in parentheses in the legend. We restrict the sample to the top 40% of Census block groups in terms of rural population share.

that welfare is higher in later periods. Further, the quality of the data is better for the latest two time periods. In particular, the 2015 Electronic Reporting Rule drastically changed state reporting requirements to EPA for certain facilities, potentially improving data quality.[18] Thus, although we continue to discuss changes over time, we emphasize that these changes may be attributable to changes in data quality rather than changes in the distribution of outfalls and that we cannot make any conclusions about welfare from this approach.

Outfalls tend to be located disproportionately in areas with a higher rural population share. In fact, in the first 50% of Census block groups in terms of rural population share (i.e., the least rural 50% of Census block groups), there are zero outfalls, which is why the pseudo-Lorenz curves in figure 2*d* are horizontal at the lower end of the support. Contrary to the findings for race, poverty, and education, the tendency for outfalls to be located disproportionately in rural areas has persisted over time. In all time periods, an overwhelming number of outfalls are located in the top 40% of Census block groups in terms of rural population share. Given this finding, we further examine the distribution of outfalls across race, poverty, and education among the top 40% of Census block groups in terms of rural population share. Figure 3 presents pseudo-Lorenz curves for these three indicators, conditioning on rurality. One notable finding is that the pseudo-Lorenz curves for the share of the population that is non-White are closer to the 45-degree line (i.e., the Gini coefficients are closer to 0), indicating that rurality may partly drive the pattern we observe when including all Census block groups. In fact, during the 2013–18 and 2019–22 periods, the distribution of outfalls is almost completely even in terms of the share of the population that is non-White. We observe a similar pattern for the share in poverty and share without a college degree, though the difference between the Gini coefficients for all Census block groups and more rural Census block groups is less stark during earlier periods.

Although figures 2 and 3 provide an overall snapshot of all outfalls, they may mask industry-specific heterogeneity that may be important, because the type, toxicity, and quantity of discharges vary across industries. For example, there is substantial heterogeneity in the amount of TRI chemicals discharged across industries, with electric, gas, and sanitary services; services, finance, insurance, and real estate; and manufacturing accounting for most TRI discharges. Similarly, when examining discharges of CWA priority pollutants—a list of 126 pollutants that are deemed to be toxic—facilities in manufacturing or electric, gas, and sanitary services are responsible for most of the discharges. As industrial patterns in the toxicity and amount of discharge exist, it may also be the case that the relationship between outfalls and demographic and socioeconomic characteristics is heterogeneous across industries. We also explore heterogeneity by industry to help inform future rules or regulations that may target industries.

In figures 4–7, we display bar graphs depicting Gini coefficients across different industrial sectors for our four main demographic and socioeconomic variables. For each time period, the width of the bar corresponds to the magnitude of the Gini coefficient, with positive Gini coefficients appearing to the right and negative Gini coefficients appearing to the left of 0, which is delineated by a vertical dashed line. In each bar graph, we order industries by the average size of the Gini coefficient across the four time periods so that industries most concentrated in areas with a higher share of traditionally underserved populations appear first. In these figures, we also show the Gini coefficient across all industries as a useful point of comparison. As a reminder, this category includes outfalls regardless of whether there is a reported industrial classification.

We first examine how outfalls are distributed across industries by the share of the population that is non-White (fig. 4). As with figure 2, we see

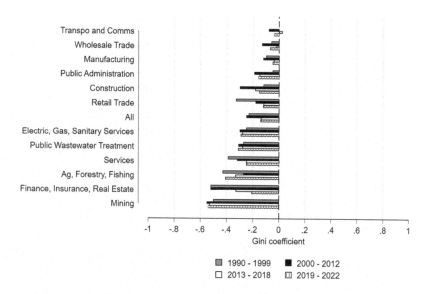

Fig. 4. Gini coefficients for distribution of outfalls by race and by industry. Color version available as an online enhancement.

Notes: This graph presents Gini coefficients by industry for the share of the population that is non-White. The category "All" depicts Gini coefficients across outfalls at all facilities, regardless of the availability of the industrial code. Gray bars are for the 1990–99 period, black bars are for the 2000–12 period, white bars are for the 2013–18 period, and patterned bars are for the 2019–22 period.

a similar pattern across most industrial classifications: outfalls tend to be located in areas with a greater fraction of the population that is White (i.e., negative Gini coefficients). We focus on (1) construction; (2) electric, gas, and sanitary services; (3) manufacturing; (4) mining; (5) public wastewater treatment; and (6) wholesale trade given the large number of these facilities (table 2). Three of these industrial categories—mining, public wastewater treatment, and electric, gas, and sanitary services—show a large number of outfalls in areas with a larger share of the population that is White, even more so than across all sectors. Contrary to the Gini coefficients computed using all sectors, the distribution for these industries is similar in all time periods.

Turning to figure 5, we examine how these outfalls vary by industrial classification and by the share of the population below the poverty line. Many industries follow a similar pattern that we see in the average across all sectors. However, mining, wholesale trade, and manufacturing in particular have more outfalls in areas with higher poverty. Unlike the overall picture, certain industries such as mining, public wastewater treatment,

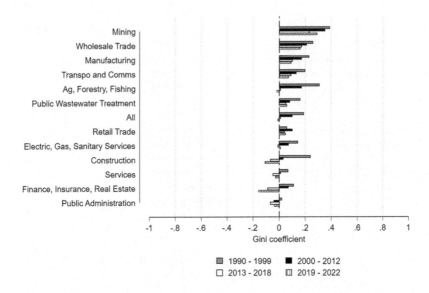

Fig. 5. Gini coefficients for distribution of outfalls by poverty and by industry. Color version available as an online enhancement.

Notes: This graph presents Gini coefficients by industry for the share of the population below the poverty line. The category "All" depicts Gini coefficients across outfalls at all facilities, regardless of the availability of the industrial code. Gray bars are for the 1990–99 period, black bars are for the 2000–12 period, white bars are for the 2013–18 period, and patterned bars are for the 2019–22 period.

and wholesale trade have changed relatively little over the study period. In contrast, industrial divisions such as construction, public administration, services, and finance, insurance, and real estate exhibit changes over time and are even slightly concentrated in lower-poverty areas during later time periods. A similar story appears in figure 6, where we display these results by industrial sector for the share of the population without a college degree. Similar to the overall picture, outfalls are located predominantly in areas with a larger share of the population without a college degree. This appears to largely be driven by outfalls from mining; wholesale trade; agriculture, forestry, and fishing; manufacturing; public wastewater treatment; and electric, gas, and sanitary services. This pattern has largely persisted over time for these industrial divisions. These results highlight these industries as potential focal points for future, or more in-depth, EJ analyses by the EPA and academic researchers. For the remaining industrial divisions, the distribution of outfalls has become more evenly distributed over time. Interestingly, for construction, outfalls are slightly concentrated in more educated areas during the latest two time periods.

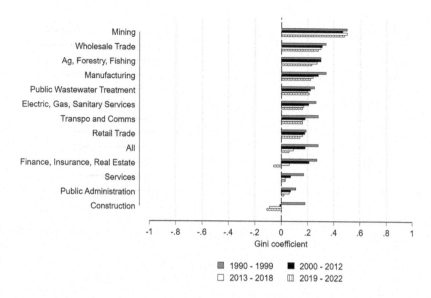

Fig. 6. Gini coefficients for distribution of outfalls by education and by industry. Color version available as an online enhancement.

Notes: This graph presents Gini coefficients by industry for the share of the population without a college degree or higher. The category "All" depicts Gini coefficients across outfalls at all facilities, regardless of the availability of the industrial code. Gray bars are for the 1990–99 period, black bars are for the 2000–12 period, white bars are for the 2013–18 period, and patterned bars are for the 2019–22 period.

Last, we examine how outfalls are distributed by the rural population share. Similar to the overall results, we find that outfalls are heavily concentrated in areas with a higher rural population share for all industries, and this pattern is highly persistent over time, regardless of industry (fig. 7). This prompts us to consider the distribution of outfalls across race, poverty, and education within more-rural areas. In figures A1–A3, we present bar graphs with Gini coefficients for the distribution of outfalls across dimensions of race, poverty, and education in the top 40% of Census block groups in terms of rural population share. Generally, even among rural Census block groups, outfalls tend to be located in areas that are predominantly White, though the Gini coefficients are much smaller in magnitude, indicating a relatively more even distribution (fig. A1).[19] For manufacturing and transportation and communications, however, the Gini coefficients are positive but small, indicating that outfalls from those industrial divisions somewhat tend to be located in areas with a higher share of the population that is non-White. For poverty and education, the overall industrial patterns largely hold, though the Gini coefficients

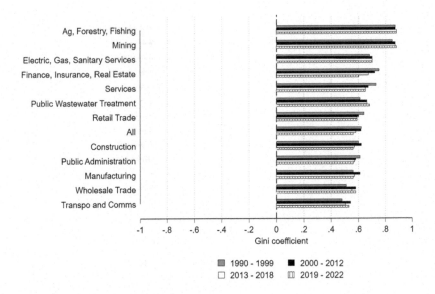

Fig. 7. Gini coefficients for distribution of outfalls by rurality and by industry. Color version available as an online enhancement.

Notes: This graph presents Gini coefficients by industry for the rural population share. The category "All" depicts Gini coefficients across outfalls at all facilities, regardless of the availability of the industrial code. Gray bars are for the 1990–99 period, black bars are for the 2000–12 period, white bars are for the 2013–18 period, and patterned bars are for the 2019–22 period.

are somewhat smaller (figs. A2 and A3). For three of the industries (construction, public administration, and finance, insurance, and real estate), outfalls are slightly concentrated in areas with lower poverty and a lower share of the population without a college degree. Interestingly, for mining and agriculture, forestry, and fishing, the Gini coefficients for the share in poverty are larger when conditioning on rurality. These results underscore the need for analyses that separately examine different industries; the distribution of outfalls across demographics and socioeconomics is heterogeneous.

As we demonstrate, there are some differences in locational patterns across industries. This is important because certain industries tend to discharge more toxic pollutants with greater potential harm to the surrounding community. The literature identifies two major industrial groups within the manufacturing industrial division as having a higher potential for harm: (1) Chemicals and Allied Products and (2) Petroleum Refining and Related Industries (Liévanos 2017). In figures A4 and A5, we present pseudo-Lorenz curves for the distribution of outfalls from these two industries for our four main demographic and socioeconomic variables. In general, the patterns are similar to what we observe for all industries. The results only diverge for the distribution of outfalls from Chemicals and Allied Products along racial lines; the pseudo-Lorenz curves are very close to the 45-degree line, indicating a relatively even distribution. Once we condition on the top 40% of Census block groups in terms of rural population share, however, outfalls from this industry are located disproportionally in areas with a higher share of the population that is non-White (fig. A6). For Petroleum Refining and Related Industries, however, we find that outfalls are more evenly distributed across racial lines once we condition on rurality (fig. A7). Again, this highlights the importance of performing industry-specific analyses, because ignoring these differences may mask potential EJ concerns.

We turn next to other measures of the presence of pollution. In figure 8, we display bar graphs depicting Gini coefficients for monthly average flow, outfalls at facilities deemed "Major" by the EPA, the number of permitted dischargers that also appear on the TRI, and the total length of impaired waterways within a HUC12 region.[20] Panel A presents the results for the non-White population share, panel B for the share below the poverty line, and panel C for the share without a college degree. When using monthly average flow as our measure of pollution, the results appear similar to the number of outfalls, with more equal distribution in terms of poverty. The results for outfalls from "Major" facilities and facilities that appear on the TRI are largely consistent with the overall number of outfalls. Last, we examine the total length of impaired waterways within

Fig. 8. Gini coefficients for other measures of pollution. (A) Share non-White. (B) Share poverty. (C) Share non-college. Color version available as an online enhancement.

Note: This figure displays bar graphs depicting Gini coefficients using the following measures: (1) monthly average flow, (2) outfalls at facilities deemed "Major" by EPA, (3) outfalls at facilities on the Toxic Release Inventory (TRI) with a water pollution discharge permit, and (4) total impaired waterway length. For each measure of pollution, we examine the distribution across the share of the population non-White (fig. 8A), the share of the population below the poverty line (fig. 8B), and the share of the population without a college degree (fig. 8C).

a subwatershed. Here, we find a departure from the prior results. This measurement of impaired waterways appears relatively evenly distributed across these demographic variables. One possibility is that richer and more educated areas are able to direct attention and funding toward listing polluted areas, as a first step toward remediation. However, we advise caution in relying too heavily on these impairment results, because they reflect state processes that do not necessarily capture the ambient status of all waterways.[21]

When we examine these other measures of the presence of pollution within the top 40% of Census block groups in terms of rural population share, some of the patterns in terms of race, poverty, and education change (fig. A8). The distribution of monthly average flow in terms of race, poverty, and education is more even within more rural Census block groups compared with all Census block groups. The distribution of outfalls from Major facilities is more even in terms of race, poverty, and education, though the Gini coefficients for race are now positive but small. Departing from previous results, the distribution of outfalls from facilities on the TRI is more concentrated in rural areas with a larger non-White population share. This is consistent with our findings for outfalls from Chemicals and Allied Products. With respect to poverty and education, outfalls from facilities on the TRI within the most rural Census block groups are slightly more evenly distributed compared with all Census block groups, though the overall patterns persist. Last, within rural Census block groups, impaired waterways are more concentrated in areas with larger White and non-college educated population shares but evenly distributed in terms of poverty. Again, we interpret the impairment results with caution.

We also investigated the distribution of wastewater discharge as collected by EPA and compiled in the Climate and Economic Justice Screening Tool. One would expect that the number of outfalls would roughly correspond to the amount of wastewater discharge within the same Census block group. Figure A9 plots a pseudo-Lorenz curve for the number of outfalls for all facilities ranked by the percentile of wastewater discharge. Here, we see that wastewater discharge corresponds nearly one to one with the number of outfalls.[22]

B. Regression Results

We complement the analysis in Subsection IV.A with regression results that examine how facility outfalls are correlated with socioeconomic characteristics. We examine the association between outfalls and the share of the population below the poverty line as well as the share of the population without a college degree. We split out our variable that captures one measure of race (share non-White) to examine the correlations between the number of outfalls and more specific measures of race and ethnicity such as share Black and share non-White Hispanic. We also add the rural population share to further examine how water pollution outfalls are distributed across the country.

Figure 9 summarizes our results across each of these six variables from regressions using all four time periods. These plots display coefficient estimates (solid dots) and 95% confidence intervals for each industrial classification for each particular variable of interest. No other controls are included in this specification, which allows us to examine the

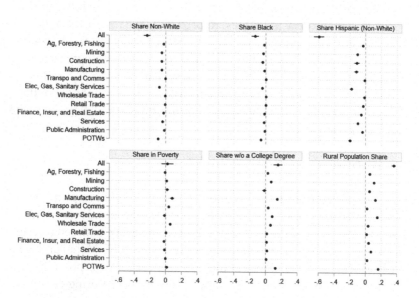

Fig. 9. Cross-sectional results between presence of outfalls and demographics. Color version available as an online enhancement.

Notes: This figure displays results from cross-sectional regressions of an indicator for the presence of outfalls in a Census block group versus a given measure of demographics. The outcome variable for the category "All" is an indicator for the presence of an outfall in a Census block group, regardless of industrial classification. This category includes facilities with and without Standard Industrial Classification information. For the remaining categories, we use industry-specific indicators for the presence of an outfall in a Census block group as the outcome variable. Coefficient estimates are shown in solid dots, and 95% confidence intervals are shown by the corresponding lines. Standard errors are clustered at the county level. Results are grouped by demographic variable and by industrial classification. The sample includes all four time periods. POTWs = publicly owned treatment works (i.e., public wastewater treatment).

cross-sectional variation in outfalls across the entire United States. Consistent with the pseudo-Lorenz curves, we find that outfalls are concentrated in areas of the country with a higher share of the population that is White, below the poverty line, and without a college education. We also find that outfalls are less likely to be in areas with a higher share of the population that is Black or non-White Hispanic. When we examine the variable for rural population share, we find a strong association with the presence of outfalls across all industries. The results are similar when we include state fixed effects (fig. A10), which suggests these associations hold within states as well as across states.

As with the pseudo-Lorenz curves, we examine correlations with other potential indicators of the quantity and toxicity from these outfalls. Figures A11 and A12 show results for outfalls at Major facilities and the monthly average flow at outfalls, respectively. The results for outfalls at Major facilities are qualitatively similar to those using the number of outfalls, though there is arguably less variation across demographics. The magnitude of the differences is also much smaller. The results for monthly average flow are also qualitatively similar to the total number of outfalls, though flow is very strongly correlated with rural population share and lower education levels.

V. Discussion

Our analysis contributes to an understanding of the EJ implications of federal regulatory policy. Decades of individual studies and meta-analyses have demonstrated statistically significant relationships between race and many types of environmental hazards (Ringquist 2005; Mohai and Saha 2007). However, the majority of these studies focus on air pollution and hazardous waste disposal, with relatively few studies focusing on the distribution of point source water pollution.

We aimed to address this gap through a two-pronged approach. First, we conducted a qualitative assessment of the implementation of EO 12898 in CWA rules and associated economic analyses by EPA. Second, we used data on the locations of permitted point source facilities to evaluate the distribution of outfalls across different demographic variables of interest. Our goal was to describe the content and quality of current EJ analyses in clean water rules, evaluate alternative approaches to assess disparities in the location of water pollution sources, and inform future analyses of EJ in proposed rules or regulations designed to protect or restore water quality.

In the review of existing water quality rules, we come to similar conclusions as previous assessments of the implementation of EO 12898 in federal regulatory review. Geltman, Gill, and Jovanovic (2016) and Banzhaf (2011) have strongly suggested the need for more rigorous distributional analysis. After reviewing all rules since 1992, we found that EPA never determined a clean water regulation to have disproportionately high and adverse impacts on low-income or minority communities. Although these findings could be correct, a lack of quantitative analysis within these reviews may leave one skeptical about the lack of EJ concerns. Further, the fact that a rule may not lead to adverse changes in low-income or minority communities does not necessarily imply that current EJ concerns are not important. In this regard, we also observed that EPA did not include publicly available data on baseline pollution exposure in their analyses. For example, in the regulatory impact assessment evaluating the 2003 Effluent Limitation Guidelines and Standards for Concentrated Animal Feeding Operations, EPA determined the rule would have no disproportionate effect on minority or low-income communities. In this case, EPA could have cited research on the distribution of CAFOs, which have been shown to be disproportionately located in minority communities and low-income communities (Wilson et al. 2002; Son et al. 2021). However, no further analysis or research was conducted, based on the justification that the rule would "benefit all of society."[23]

In our assessment of the baseline distribution of water polluting facilities in the United States, we found that water pollution sources are more likely to be located in areas with a larger share of the population that is White, below the poverty line, and without a college education. Overall, this pattern holds for most industries, though the extent of the disproportionate siting is heterogeneous. In later time periods, we observe more even distributions across these characteristics and across most industries. We also found that block groups with the greatest number of outfalls are more likely to be rural. Within the most-rural Census block groups, however, the demographic and socioeconomic patterns are a bit more mixed. For the share of the population that is non-White, depending on industry and toxicity, the distribution remains the same, becomes more evenly distributed, or even slightly concentrated in areas with higher non-White population shares. Of note, facilities discharging more toxic pollutants tend to be located in rural areas with higher non-White population shares. In general, the concentration of outfalls in areas with higher poverty and lower education is slightly lower within rural areas, regardless of industry or toxicity of discharges. Overall, our results suggest that rurality partly drives the observed patterns for the other demographic and socio-economic variables. However, we reiterate that our analysis does not address causal reasons for the location of these outfalls, but rather documents how they vary across space and socioeconomic characteristics.

We present a few takeaways from our assessment of the baseline distribution of polluting facilities that may be helpful for future EJ analyses. We found disparities across educational attainment, with greater numbers of pollution outfalls in Census block groups with lower levels of education. EO 12898 only requires analysts to assess impacts on "minority and low-income populations." Our analysis suggests that education may be an important factor to consider in future distributional assessments, especially because education attainment may be related to awareness of environmental hazards (Meyer 2015). In addition, the heterogeneity we observed across industries highlights the importance of performing industry-specific EJ analyses; our findings revealed greater EJ concerns for certain industries such as mining, public wastewater treatment, and manufacturing.

Relatedly, not all outfalls pose equal risks to adjacent populations, and examining outfalls with more harmful discharges in combination with those with relatively benign discharges may mask EJ concerns. Our analysis focusing on facilities with more toxic discharges is an imperfect exercise, as it uses a facility's industrial codes and appearance on the TRI to capture the toxicity of discharges. A more refined approach that uses the type, quantity, and concentration of the discharged pollutants could provide a more accurate picture of the distribution of water pollution (see Liévanos 2017 for an example of an approach that accounts for toxicity). To this end, recent agency investments such as the EPA's Risk-Screening Environmental Indicators (RSEI) database and the P2 EJ Facility Mapping Tool could increase the ease of future EJ analyses and the identification of toxic discharges.[24] Future work using more finely defined industrial categories focusing on specific pollutants may also improve our understanding of the distribution of water polluting facilities. Last, improved data collection on polluting facilities would greatly facilitate EJ analyses. The data sets we use are missing industrial codes for a substantial fraction of facilities, which could alter our industry-specific conclusions.

A. Limitations and Caveats

We acknowledge several limitations to our analysis that may affect the interpretation of our findings. A challenge in conducting distributional assessments is enumerating the affected population and associated baseline group. In our analysis, we assumed the affected population was all households within a Census block group containing a permitted facility. Some Census block groups with high concentrations of polluting facilities may not have demographic data associated with them because they are in unpopulated industrial areas. Adjacent populated block groups may be negatively affected by pollution from nearby facilities but would not be recorded in our analysis. An alternative would be to assess the affected population based on a proximity analysis (e.g., Mohai et al. 2009 assessed demographic characteristics within 1 mile of polluting facilities). As noted by Mansur and Sheriff (2021), facility-based analyses are not direct measures of welfare, because the unit of analysis is not the individual. The movement of water pollutants through surface water and groundwater is complex and requires more data-intensive hydrologic modeling to link outfalls with concentrations and transport pollutants downstream. In addition, it is important to determine the exposure of communities to pollution via direct or indirect consumption or water-contact recreation and the relative risk of certain subpopulations. Furthermore, a cumulative impacts framework requires that exposure to a particular pollutant is considered along with exposure to other pollutants, as well as factors that moderate exposure and damages including access to health care or resources to invest in avoidance behaviors (Hsiang, Oliva, and Walker 2019). Indeed, EPA notes that cumulative impacts are an important area for future focus (USEPA 2022b).

Inconsistent methodologies across distributional analyses also make it difficult to compare our results with previous studies. We know that selection of affected communities, reference populations, spatial unit of analysis, assumptions about exposure and health impacts, and the ability to control for other contributing factors have been found to affect the conclusions of past EJ studies (Anderton 1996; Mohai et al. 2009). As others have noted (Keeler et al. 2012; Keiser et al. 2019), water quality–related benefits remain difficult to quantify and monetize, making it challenging to assess net benefits of proposed rules or regulations. Welfare impacts of exposure to water pollution can be moderated or exacerbated by infrastructure, adoption of avoidance behaviors, preexisting health conditions, and baseline exposure to other contaminants, among other factors.

Our analysis offers limited insight into how changes in water pollution will affect other types of valued benefits, including recreation, cultural resources, nonuse benefits, or other aspects of human well-being. Water quality–related benefits, including the destruction of culturally valued species, loss of access to ceremonial springs, mercury contamination of fish, and polluted beaches and swimming places, can have a particular significance for EJ communities (EJCW 2005) but were beyond the scope of this analysis.

B.   Future Directions

Our retrospective analysis of the implementation of EO 12898 suggests that more work is needed to come to a shared definition of what constitutes a "disproportionately high and adverse human health or environmental effect" as it relates to water quality. Consistency across methodologies and their application will allow for more systematic assessment of impacts of proposed water quality rules or regulations. Agency analysis aside, there is also no agreed-upon methodology in the academic literature to assess disproportionality of environmental benefits and burdens. The draft updated Circular A-4 guidance from OMB calls for increased investment in distributional analysis but stops short of prescribing a standardized approach. Access to publicly available data on the location of polluting facilities and outfalls opens opportunities for analysis that could greatly improve on past assessments of water quality rules and regulations. Here, we demonstrate how analysts can use these data, along with sociodemographic information and other environmental variables, to assess potential distributional effects of changes that affect permitted facilities. Future analyses could assess the sensitivity of assumptions about the appropriate spatial unit to determine affected population, focus on specific industries or regulated contaminants, assess compliance records of regulated facilities, or link outfall data with toxicity information to understand relative levels of harm from water pollution. All of these approaches would increase the salience of environmental justice considerations in analyses of clean water rules.

Appendix

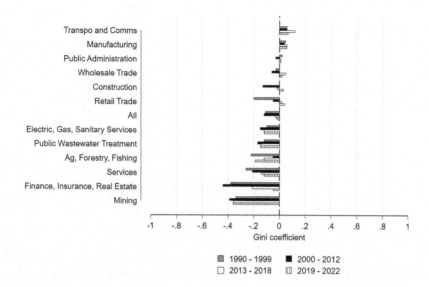

Fig. A1. Gini coefficients for distribution of outfalls by industry and by race for the top 40% of Census block groups in terms of rural population share. Color version available as an online enhancement.

Notes: This graph presents Gini coefficients by industry for the share of the population that is non-White. The category "All" depicts Gini coefficients across all facilities, regardless of the availability of the industrial code. Gray (or blue in the online version) bars are for the 1990–99 period, black bars are for the 2000–12 period, white bars are for the 2013–18 period, and patterned bars are for the 2019–22 period. We restrict the sample to the top 40% of Census block groups in terms of rural population share.

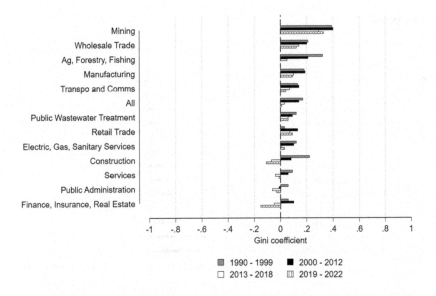

Fig. A2. Gini coefficients for distribution of outfalls by industry and by poverty for the top 40% of Census block groups in terms of rural population share. Color version available as an online enhancement.

Notes: This graph presents Gini coefficients by industry for the share of the population that is below the poverty line. The category "All" depicts Gini coefficients across outfalls at all facilities, regardless of the availability of the industrial code. Gray bars are for the 1990–99 period, black bars are for the 2000–12 period, white bars are for the 2013–18 period, and patterned bars are for the 2019–22 period. We restrict the sample to the top 40% of Census block groups in terms of rural population share.

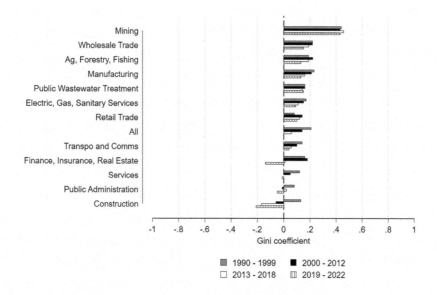

Fig. A3.   Gini coefficients for distribution of outfalls by industry and by education for the top 40% of Census block groups in terms of rural population share. Color version available as an online enhancement.

Notes: This graph presents Gini coefficients by industry for the share of the population without a college degree or higher. The category "All" depicts Gini coefficients across outfalls at all facilities, regardless of the availability of the industrial code. Gray bars are for the 1990–99 period, black bars are for the 2000–12 period, white bars are for the 2013–18 period, and patterned bars are for the 2019–22 period. We restrict the sample to the top 40% of Census block groups in terms of rural population share.

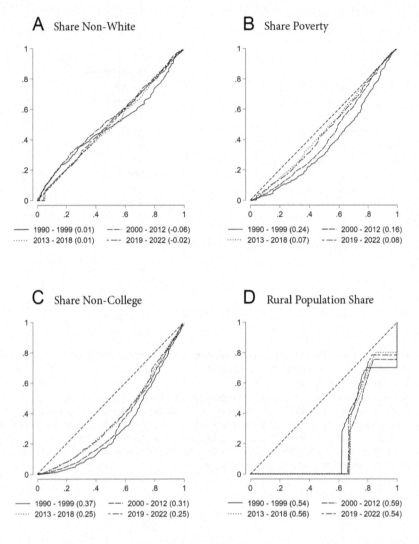

Fig. A4. Pseudo-Lorenz curves for the count of all outfalls by race, poverty, education, and rurality for facilities in Chemicals and Allied Products. (*A*) Share non-White. (*B*) Share poverty. (*C*) Share non-college. (*D*) Rural population share. Color version available as an online enhancement.

Notes: This figure displays pseudo-Lorenz curves for the count of all outfalls from Chemicals and Allied Products (SIC 28) by the share of the population non-White (fig. A4*A*), the share of the population below the poverty line (fig. A4*B*), the share of the population without a college education or higher (fig. A4*C*), and the share of the population living in rural areas (fig. A4*D*). The 45-degree line represents equal distribution. Each figure shows pseudo-Lorenz curves for the 1990–99 period (solid line), 2000–12 period (even-dashed line), 2013–18 period (dotted line), and 2019–22 period (uneven dashed line). Gini coefficients for each period are in parentheses in the legend.

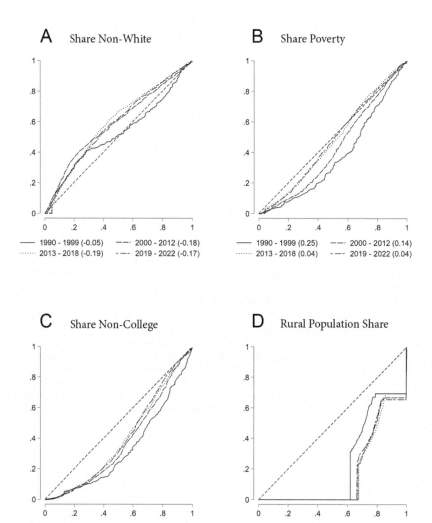

Fig. A5. Pseudo-Lorenz curves for the count of all outfalls by race, poverty, education, and rurality for facilities in Petroleum Refining and Related Industries. (*A*) Share non-White. (*B*) Share poverty. (*C*) Share non-college. (*D*) Rural population share. Color version available as an online enhancement.

Notes: This figure displays pseudo-Lorenz curves for the count of all outfalls from Petroleum Refining and Related Industries (SIC 29) by the share of the population non-White (fig. A5*A*), the share of the population below the poverty line (fig. A5*B*), the share of the population without a college education or higher (fig. A5*C*), and the share of the population living in rural areas (fig. A5*D*). The 45-degree line represents equal distribution. Each figure shows pseudo-Lorenz curves for the 1990–99 period (solid line), 2000–12 period (even-dashed line), 2013–18 period (dotted line), and 2019–22 period (uneven dashed line). Gini coefficients for each period are in parentheses in the legend.

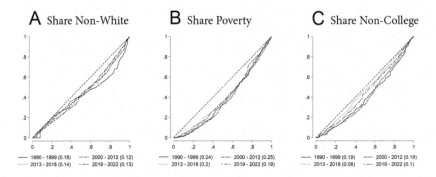

Fig. A6. Pseudo-Lorenz curves for the count of all outfalls by race, poverty, and education for facilities in Chemicals and Allied Products for the top 40% of Census block groups in terms of rural population share. (*A*) Share non-White. (*B*) Share poverty. (*C*) Share non-college. Color version available as an online enhancement.

Notes: This figure displays pseudo-Lorenz curves for the count of outfalls from Chemicals and Allied Products (SIC 28) by the share of the population non-White (fig. A6*A*), the share of the population below the poverty line (fig. A6*A*), and the share of the population without a college education or higher (fig. A6*C*). The 45-degree line represents equal distribution. Each figure shows pseudo-Lorenz curves for the 1990–99 period (solid line), 2000–12 period (even-dashed line), 2013–18 period (dotted line), and 2019–22 period (uneven dashed line). Gini coefficients for each period are in parentheses in the legend. We restrict the sample to the top 40% of Census block groups in terms of rural population share.

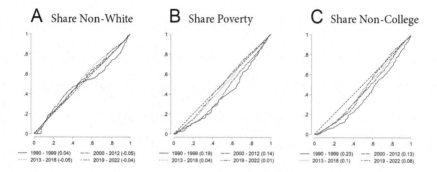

A Share Non-White **B** Share Poverty **C** Share Non-College

Fig. A7. Pseudo-Lorenz curves for the count of all outfalls by race, poverty, and education for facilities in Petroleum Refining and Related Industries for the top 40% of Census block groups in terms of rural population share. (*A*) Share non-White. (*B*) Share poverty. (*C*) Share non-college. Color version available as an online enhancement.

Notes: This figure displays pseudo-Lorenz curves for the count of outfalls from Petroleum Refining and Related Industries (SIC 29) by the share of the population non-White (fig. A7*A*), the share of the population below the poverty line (fig. A7*B*), and the share of the population without a college education or higher (fig. A7*C*). The 45-degree line represents equal distribution. Each figure shows pseudo-Lorenz curves for the 1990–99 period (solid line), 2000–12 period (even-dashed line), 2013–18 period (dotted line), and 2019–22 period (uneven dashed line). Gini coefficients for each period are in parentheses in the legend. We restrict the sample to the top 40% of Census block groups in terms of rural population share.

A Share Non-White **B** Share Poverty **C** Share Non-College

Fig. A8. Gini coefficients for other measures of pollution for the top 40% of Census block groups in terms of rural population share. (*A*) Share non-White. (*B*) Share poverty. (*C*) Share non-college. Color version available as an online enhancement.

Notes: This figure displays bar graphs depicting Gini coefficients using the following measures: (1) monthly average flow, (2) outfalls at facilities deemed "Major" by EPA, (3) outfalls at facilities on the Toxic Release Inventory (TRI) with a water pollution discharge permit, and (4) total impaired waterway length. For each measure of pollution, we examine the distribution across the share of the population non-White (fig. A8*A*), the share of the population below the poverty line (fig. A8*B*), and the share of the population without a college degree (fig. A8*C*). We restrict the sample to the top 40% of Census block groups (HUC12s for impaired length) in terms of rural population share.

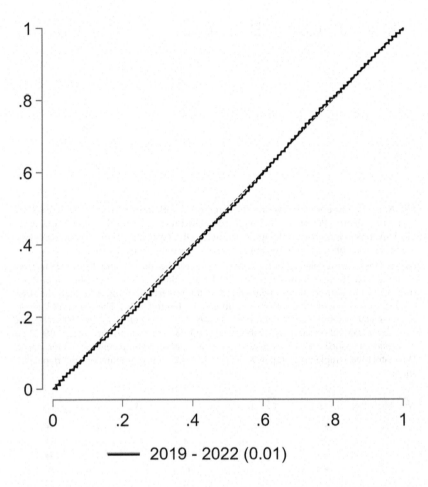

Fig. A9. Pseudo-Lorenz curves and wastewater discharge. Color version available as an online enhancement.

Notes: This figure displays a pseudo-Lorenz curve for the count of outfalls for the period 2019–22 by the percentile of wastewater discharge (solid line) from the Climate and Economic Justice Screening Tool (version 1). The 45-degree dashed line represents equal distribution. The Gini coefficient is in parentheses in the legend.

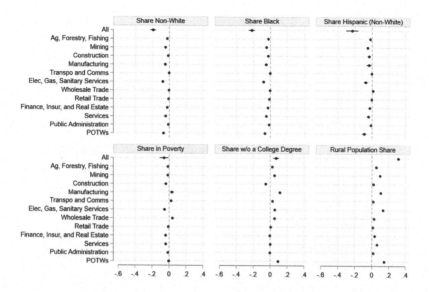

Fig. A10. Cross-sectional results between presence of outfalls and demographics and state fixed effects. Color version available as an online enhancement.

Notes: This figure displays results from cross-sectional regressions of an indicator for the presence of outfalls in a Census block group versus a given measure of demographics and state fixed effects. The outcome variable for the category "All" is an indicator for the presence of an outfall in a Census block group regardless of industrial classification. This category includes facilities with and without Standard Industrial Classification information. For the remaining categories, we use industry-specific indicators for the presence of an outfall in a Census block group as the outcome variable. Coefficient estimates are shown in solid dots, and 95% confidence intervals are shown by the corresponding lines. Standard errors are clustered at the county level. Results are grouped by demographic variable and by industrial classification. The sample includes all four time periods. POTWs = publicly owned treatment works (i.e., public wastewater treatment).

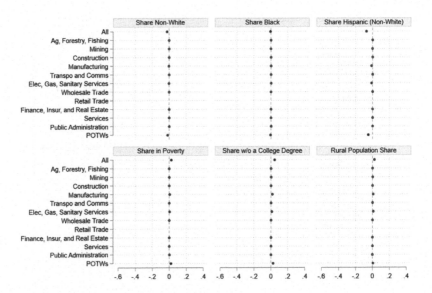

Fig. A11. Cross-sectional results between presence of outfalls from Major dischargers and demographics. Color version available as an online enhancement.

Notes: This figure displays results from cross-sectional regressions of an indicator of an outfall at Major water pollution dischargers in a Census block group versus a given measure of demographics. The outcome variable for the category "All" is an indicator for the presence of an outfall at a Major facility in a Census block group regardless of industrial classification. This category includes Major facilities with and without Standard Industrial Classification information. For the remaining categories, we use industry-specific indicators for the presence of an outfall at a Major facility in a Census block group as the outcome variable. Coefficient estimates are shown in solid dots, and 95% confidence intervals are shown by the corresponding lines. Standard errors are clustered at the county level. Results are grouped by demographic variable and industrial classification. The sample includes all four time periods. There are no Major dischargers in the retail trade industrial division. POTWs = publicly owned treatment works (i.e., public wastewater treatment).

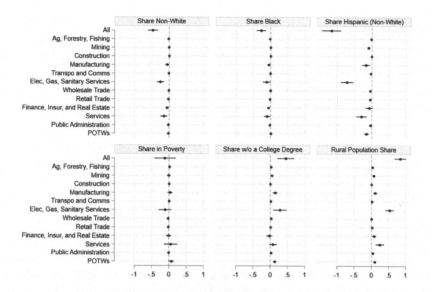

Fig. A12. Cross-sectional results between mean monthly average flow and demographics. Color version available as an online enhancement.

Notes: This figure displays results from cross-sectional regressions of the mean of monthly average flow at outfalls versus a given measure of demographics. The outcome variable for the category "All" is the mean of monthly average flow from outfalls in a Census block group regardless of industrial classification. This category includes facilities with and without Standard Industrial Classification information. For the remaining categories, we use the mean of monthly average flow from industry-specific outfalls in a Census block group as the outcome variable. Coefficient estimates are shown in solid dots, and 95% confidence intervals are shown by the corresponding lines. Standard errors are clustered at the county level. Results are grouped by demographic variable and industrial classification. The sample includes all four time periods. POTWs = publicly owned treatment works (i.e., public wastewater treatment).

Table A1
List of Regulatory Impact Assessments in Data Set

Date	Title	ID #
1992	Water Quality Standards; Establishment of Numeric Criteria for Priority Toxic Pollutants; States' Compliance	40 CFR Part 131
1993	Oil and Gas Extraction Point Source Category; Off-shore Subcategory Effluent Limitations Guidelines and New Source Performance Standards	RIN 2040-AA12
1995	Water Quality Standards for Surface Waters of the Sacramento River, San Joaquin River, and San Francisco Bay and Delta of the State of California	60 FR 4664
1998	National Emission Standards for Hazardous Air Pollutants for Source Category: Pulp and Paper Production; Effluent Limitations Guidelines, Pretreatment Standards, and New Source Performance Standards: Pulp, Paper, and Paperboard Category	RIN 2040–AB53
1999	National Pollutant Discharge Elimination System—Regulations for Revision of the Water Pollution Control Program Addressing Storm Water Discharges	RIN 2040–AC82
2003	Effluent Limitations Guidelines and New Source Performance Standards for the Metal Products and Machinery Point Source Category	RIN 2040-AB79
2003	National Pollutant Discharge Elimination System Permit Regulation and Effluent Limitation Guidelines and Standards for Concentrated Animal Feeding Operations (CAFOs)	RIN 2040–AD19
2004	Effluent Limitations Guidelines and New Source Performance Standards for the Meat and Poultry Products Point Source Category	RIN 2040–AD56
2004	National Pollutant Discharge Elimination System—Final Regulations to Establish Requirements for Cooling Water Intake Structures at Phase II Existing Facilities	RIN 2040–AD62
2006	Oil Pollution Prevention; Spill Prevention, Control, and Countermeasure Plan Requirements—Amendments	RIN 2050–AG23
2009	Construction and Development Effluent Guidelines	RIN 2040-AE91
2009	Oil Pollution Prevention; Spill Prevention, Control, and Countermeasure (SPCC) Rule—Amendments	RIN 2050–AG16
2010	Water Quality Standards for the State of Florida's Lakes and Flowing Waters	RIN 2040–AF11
2011	Oil Pollution Prevention; Spill Prevention, Control, and Countermeasure (SPCC) Rule—Amendments for Milk and Milk Product Containers	RIN 2050–AG50

Table A1
(Continued)

Date	Title	ID #
2014	National Pollutant Discharge Elimination System—Final Regulations to Establish Requirements for Cooling Water Intake Structures at Existing Facilities and Amend Requirements at Phase I Facilities	RIN 2040–AE95
2015	Effluent Limitations Guidelines and Standards for the Steam Electric Power Generating Point Source Category	RIN 2040–AF77
2015	Clean Water Rule: Definition of "Waters of the United States"	RIN 2040–AF30
2019	Definition of "Waters of the United States"—Recodification of Preexisting Rule	RIN 2040-AF74

Table A2
Definitions of Industrial Divisions in Data Set

Industrial Division	Major Group (Two-Digit SIC Code)
A: Agriculture, Forestry, and Fishing	01: Agricultural Production Crops
	02: Agriculture Production Livestock and Animal Specialties
	07: Agricultural Services
	08: Forestry
	09: Fishing, Hunting, and Trapping
B: Mining	10: Metal Mining
	12: Coal Mining
	13: Oil and Gas Extraction
	14: Mining and Quarrying of Nonmetallic Minerals, Except Fuels
C: Construction	15: Building Construction General Contractors and Operative Builders
	16: Heavy Construction other than Building Construction Contractors
	17: Construction Special Trade Contractors
D: Manufacturing	20: Food and Kindred Products
	21: Tobacco Products
	22: Textile Mill Products
	23: Apparel and other Finished Products Made from Fabrics and Similar Materials
	24: Lumber and Wood Products, Except Furniture
	25: Furniture and Fixtures
	26: Paper and Allied Products
	27: Printing, Publishing, and Allied Industries
	28: Chemicals and Allied Products
	29: Petroleum Refining and Related Industries
	30: Rubber and Miscellaneous Plastics Products

Industrial Division	Major Group (Two-Digit SIC Code)
	31: Leather and Leather Products
	32: Stone, Clay, Glass, and Concrete Products
	33: Primary Metal Industries
	34: Fabricated Metal Products, Except Machinery and Transportation Equipment
	35: Industrial and Commercial Machinery and Computer Equipment
	36: Electronic and Other Electrical Equipment and Components, Except Computer Equipment
	37: Transportation Equipment
	38: Measuring, Analyzing, and Controlling Instruments; Photographic, Medical and Optical Goods; Watches and Clocks
	39: Miscellaneous Manufacturing Industries
E1: Transportation and Communications	40: Railroad Transportation
	41: Local and Suburban Transit and Interurban Highway Passenger Transportation
	42: Motor Freight Transportation and Warehousing
	43: United States Postal Service
	44: Water Transportation
	45: Transportation by Air
	46: Pipelines, Except Natural Gas
	47: Transportation Services
	48: Communications
E2: Electric, Gas, and Sanitary Services	49: Electric, Gas, and Sanitary Services
F: Wholesale Trade	50: Wholesale Trade-Durable Goods
	51: Wholesale Trade-Non-durable Goods
G: Retail Trade	52: Building Materials, Hardware, Garden Supply, and Mobile Home Dealers
	53: General Merchandise Stores
	54: Food Stores
	55: Automotive Dealers and Gasoline Service Stations
	56: Apparel and Accessory Stores
	57: Home Furniture, Furnishings, and Equipment Stores
	58: Eating and Drinking Places
	59: Miscellaneous Retail
H: Finance, Insurance, and Real Estate	60: Depository Institutions
	61: Non-depository Credit Institutions
	62: Security and Commodity Brokers, Dealers, Exchanges, and Services
	63: Insurance Carriers
	64: Insurance Agents, Brokers, and Service
	65: Real Estate
	67: Holding and Other Investment Offices

Table A2
(Continued)

Industrial Division	Major Group (Two-Digit SIC Code)
I: Services	70: Hotels, Rooming Houses, Camps, and Other Lodging Places
	72: Personal Services
	73: Business Services
	75: Automotive Repair, Services, and Parking
	76: Miscellaneous Repair Services
	78: Motion Pictures
	79: Amusement and Recreation Services
	80: Health Services
	81: Legal Services
	82: Educational Services
	83: Social Services
	84: Museums, Art Galleries, and Botanical and Zoological Gardens
	86: Membership Organizations
	87: Engineering, Accounting, Research, Management, and Related Services
	88: Private Households
	89: Miscellaneous Services
J: Public Administration	91: Executive, Legislative, and General Government, Except Finance
	92: Justice, Public Order, and Safety
	93: Public Finance, Taxation, and Monetary Policy
	94: Administration of Human Resource Programs
	95: Administration of Environmental Quality and Housing Programs
	96: Administration of Economic Programs
	97: National Security and International Affairs
	99: Nonclassifiable Establishments

Note: This table presents the names of the major groups, identified by the two-digit Standard Industrial Classification (SIC) code, within each industrial division. We split industrial Division E (Transportation, Communications, Electric, Gas, and Sanitary Services) into two: (1) E1: Transportation and Communications and (2) E2: Electric, Gas, and Sanitary Services. For additional information on these industries, please refer to https://www.osha.gov/data/sic-manual.

Table A3

Number of Outfalls by Industrial Classifications and Corresponding Demographics (1990–1999)

Industry	No. of Outfalls	No. of CBGs	Non-White (%)	Non-College (%)	Poverty (%)	Rural Population (%)
Agriculture, Forestry, Fishing	1,754	776	8	87	15	86
Construction	743	460	13	84	16	55
Electric, Gas, Sanitary Services	15,247	7,662	11	85	14	66
Finance, Insurance, Real Estate	3,465	2,253	6	86	13	79
Manufacturing	22,793	8,253	14	88	16	53
Mining	12,448	2,923	8	89	17	80
Public Administration	2,528	1,247	13	84	14	59
Retail Trade	1,022	839	10	85	12	57
Wholesale Trade	3,817	2,092	16	88	17	47
Services	5,132	3,514	8	85	14	78
Transportation and Communications	3,779	1,873	18	87	16	42
POTWs	17,666	11,102	11	86	15	62
All industries w/ SIC code	68,366	22,865	12	86	15	60
All industries	92,761	32,957	12	86	14	59
All CBGs (CONUS average)	92,761	216,330	18	80	13	28

Note: This table provides summary statistics of the total number of outfalls and the distribution of outfalls by industrial classification for the 1990–99 period. The table also shows corresponding Census block group demographic information for all Census block groups and by industrial classification. A given facility may belong to multiple industries. "All industries w/ SIC code" summarizes these statistics for outfalls that correspond to facilities with at least one Standard Industrial Classification code. "All industries" summarizes these statistics for all outfalls, regardless of the availability of the code. "All CBGs" summarizes these statistics for all Census block groups in the conterminous United States (CONUS) for comparison purposes. POTWs = publicly owned treatment works (i.e., public wastewater treatment).

Table A4

Number of Outfalls by Industrial Classifications and Corresponding Demographics (2000–2012)

Industry	No. of Outfalls	No. of CBGs	Non-White (%)	Non-College (%)	Poverty (%)	Rural Population (%)
Agriculture, Forestry, Fishing	9,210	3,665	11	85	13	84
Construction	47,263	12,844	13	77	13	42
Electric, Gas, Sanitary Services	38,125	16,274	13	81	12	60
Finance, Insurance, Real Estate	7,785	4,092	11	80	11	61
Manufacturing	55,881	20,005	17	83	14	49
Mining	42,304	7,451	12	85	14	75
Public Administration	10,158	4,889	14	78	12	42
Retail Trade	4,183	3,245	16	82	13	44
Wholesale Trade	11,257	6,034	18	84	15	46
Services	13,079	8,069	13	78	12	58
Transportation and Communications	13,784	6,714	18	81	14	38
POTWs	26,857	16,419	12	82	13	60
All industries w/ SIC code	238,203	52,437	15	80	13	47
All industries	338,288	72,952	16	79	12	43
All CBGs (CONUS average)	338,288	216,330	22	75	13	23

Note: This table provides summary statistics of the total number of outfalls and the distribution of outfalls by industrial classification for the 2000–12 period. The table also shows corresponding Census block group demographic information for all Census block groups and by industrial classification. A given facility may belong to multiple industries. "All industries w/ SIC code" summarizes these statistics for outfalls that correspond to facilities with at least one Standard Industrial Classification code. "All industries" summarizes these statistics for all outfalls, regardless of the availability of the code. "All CBGs" summarizes these statistics for all Census block groups in the conterminous United States (CONUS) for comparison purposes. POTWs = publicly owned treatment works (i.e., public wastewater treatment).

Table A5
Number of Outfalls by Industrial Classifications and Corresponding Demographics
(2013–2018)

Industry	No. of Outfalls	No. of CBGs	Non-White (%)	Non-College (%)	Poverty (%)	Rural Population (%)
Agriculture, Forestry, Fishing	10,806	4,166	12	82	14	82
Construction	89,534	21,192	18	74	16	35
Electric, Gas, Sanitary Services	47,016	17,967	16	78	15	55
Finance, Insurance, Real Estate	10,340	4,983	15	75	13	50
Manufacturing	87,741	26,982	21	80	17	41
Mining	76,632	10,098	14	81	15	70
Public Administration	12,186	5,934	18	75	15	35
Retail Trade	4,845	3,427	20	79	17	41
Wholesale Trade	19,291	9,340	23	82	19	38
Services	14,400	8,595	16	75	14	51
Transportation and Communications	26,488	11,287	24	78	18	30
POTWs	27,512	16,777	14	80	16	58
All industries w/ SIC code	379,964	66,881	19	77	16	40
All industries	631,160	96,629	20	75	16	35
All CBGs (CONUS average)	631,160	216,330	25	73	16	21

Note: This table provides summary statistics of the total number of outfalls and the distribution of outfalls by industrial classification for the 2013–18 period. The table also shows corresponding Census block group demographic information for all Census block groups and by industrial classification. A given facility may belong to multiple industries. "All industries w/ SIC code" summarizes these statistics for outfalls that correspond to facilities with at least one Standard Industrial Classification code. "All industries" summarizes these statistics for all outfalls, regardless of the availability of the code. "All CBGs" summarizes these statistics for all Census block groups in the conterminous United States (CONUS) for comparison purposes. POTWs = publicly owned treatment works (i.e., public wastewater treatment).

Endnotes

Authors' email addresses: Andarge (tandarge@umass.edu), Ji (yongjiej@iastate.edu), Keeler (keel0041@umn.edu), Keiser (dkeiser@umass.edu), McKenzie (mcken451@umn.edu). We thank Tatyana Deryugina, Matthew Kotchen, seminar participants at UMass Amherst, Jonathan Adler and participants at the Clean Water Act at 50: An Interdisciplinary Symposium at Case Western Reserve University, and participants at the NBER Environmental and Energy Policy and the Economy Conference for helpful comments and suggestions. We thank William Wheeler, Bryan Parthum, Chris Moore, and Joel Corona at EPA for helpful discussions, particularly related to the use of EPA data sets and Clean Water Act regulatory impact assessments. For acknowledgments, sources of research support, and disclosure of the authors' material financial relationships, if any, please see https://www.nber.org/books-and-chapters

/environmental-and-energy-policy-and-economy-volume-5/environmental-justice-and
-clean-water-act-implications-economic-analyses-clean-water-regulations.

1. The Justice40 Initiative is part of a broader Executive Order, EO 14008. In addition, the Biden administration has promoted several related efforts, including 2021's EO 13985 that promotes "Racial Equity and Underserved Communities through the Federal Government," an additional EO in February 2023 on "Further Advancing Racial Equity and Support for Underserved Communities through the Federal Government," and numerous other EOs on diversity, equity, inclusion, and accessibility (see, e.g., https://www.usaid .gov/equity/executive-orders-deia).

2. In a similar vein, except for conditioning on rurality, all of our analyses are unconditional, meaning that we examine the pure correlation between pollution outfalls and demographic information without controlling for other factors. We believe this provides important information on the current distribution of outfalls across space but does not attempt to explain why the variation in outfalls arises or whether this distribution is unequal when conditioning on other factors. For example, in the air-pollution literature, some studies include factors such as population density, employment patterns, and land use to explain observed pollution-exposure patterns (Mennis 2003; Ash and Boyce 2018). We leave these important questions with respect to surface water pollution to future work.

3. Lorenz curves or variations of Lorenz curves have been used in the EJ literature to depict the distribution of a given outcome along demographic and socioeconomic lines (Mehta et al. 2014; Mohammed et al. 2021).

4. These pseudo-Lorenz curves are similar to concentration curves used in the inequality literature (Maguire and Sheriff 2011). They depict the level of dispersion in the outcome variable across socioeconomic characteristics. For two distributions with different means, we cannot use these curves to rank distributions of the number of outfalls; although one distribution may have a more equal distribution, the other may have a lower mean (Mansur and Sheriff 2021). There are other approaches to visually represent inequality. For example, generalized Lorenz curves, which scale up the Lorenz curve by the mean of the distribution, have been used to depict income and environmental inequality (Shorrocks 1983; Mansur and Sheriff 2021; Sheriff 2023). The advantage of generalized Lorenz curves is that they take into account both the mean of the distribution and the level of dispersion, allowing for at least a partial ranking of distributions, even if they have different means. However, in this paper, the use of pseudo-Lorenz curves is sufficient as our goal is only to describe how the number of outfalls (and other pollution measures) varies with socioeconomic and demographic characteristics, not to rank distributions or make claims regarding social welfare.

5. Gini coefficients are just one of several metrics used to compare distributions of pollution outcomes (Mansur and Sheriff 2021). Other indices include the Atkinson inequality index, equally distributed equivalents, and the generalized entropy index.

6. Specifically, we define the date of first activity as the minimum of the original issue date and issue date.

7. Dropping facilities without start and end dates and geographic coordinates may lead to sample selection bias if incompleteness of this information is nonrandom.

8. Facilities may belong to multiple industrial sectors. Thus, a given facility may belong to more than one of these 11 categories. We place facilities into industrial categories largely along the lines of the SIC divisions. However, we split the Transportation, Communications, Electric, Gas, and Sanitary Services industrial division into two separate subdivisions given the importance of the Electric, Gas, and Sanitary Services as major sources of water pollution.

9. EPA typically designates Major sources as POTWs with a total design flow greater than 1 MGD, industrial sources with a score greater than 80 on the NPDES Permit Rating Worksheet, or sources designated as "Major" by the regulator. Note that the NPDES Permit Rating Worksheet takes into account six factors to determine the score: toxicity potential, flow, amount of conventional pollutants that would be discharged, public health impact, characteristics of the receiving stream and potential for violation of water quality standards, and proximity to coastal waters.

10. Most large point sources, but not all, are required to submit DMRs. Most standard industrial dischargers (i.e., those that discharge directly to surface waters), POTWs, and Major facilities in the municipal stormwater subprogram regularly submit DMRs. Some industrial stormwater facilities, such as those regulated under EPA's Multi-Sector General Permit,

regularly submit DMRs. In general, most construction stormwater facilities and nonmajor municipal stormwater facilities are not required to submit DMRs. A small percentage of these facilities may have to submit DMRs due to a violation and subsequent enforcement action. CAFOs submit DMRs quite irregularly (e.g., after a major storm event). For more information, see section 2 of EPA's Economic Analysis of the National Pollution Discharge Elimination System Electronic Reporting Final Rule.

11. The number of measurements required may vary across permits. We follow the approach used in the EPA DMR Loading Tool to correct outliers for reported flow. See https://echo.epa.gov/system/files/Technical_Users_Background_Doc.pdf.

12. We downloaded version 1.0 from the "Downloads" section of https://screeningtool .geoplatform.gov/en/#3/33.47/-97.5. As the data are available only at the Census tract level, we assume that all Census block groups within a Census tract have the same percentile of wastewater discharge.

13. The IPUMS NHGIS website provides additional information (https://www.nhgis.org).

14. We calculate this as the share of population living in rural Census blocks within the corresponding Census block group. Because we standardize Census block group–level demographics using 2010 Census block groups, we also standardize 1990, 2000, and 2013 Census block–level demographic data using 2010 Census blocks from the NHGIS database (see http://www.ipums.org). For 2019, we use the rural designation information from the 2020 census along with the crosswalk matrix between 2010 and 2020 Census blocks to standardize these statistics to 2010 Census block groups.

15. Unfortunately, the 2010 and 2020 Censuses do not provide poverty and education data at the Census block group level, which prevents us from using decades starting with Census years to construct our panel. As a result, we rely on 2013 and 2019 ACS 5-year averages and adjust our time periods accordingly.

16. EnviroAtlas is an online tool developed by the EPA that provides geospatial data and other information on the nation's ecosystems and their services. It allows users to explore and analyze environmental and socioeconomic factors at various scales. We obtained impaired waterway length from the September 2021 version of EnviroAtlas. For more information about downloading the data set, visit https://www.epa.gov/enviroatlas/forms /enviroatlas-data-download.

17. The subwatershed is identified by the 12-digit hydrologic unit code (HUC12).

18. Data reporting may have improved over time. In particular, the 2013–18 and 2019–22 time periods coincide with the implementation of the 2015 Electronic Reporting (eReporting) Rule by EPA. This rule changed state reporting requirements to EPA for nonmajor facilities. Prior to this rule, states were required to report only basic facility information about nonmajor facilities to EPA. Some states did, however, voluntarily report on nonmajors even before the implementation of the rule. Given that the universe of permits overwhelmingly consists of nonmajor facilities, the implementation of this rule potentially improves overall data quality.

19. Our discussion of patterns in all Census block groups versus the most-rural Census block groups focuses on the evenness of the distribution of outfalls along social and demographic lines. However, the average number of outfalls may also differ between rural and urban areas.

20. We follow the procedures in one EPA document to convert demographic information from block groups to each HUC12 (https://www.epa.gov/system/files/documents /2022-03/demographics-indicator-reference-sheet-20220306.pdf). Because we do not have information on which year's impaired status was used in the EnviroAtlas database, we construct the pseudo-Lorenz curve only with 2019 demographic information.

21. Although EPA guidelines contain a list of information that must be considered, the specific framework for assessing water quality widely differs across states (National Research Council 2001). Thus, a given water body may be deemed impaired by one state but not impaired by another due to differences in their assessment framework.

22. Note that it may be the case that discharge data are not always available or completely reported to the federal government.

23. Guidance on best practices for conducting distributional analyses of regulations is beyond the scope of this paper. However, we point readers to Ando et al. (2023), Lienke et al. (2021), and Banzhaf, Ma, and Timmins (2019) as resources for best practices in assessing equity and distributional impacts of federal policies.

24. The EPA's RSEI database links potential chemical releases from facilities on the TRI to surface water "flowlines" up to 300 kilometers downstream from a facility. The RSEI method also attempts to link pollution to exposure via pathways of drinking water and recreational and subsistence fish consumption (USEPA 2023). The P2 EJ Facility Mapping Tool allows users to identify industrial facilities located in or adjacent to communities with EJ concerns, including facilities included in the TRI and Resource Conservation and Recovery Act.

References

Anderton, D. L. 1996. "Methodological Issues in the Spatiotemporal Analysis of Environmental Equity." *Social Science Quarterly* 77 (3): 508–15. http://www.jstor.org/stable/42863497.

Ando, A., T. O. Awokuse, N. W. Chan, J. González-Ramírez, S. Gulati, M. G. Interis, S. Jacobson, D. T. Manning, and S. Stolper. 2023. "Environmental and Natural Resource Economics and Systemic Racism." Working Paper no. 23-06, Resources for the Future, Washington, DC. https://media.rff.org/documents/WP_23-06.pdf.

Ash, M., and J. K. Boyce. 2018. "Racial Disparities in Pollution Exposure and Employment at US Industrial Facilities." *Proceedings of the National Academy of Sciences of the USA* 115 (42): 10636–41. https://doi.org/10.1073/pnas.1721640115.

Balazs, C., and I. Ray. 2014. "The Drinking Water Disparities Framework: On the Origins and Persistence of Inequities in Exposure." *American Journal of Public Health* 104 (4): 603–11. https://doi.org/10.2105/AJPH.2013.301664.

Banzhaf, H. 2011. "Regulatory Impact Analyses of Environmental Justice Effects." *Journal of Land Use and Environmental Law* 27 (1): 1–30.

Banzhaf, H., L. Ma, and C. Timmins. 2019. "Environmental Justice: Establishing Causal Relationships." *Annual Review of Resource Economics* 11 (1): 377–98. https://doi.org/10.1146/annurev-resource-100518-094131.

Benz, S. A., and J. A. Burney. 2021. "Widespread Race and Class Disparities in Surface Urban Heat Extremes across the United States." *Earth's Future* 9 (7): e2021EF002016. https://doi.org/10.1029/2021EF002016.

Bullard, R. D., P. Mohai, R. Saha, and B. Wright. 2008. "Toxic Wastes and Race at Twenty: Why Race Still Matters after All of These Years." *Environmental Law* 38 (1): 371.

Cecot, C., and R. W. Hahn. 2022. "Incorporating Equity and Justice Concerns in Regulation." Law and Economics Research Paper no. 22-19, George Mason University. https://doi.org/10.1111/rego.12508.

Colmer, J., I. Hardman, J. Shimshack, and J. Voorhies. 2020. "Disparities in $PM_{2.5}$ Air Pollution in the United States." *Science* 369 (6503): 575–78. https://doi.org/10.1126/science.aaz9353.

Deitz, S., and K. Meehan. 2019. "Plumbing Poverty: Mapping Hot Spots of Racial and Geographic Inequality in US Household Water Insecurity." *Annals of the American Association of Geographers* 109 (4): 1092–109. https://doi.org/10.1080/24694452.2018.1530587.

EJCW (Environmental Justice Coalition for Water). 2005. *Thirsty for Justice: A People's Blueprint for California Water.* Oakland, CA: Environmental Justice Coalition for Water.

Executive Order 12898 of February 11, 1994. "Federal Actions to Address Environmental Justice in Minority Populations and Low-Income Populations." Fed Reg 59:FR7629. https://www.federalregister.gov/documents/1994/02/16

/94-3685/federal-actions-to-address-environmental-justice-in-minority-popu
lations-and-low-income-populations.
Geltman, E. G., G. Gill, and M. Jovanovic. 2016. "Beyond Baby Steps: An Empirical Study of the Impact of Environmental Justice Executive Order 12898."
Family and Community Health 39 (3): 143–50. https://doi.org/10.1097/fch
.0000000000000113.
Hsiang, S., P. Oliva, and R. Walker. 2019. "The Distribution of Environmental
Damages." *Review of Environmental Economics and Policy* 13 (1): 83–103. https://
doi.org/10.1093/Reep/Rey024.
Keeler, B. L., S. Polasky, K. Brauman, K. Johnson, J. Finlay, A. O'Neill, K. Kovacs,
and B. Dalzell. 2012. "Linking Water Quality and Well-Being for Improved
Assessment and Valuation of Ecosystem Services." *Environmental Science*
109 (45): 18619–24. https://doi.org/10.1073/pnas.1215991109.
Keiser, D. A., C. L. Kling, and J. S. Shapiro. 2019. "The Low but Uncertain Mea-
sured Benefits of US Water Quality Policy." *Proceedings of the National Academy
of Sciences of the United States of America* 116 (12): 5262–69. https://doi.org/10
.1073/pnas.1802870115.
Keiser, D. A., and J. S. Shapiro. 2019. "US Water Pollution Regulation over the
Last Half Century: Burning Waters to Crystal Springs?" *Journal of Economic
Perspectives* 33 (4): 51–75. https://doi.org/10.1257/jep.33.4.51.
Konisky, D. M., C. Reenock, and S. Conley. 2021. "Environmental Injustice in
Clean Water Act Enforcement: Racial and Income Disparities in Inspection
Time." *Environmental Research Letters* 16 (8): 084020. https://doi.org/10
.1088/1748-9326/ac1225.
Lee, C. 2002. "Environmental Justice: Building a Unified Vision of Health and
the Environment." *Environmental Health Perspectives* 110 (2, suppl): 141–44.
https://doi.org/10.1289/ehp.02110s2141.
Lienke, J., I. Paul, M. Sarinsky, B. Ünel, and A. V. Varela. 2021. "Making Regu-
lations Fair: How Cost-Benefit Analysis Can Promote Equity and Advance
Environmental Justice." Report, Institute for Policy Integrity, New York University School of Law.
Liévanos, R. S. 2017. "Sociospatial Dimensions of Water Injustice: The Distribu-
tion of Surface Water Toxic Releases in California's Bay-Delta." *Sociological
Perspectives* 60 (3): 575–99. https://doi.org/10.1177/0731121416648935.
Maguire, K., and G. Sheriff. 2011. "Comparing Distributions of Environmental
Outcomes for Regulatory Environmental Justice Analysis." *International Jour-
nal of Environmental Research and Public Health* 8 (5): 1707–26. https://doi.org
/10.3390/ijerph8051707.
Mansur, E. T., and G. Sheriff. 2021. "On the Measurement of Environmental
Inequality: Ranking Emissions Distributions Generated by Different Policy
Instruments." *Journal of the Association of Environmental and Resource Econo-
mists* 8 (4). https://doi.org/10.1086/713113.
Mehta, V. K., R. Goswami, E. Kemp-Benedict, S. Muddu, and D. Malghan. 2014.
"Metabolic Urbanism and Environmental Justice: The Water Conundrum in
Bangalore, India." *Environmental Justice* 7 (5): 130–7. https://doi.org/10.1089
/env.2014.0021.
Mennis, J. L. 2003. "The Distribution and Enforcement of Air Polluting Facilities
in New Jersey." *Professional Geographer* 57 (3): 411–22. https://doi.org/10
.1111/j.0033-0124.2005.00487.x.
Meyer, A. 2015. "Does Education Increase Pro-Environmental Behavior? Evidence from Europe." *Ecological Economics* 116:108–21. https://doi.org/10
.1016/j.ecolecon.2015.04.018.

Mohai, P., and R. Saha. 2007. "Racial Inequality in the Distribution of Hazardous Waste: A National-Level Reassessment." *Social Problems* 54 (3): 343–70.
https://doi.org/10.1525/sp.2007.54.3.343.

Mohai, P., P. M. Lantz, J. Morenoff, J. S. House, and R. P. Mero. 2009. "Racial and
Socioeconomic Disparities in Residential Proximity to Polluting Industrial Facilities: Evidence from the Americans' Changing Lives Study." *American Journal
of Public Health* 99 (3): S649–S656. https://doi.org/10.2105/ajph.2007.131383.

Mohammed, M., S. J. Dukku, Y. Y. Babanyara, I. Muhammad, and J. K. Mohammed. 2021. "A Comparative Analysis of Environmental Justice between Urban
Neighbourhoods." *Journal of Inclusive Cities and Built Environment* 1 (2): 27–40.
https://doi.org/10.54030/2788-564X/2021/v1i2a4.

Mueller, J. T., and S. Gasteyer. 2021. "The Widespread and Unjust Drinking Water
and Clean Water Crisis in the United States." *Nature Communications* 12 (1):
3544. https://doi.org/10.1038/s41467-021-23898-z.

National Research Council. 2001. *Assessing the TMDL Approach to Water Quality
Management*. Atlanta: National Academies Press.

NEJAC (National Environmental Justice Advisory Council). 2020. "EJ 2020 Action Agenda." Environmental Protection Agency. https://www.epa.gov/sites
/default/files/2017-10/documents/ej_2020_action_agenda.pdf.

Revesz, R. L., and S. Yi. 2022. "Distributional Consequences and Regulatory Analysis." *Environmental Law* 52 (1): 53–98. https://www.jstor.org/stable/48657962.

Ringquist, E. J. 2005. "Assessing Evidence of Environmental Inequities: A Meta-
analysis." *Journal of Policy Analysis and Management* 24 (2): 223–47. https://
doi.org/10.1002/pam.20088.

Robinson, L. A., J. K. Hammitt, and R. J. Zeckhauser. 2016. "Attention to Distribution in US Regulatory Analyses." *Review of Environmental Economics and
Policy* 10 (2): 308–28.

Sheriff, G. 2023. "California's GHG Cap and Trade Program and the Equity
of Air Toxic Releases." *Journal of the Association of Environmental and Resource
Economists*. https://doi.org/10.1086/725699.

Shorrocks, A. F. 1983. "Ranking Income Distributions." *Economica* 50 (197): 3–17.
https://doi.org/10.2307/2554117.

Son, J. Y., R. L. Muenich, D. Schaffer-Smith, M. L. Miranda, and M. L. Bell. 2021.
"Distribution of Environmental Justice Metrics for Exposure to CAFOs in
North Carolina, USA." *Environmental Research* 195:110862. https://doi.org
/10.1016/j.envres.2021.110862.

Tate, E., M. A. Rahman, C. T. Emrich, and C. C. Sampson. 2021. "Flood Exposure
and Social Vulnerability in the United States." *Natural Hazards* 106 (1): 1–23.
https://doi.org/10.1007/s11069-020-04470-2.

Tessum, C. W., D. A. Paolella, S. E. Chambliss, J. S. Apte, J. D. Hill, and J. D. Marshall. 2021. "$PM_{2.5}$ Polluters Disproportionately and Systemically Affect People of Color in the United States." *Science Policy* 7 (18). https://doi.org/10
.1126/sciadv.abf4491.

USEPA (US Environmental Protection Agency). 2004a. "Effluent Limitations
Guidelines and New Source Performance Standards for the Meat and Poultry
Products Point Source Category." https://www.federalregister.gov/documents
/2004/09/08/04-12017/effluent-limitations-guidelines-and-new-source-per
formance-standards-for-the-meat-and-poultry.

———. 2004b. "EPA Needs to Consistently Implement the Intent of the Executive
Order on Environmental Justice." Report No. 2004-P-00007. https://www.epa
.gov/office-inspector-general/report-epa-needs-consistently-implement-intent
-executive-order.

———. 2022a. "Justice40 at EPA." https://www.epa.gov/environmentaljustice /justice40-epa.

———. 2022b. "Cumulative Impacts: Recommendations for ORD Research." White paper. https://www.epa.gov/system/files/documents/2022-01/ord -cumulative-impacts-white-paper_externalreviewdraft-_508-tagged_0.pdf.

———. 2023. "EPA's Risk-Screening Environmental Indicators (RSEI) Methodology: RSEI Version 2.3.11." March. https://www.epa.gov/system/files/doc uments/2023-04/rsei-methodology-document-v2311-March2023.pdf.

Vajjhala, S. P., S. Szambelan, and A. van Epps. 2008. "Integrating EJ into Federal Policies and Programs: Examining the Role of Regulatory Impact Analyses and Environmental Impact Statements." Discussion Paper no. 04-45, Resources for the Future, Washington, DC. https://doi.org/10.2139/ssrn.1299062.

Wang, Y., J. S. Apte, and J. Marshall. 2022. "Location-Specific Strategies for Eliminating US National Racial-Ethnic $PM_{2.5}$ Exposure Inequality." *Environmental Sciences* 119 (44): e2205548119. https://doi.org/10.1073/pnas.2205548119.

White House. 2003. "Circular A-4." https://obamawhitehouse.archives.gov /omb/circulars_a004_a-4/.

White House. 2021. "Modernizing Regulatory Review." Memorandum (January). https://www.whitehouse.gov/briefing-room/presidential-actions/2021/01 /20/modernizing-regulatory-review.

White House. 2023. "Circular A-4: Regulatory Analysis." Draft for Public Review (April 6). https://www.whitehouse.gov/wp-content/uploads/2023/04 /DraftCircularA-4.pdf.

Wilson, S. M., F. Howell, S. Wing, and M. Sobsey. 2002. "Environmental Injustice and the Mississippi Hog Industry." *Environmental Health Perspectives* 110:195–201. https://doi.org/10.1289/ehp.02110s2195.

Workers and the Green-Energy Transition: Evidence from 300 Million Job Transitions

E. Mark Curtis, *Wake Forest University,* United States of America

Layla O'Kane, *Lightcast,* United States of America

R. Jisung Park, *University of Pennsylvania,* United States of America, *and Institute of Labor Economics (IZA),* Germany

Executive Summary

Using microdata representing more than 130 million online work profiles, we explore transitions into and out of jobs most likely to be affected by a transition away from carbon-intensive production technologies. Exploiting detailed textual data on job title, firm name, occupation, and industry to focus on workers employed in carbon-intensive ("dirty") and non–carbon-intensive ("green") jobs, we find that the rate of transition from dirty to green jobs is rising rapidly, increasing 10-fold over the period 2005–21, including a significant uptick in electric vehicle–related jobs in recent years. Overall, however, less than 1% of all workers who leave a dirty job appear to make the transition to a green job. We find that the persistence of employment within dirty industries varies enormously across local labor markets; in some states, more than half of all transitions out of dirty jobs are into other dirty jobs. Older workers and those without a college education appear less likely to make transitions to green jobs and more likely to other dirty jobs, other jobs, or nonemployment. When accounting for the fact that green jobs tend to have later start dates, it appears that green and dirty jobs have roughly comparable job durations.

JEL Codes: Q55, Q52, J21, J23

Keywords: green jobs, green-energy transition, fossil fuel jobs, labor-market dynamics, job transitions

Environmental and Energy Policy and the Economy, volume 5, 2024.

I. Introduction

What are the consequences for workers of making the transition away from fossil fuels? The answer depends in part on the outside options that are available to potentially displaced workers, including in cleaner industries and in other local industries for which current carbon-intensive workers' skills provide a good match. This paper explores the potential labor-market implications of the clean-energy transition, focusing on employment flows observed in data from roughly 130 million online employment profiles, representing approximately 300 million job-to-job transitions.

Climate-mitigation policy can be thought of as a form of directed technical change away from carbon-intensive production processes.[1] Under perfectly competitive markets, the associated reallocation of labor (and capital) inputs has minimal efficiency costs, as workers frictionlessly and instantaneously adjust to new optimal input mixes by switching jobs and moving to areas with greater labor demand. In practice, search frictions, human capital acquisition costs, or ties to particular geographies may give rise to significant transition costs for workers (Manning 2021).

Understanding the distributional consequences of the clean-energy transition may be especially important in light of recent trends in labor-market inequality, where workers with and without access to higher education have seen increasing "polarization" in wage and nonwage outcomes across many Organisation for Economic Co-operation and Development (OECD) countries (Hamermesh 1999; Goos, Manning, and Salomons 2009; Autor 2014; Katz and Krueger 2017). Making the transition away from fossil fuels may have distributional implications if some workers are better able to respond to changes in labor demand induced by changes in policy. Employment dislocations associated with labor-demand shocks such as globalization and skill-biased technical change have been shown to be highly localized, scarring, and concentrated among noncollege workers (Autor, Levy, and Murnane 2003; Autor, Dorn, and Hanson 2013).[2]

The magnitude of the shifts in product and labor demand arising from fully correcting the climate externality is likely to be large. Recent estimates of the social cost of carbon (Rennert et al. 2021; Carleton and Greenstone 2022) suggest that the present value of marginal damages created by greenhouse gases in a given year may be on the order of several trillion dollars globally.[3] Available estimates suggest that the US Inflation Reduction Act, passed in 2022, may cost up to $900 billion over the following

10 years (Bistline, Mehrotra, and Wolfram 2023). Both facts suggest that the labor-market impacts of shifts in policy-induced investment flows could have nontrivial welfare consequences.

In this paper, we use detailed job-to-job transition data to provide new descriptive evidence on this question. We develop novel, text-based measures of carbon-intensive "dirty" and non–carbon-intensive "green" jobs, which are generated on the basis of worker-job-level information on job title, firm name, industry, and occupation. This allows us to construct a broader measure of relevant jobs, particularly in emerging green sectors such as electric vehicles (EVs), than many previous analyses. It also allows us to measure the rate of transition out of and into dirty and green jobs in a way that permits an exploration of heterogeneity across geographies, educational attainment, and age.

We find that the rate of transition from dirty to green jobs is growing rapidly, increasing nearly 10-fold over the period 2005–2021. A growing share of these transitions appears to be driven in particular by EV-related jobs. At the same time, the vast majority of workers in carbon-intensive jobs have not historically found work in green jobs. In 2021, 0.7% of workers who transitioned out of a dirty job transitioned into a green job. Conversely, the vast majority of workers obtaining green jobs does not come from carbon-intensive industries, but from a wide range of other industries and occupations (e.g., Sales Managers, Software Developers, Marketing Managers). Approximately a quarter (26.7%) of green jobs appear to be taken by first-time job holders, and more than 20,000 workers are observed entering green jobs from overseas.

Some workers appear to be far better able to make—and some local economies much more likely to benefit from—these transitions than others. Overall, workers without a bachelor's degree are significantly less likely to transition into green jobs, as are older workers (e.g., workers in their forties and fifties). In some local labor markets, such transitions appear exceedingly rare, despite a large number of workers in dirty jobs who may increasingly face declining labor-market prospects due to climate-mitigation policies. Whereas some states, such as California, feature relatively high rates of transition from dirty to green jobs, others, like West Virginia, appear to have low rates of dirty-to-green transitions despite a high density of existing dirty jobs.

Given the relatively low share of "dirty workers" who appear able to transition to green jobs, this begs an important question of where such workers might find alternative employment as labor demand in fossil fuel–intensive industries declines. Our data allow us to assess the likelihood that workers who previously held dirty jobs are likely to transition into other dirty jobs, both within and outside of local labor markets. We find that on average, approximately 20% of transitions out of dirty jobs are into other dirty jobs, including transitions within and out of local labor markets. The sector to which dirty workers are most likely to transition is manufacturing, which accounts for more than 25% of all transitions out of dirty jobs.

The degree of persistence of employment within carbon-intensive sectors (dirty-to-dirty job transitions) varies considerably across educational attainment, age, and geography. The proportion of dirty-to-dirty transitions is 44% (8 percentage points) higher for workers with only a high school degree or less compared with those with at least an associate's degree. Older workers are also significantly more likely to remain in a dirty job; workers ages 55–64 are 25% (5 percentage points) more likely to transition into another dirty job compared with workers ages 18–34. In some cities, the share of dirty-to-dirty transitions can be as high as 90%, suggesting that nearly all workers in carbon-intensive sectors stay within such sectors, with limited attractive options in non–carbon-intensive industries.

One way to assess the potential welfare implications of a sustained transition away from fossil fuels is to look at how outside-option wage values for dirty workers vary as other dirty jobs become more limited in a local labor market. We provide novel estimates of empirically observed outside-option wage values for fossil fuel–intensive workers by geography, educational attainment, and age, following methods pioneered by Schubert, Stansbury, and Taska (2021). Our data suggest that non–bachelor's degree workers are likely to experience a much larger decline in local outside options as fossil fuel–intensive jobs become more limited. The drop-off is far more pronounced in places where alternative jobs outside of fossil fuel–intensive industries appear to be more limited (e.g., Wilmington, Delaware, and Oklahoma City, Oklahoma).

Research increasingly shows that workers place significant value on nonwage aspects of work (Maestas et al. 2018), including job stability (Hyatt and Spletzer 2016). An important unanswered question pertains to the relative duration of dirty versus green jobs, regarding which our data provide novel evidence. For instance, an oft-cited concern has been that, even if wind and solar jobs are numerically plentiful, they may be relatively short-lived. We find that, although many green jobs appear to have shorter durations than dirty jobs in the cross section, controlling for job-specific start and end dates erases much of the difference. In other words, controlling for the fact that green jobs will tend to be mechanically shorter in the cross section due to their relatively recent emergence, we find relatively small duration differences between green and dirty jobs. Solar jobs appear to last 0.26 fewer years than dirty jobs, wind jobs do not appear to be significantly different in length than dirty jobs (which on average last 4.6 years in the cross section), and EV jobs appear to be commensurate in length to the average dirty job.

Our findings contribute to a growing literature on green jobs and the labor-market consequences of environmental policies. Recent evidence suggests that the wage and employment implications of environmental regulation can vary by industry and region. For instance, Greenstone (2002) estimates that the US Clean Air Act resulted in more than 590,000 lost jobs in counties and industries that were historically heavily polluting. Curtis (2018) finds that overall employment in energy-intensive industries fell by up to 4.8% in the wake of the NOx trading program. Conversely, some analyses suggest that future green jobs could be plentiful and well-paying, resulting in net positive employment impacts (Lehr, Lutz, and Edler 2012), and that well-designed labor-market policies may help workers make the transition out of historically "brown" or "dirty" sectors.

One important knowledge gap pertains to the extent to which the skills demanded by, and geographic availability of, new green jobs overlap (or not) with those in traditionally dirty industries. Consider the following statement by former national climate adviser Gina McCarthy: "Take the US manufacturing sector . . . It has relied on a carbon-based system for nearly 200 years, so *reshaping the system means ensuring that these industrial workers get the training and resources to build the clean energy economy*" (emphasis added).

Whether the workers who are currently employed in carbon-intensive jobs can be effectively matched to the jobs that will be demanded in a clean-energy economy is not immediately obvious. Our approach is to use observed job transitions to inform this question empirically. The papers closest in spirit to ours are Vona et al. (2018) and Curtis and Marinescu (2022), who explore potential wage and skill mismatches between brown and green workers, and the number and geographic distribution of new green jobs, respectively. Our analysis features novel data that allow for a more detailed categorization of relevant jobs—including, for instance, the inclusion of new jobs in EV production and associated industries—as well as estimates of empirically observed job-to-job transitions between dirty and green jobs, as opposed to simulations based on measures of skill similarity. Our paper also provides novel measures of job length across green and dirty jobs.

The rest of the paper is organized as follows. Section II discusses the empirical approach and the data. Section III presents our descriptive analysis of transitions into green jobs. Section IV presents a discussion of transitions out of dirty jobs. Section V discusses average job length of green and dirty jobs. Section VI discusses potential policy implications and concludes.

II. Data and Empirical Approach

Understanding the labor-market implications of the clean-energy transition requires, among other things, knowledge of realistic outside options: in particular, the outside options typically on offer to workers of varying skill levels within exposed (carbon-intensive) industries. An electrical engineer employed in the fossil fuel industry may be able to find work in similar occupations in a renewable energy firm. Could the same be said for oil derrick operators? To what extent might such transitions also be constrained by geography? And how might the transition prospects of either occupational group depend on the worker's age or educational attainment?

Answering these questions requires detailed employer-employee data and the ability to observe job transitions, the characteristics of the workers that make them, and detailed data on the jobs/firms they are making the transition to and from. Even the US Census' Longitudinal Employer-Household Dynamics program does not contain the detailed job information required to ascertain whether workers are in green jobs.

A. Lightcast Job-Profile Data

A major contribution of this paper is to apply social-profile data from Lightcast, which contains data on 130 million workers and their longitudinal job history, to questions pertaining to the labor-market implications of environmental policy.[4] The data contain a unique identifier for each individual, their job title, education level, gender, occupation, and industry of their company. Start dates are reported for each job, and end dates are reported for previous jobs reported on the profile. We infer workers' age based on their education level and the start of their first job. The worker's city and state are also reported. Although our sample consists of all workers who are currently in the United States or whose most recent job was in the United States, because we observe their full work history we can view transitions that have been made from other countries.

To identify job transitions, we first order each worker's jobs according to their start dates. We define a job transition as having occurred when the start date of a worker's next job occurs simultaneously or after the end date of their previous job. Because changes in job title are also reported, we require the company name to change as well.[5]

Importantly, the data include information on a worker's job title, employer name, industry (up to six-digit North American Industry Classification System [NAICS] codes), detailed occupation (Standard Occupational Classification [SOC] codes), and, for a subset of the data, the location of each job (city, state, and country). For the vast majority of observations, the data include information on the start and end month and year for each job.

As discussed in greater detail below, one of the advantages of working with these data is that it allows us to construct job-to-job transitions, into and out of green and dirty jobs. By combining information on job titles, employer names, industries, and occupations, we are also able to generate an arguably more comprehensive measure of green and dirty jobs than existing analyses. One of the disadvantages of using these data pertains to the representativeness of the population of interest. Although our sample spans all 50 US states, most major occupation groups, and most industries, it appears to overrepresent more educated workers, particularly in managerial and technical occupations. As shown in tables A1 and A2, which compare the relative share of jobs in our data by occupation and industry group with data from the Bureau of Labor Statistics (BLS), our worker profiles data overrepresent some industries—including "Educational Services," "Finance and Insurance," and "Wholesale Trade"—as well as certain occupational groups, notably "Management Occupations" and "Architecture and Engineering Occupations." However, as shown in tables A1 and A2, our data include jobs across all major industry and occupation categories, including in such industries as Manufacturing, Mining, Utilities, and Administrative Support and Waste Management and Remediation Services, as well as such occupation categories as Construction and Extraction, Production, and Sales. If anything, our data appear to slightly overrepresent Mining, Utilities, and Construction workers relative to the US population.

Another disadvantage of our data is that it is difficult to infer whether the observed transitions reflect voluntary movements up the job ladder or involuntary separations. It is unclear how such unobserved selection affects our interpretation of observed transitions. To the extent that one is interested in understanding the wage and employment consequences of adverse shocks to local labor demand, it is important to note that our measures of transition density or outside-option wage values include a mix of "push-" and "pull-related" factors.

B. Marklines Automobile Manufacturers Data

Marklines is a private company that collects detailed information on automobile and auto supplier sales and production data. Their data include a list of all automobile plants in the United States and the models they produce. It also contains all EV battery plants in the United States. We use information on firm-specific automobile plant characteristics to identify jobs that are associated with EV production: for instance, jobs based in manufacturing plants owned and operated by EV manufacturers (e.g., Tesla) or in EV-specific plants owned by general automobile manufacturers (e.g., Toyota).

C. BLS Data

Although Lightcast data provide considerable information on both firms and workers, they do not contain a direct measure of a worker's salary or earnings. To obtain a measure of worker pay, we use data from BLS' Occupational and Employment Wage Statistics (OEWS) program. The OEWS reports average earnings for every state by six-digit SOC pairing. When calculating outside earnings option, we therefore assign workers to have the average earnings of the state by the six-digit SOC pairing to which they belong.

D. Categorizing Dirty and Green Jobs

Our conceptual object of interest is a continuous measure of the carbon intensity of the marginal revenue of labor product associated with any given job. Such a measure would allow the researcher to array all existing jobs along a spectrum of potential adverse (or beneficial) labor-demand effects associated with policies that provide incentives for less carbon-intensive production as a means of internalizing the negative externality associated with carbon pollution.

In practice, such a measure is not readily available, nor are existing standardized industry or occupation codes designed in a way that neatly partitions the labor market along these dimensions. Our categorization of jobs into carbon-intensive (dirty), non–carbon-intensive (green), and an omitted "all other" classification reflects the notion that, to understand the relevant labor-market dynamics, starting with the extremes may be most instructive. As described below, we use information on job title, firm name, occupation, and industry, as well as, in some instances, a combination of firm name and location to provide a robust definition.

We define jobs as dirty if they are associated with industries and occupations very clearly related to fossil fuel extraction and fossil energy production, as well as on the basis of text matching on job title and company name. For instance, workers are categorized as dirty if their jobs are in extraction occupations (SOC code 47-5000, Extraction Workers) and in such industries as coal (NAICS 212), mining (213), oil and natural gas (211), and petroleum refining (324). We also include workers in the top five most energy-intensive manufacturing industries: cement and nonmetallic (327); primary metals (331); paper and pulp (322); chemicals, excluding cosmetics and pharmaceuticals (325); and textiles (313). In addition, we use keywords such as "coal," "petroleum," "fossil fuel," "shale," or "petrol" to match by job title.[6]

We define jobs as green in a similar way, using information on job title, occupation, company name, and industry, focusing in particular on jobs that are clearly associated with the production of renewable energy (solar, wind, etc.) or the production of EVs.[7]

To identify jobs in renewable energy, we include job titles that feature text such as "solar," "photovoltaic," "wind turbine," or "wind energy" and occupation titles that are defined by O*NET as solar and wind jobs (five eight-digit SOC codes for solar, four eight-digit SOC codes for wind).[8] We also include worker-jobs employed in the top five wind and top five solar companies in terms of revenues and market capitalization, respectively.[9] These include such solar companies as Avangrid, First Solar, and Sunpower, and such wind companies as Vestas Wind Systems and Brookfield Renewables. Importantly, we exclude from our definition jobs based in companies such as Siemens or General Electric, which not only engage in renewable energy generation but also engage in a wide range of other activities. Despite the availability of industry codes specific to renewable power generation, we decided to exclude "Solar Electric Power Generation" and "Wind Electric Power Generation" (NAICS 221114 and 221115) on the basis of visual inspection that suggested that a nontrivial fraction of underlying data had six-digit NAICS codes that were misclassified.

An important industry that has been missing from many previous analyses of green jobs is the production of EVs, which have historically been difficult to classify. This difficulty stems in part from the strong overlap between existing internal combustion engine automobile manufacturing firms and those engaging in EV production, as well as the lack of specific occupation codes associated with EV production. We use data from Marklines to identify automobile plants and companies in the United States that are exclusively engaging in EV production, as well as those firms that are engaged in the production of EV batteries. For instance, we categorize a job as a (green) EV job if it is based in EV battery-producing firms such as Ultium, Proterra, or SK Battery, or EV-producing firms such as Tesla or Rivian. We also include jobs in such companies as Toyota or Mercedes if they are based in cities where EV plants of those firms are known to exist.

Including these jobs expands our definition of green jobs significantly. Based on these classifications, we estimate that approximately 32.4% of green jobs are in solar, 13.5% are in wind, and 37.5% are associated with the production of EVs and their batteries. However, the total number of green jobs may be higher than our definition suggests. We do not capture workers in various up- or downstream industries whose labor demand may increase, such as chip manufacturers or EV sales and maintenance jobs. In addition, we do not capture EV jobs created by many established automobile manufacturers whose plants are currently making the transition to EV production.

III. Transitions into Green Jobs

What proportion of workers successfully make the transition from dirty to green jobs? And who are these workers?

Figure 1 shows the evolution of dirty-to-green transition share over time. It plots the share of workers who ever held a dirty job and made the transition to a new job (which could be another dirty job, a green job, or something else) whose destination job was classified as green. It suggests that the rate of successful transition has been rising steadily since the early 2000s, from less than 0.1% prior to 2005, reaching nearly 0.7% of all transitions out of dirty jobs by 2021. However, it also suggests that, as an overall share of transitions out of dirty jobs, such dirty-to-green transitions are exceedingly rare.

Figure 2 reproduces panel A of figure 1 but reports the share of transitions out of dirty jobs into green jobs by job category. We report jobs into EV, wind, solar, and renewables, as defined above. EV jobs stand out as having experienced notably rapid growth in recent years; they occupied a

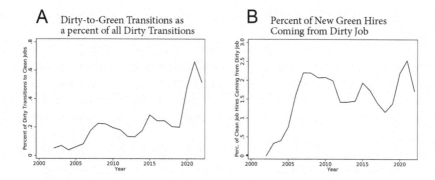

Fig. 1. Dirty-to-green transition rates. (*A*) Dirty-to-green transitions as a percentage of all dirty transitions. (*B*) Percentage of new green hires coming from dirty job. Color version available as an online enhancement.

Notes: Panel *A* of figure 1 shows a time-series plot of dirty-to-green transitions as a percentage of all transitions out of dirty jobs. Panel *B* shows a time-series plot of the percentage of hires in clean jobs that come from dirty jobs. A transition is defined as occurring if a worker leaves their company and joins another company.
Source: Worker profile data from Lightcast.

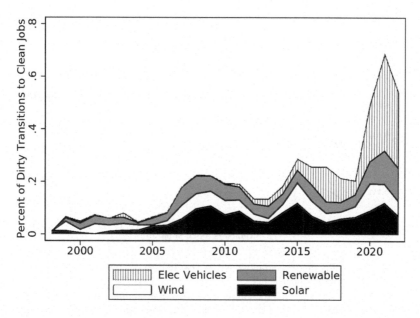

Fig. 2. Dirty-to-green transition probability by job category. Color version available as an online enhancement.

Source: Worker profile data from Lightcast.

miniscule share prior to 2010 but have undergone a significant increase, particularly since around 2015.

Workers seeking to make the transition out of declining dirty industries may not be able to find a green job immediately. Therefore, it may be important to account for the possibility that workers may hold intermediate positions—including in other jobs—before making the transition into a green job. Figure 3 shows the probability that a worker separating from a dirty job is employed in a green job as a function of the number of quarters since dirty-job separation, plotted separately by cohort, where a cohort is defined according to the year in which initial dirty-job separation occurred. For instance, across all workers who left a dirty job in 2018, 0.2% had started a green job within three quarters of initial separation, roughly 0.4% had done so within eight quarters (2 years), and more than 0.6% within 3 years. Consistent with the growing availability of green jobs, the slope of each cohort's transition rate appears to be growing steeper over time, with the exception of the 2022 cohort, for which we have limited data.[10]

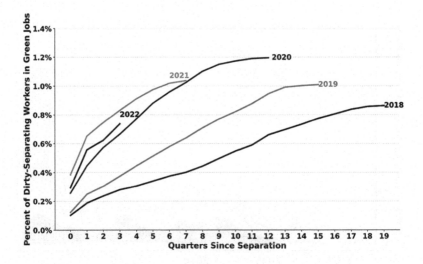

Fig. 3. Probability of green employment by year of dirty-job separation. Color version available as an online enhancement.

Notes: Figure 3 plots out the probability that a worker separating from a dirty job is employed in a green job as a function of the number of quarters since the dirty-job separation. For example, 1.2% of workers leaving a dirty job in 2020 were employed in a green job 12 quarters after their separation. The figure tracks this out separately for workers separating in 2018, 2019, 2020, 2021, and 2022.

Source: Worker profile data from Lightcast.

The rate of dirty-to-green transition varies substantially by educational attainment. Workers without a bachelor's degree are significantly less likely to successfully make the transition from dirty jobs to green ones compared with workers in our data with at least a bachelor's. Figure 4 shows the transition shares across educational-attainment categories. Workers with doctoral degrees appear to be 44% (0.15 percentage points) more likely to successfully make the transition from a carbon-intensive job to a green job than workers with a high school education or less, though only 4% (0.02 percentage points) more likely than those with associate's degrees.

Figure 4 also shows the breakdown by age group. It suggests that older workers are significantly less likely to make a dirty-to-green transition than younger workers. Workers between the ages of 55 and 64 appear to be 38% (0.16 percentage points) less likely to make the transition than workers ages 25–34. Workers ages 65 and above are 60% (0.25 percentage points) less likely to do so than workers ages 25–34.

Consistent with previous work that finds job growth in green industries to be highly geographically concentrated, we find that the rate of dirty-to-green transition varies enormously across local labor markets. Figure 5 shows the top states and cities by share of workers who made the transition out of dirty jobs into green jobs. States such as California, Oregon, and Arizona appear to have experienced higher rates of dirty-to-green transition, compared with states such as South Carolina, Louisiana, and West Virginia.

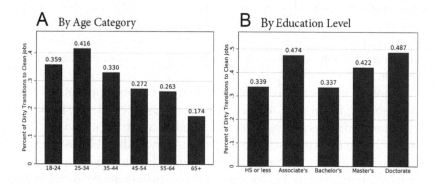

Fig. 4. Probability of dirty-to-green transition. (*A*) By age category. (*B*) By education level. Color version available as an online enhancement.

Notes: Figure 4 shows the probability that a worker leaving a dirty job enters a green job for workers of different ages and levels of education. For reference, the percentage of workers in our sample leaving a dirty job and entering a green job with a high school degree or less is 28.1 and for associate's degrees is 7.1. For bachelor's, master's, and doctoral degrees, the shares are 34, 25.2, and 5.5, respectively. Source: Worker profile data from Lightcast.

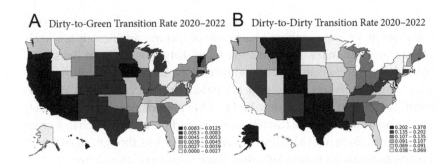

Fig. 5. Dirty-to-green and dirty-to-dirty transition rates 2020–22. (*A*) Dirty-to-green transition rate 2020–22. (*B*) Dirty-to-dirty transition rate 2020–22. Color version available as an online enhancement.

Notes: Figure 5 shows the probability that a worker leaving a dirty job enters a green job. Since 2020, more than 1% of workers leaving a dirty job in California, Iowa, Nevada, and Arizona have transitioned to a green job. Delaware, Louisiana, Texas, Oklahoma, and Wyoming are the highest dirty-to-dirty states.

Source: Worker profile data from Lightcast.

Who are the workers most likely to make the transition into green jobs? Table 1 reports the most common occupations that make the transition into each of the four green-job categories we define. Table A3 reports the occupations of noncollege workers most likely to make the transition into these categories. For example, column 2 shows the top 20 occupation groups by thickness of transition share into wind jobs, limiting to noncollege workers. Many of these workers previously worked as Maintenance and Repair Workers, General and Operations Managers, or Computer Support Specialists. Table A4 shows similar information for college workers entering wind jobs and both noncollege and college workers entering solar jobs.

A nontrivial fraction of transitions into green jobs appears to come from abroad. In our data, 4.9% of transitions into green jobs are by workers whose previous jobs were located in other countries, including Denmark, the United Kingdom, Spain, Germany, and India. Table A5 reports the top 10 countries sending workers to green jobs in the United States. We are careful to note that our data do not include information on the worker's nationality and that the nature of selection into our data may overstate the share coming from overseas, given relative overrepresentation of more highly educated workers and managerial, technical, and professional occupations. Nevertheless, it is notable that at least 14,066 green jobs during our study period were taken by individuals whose previous jobs were located overseas.

Table 1
Top Green Entering Occupations

Top Occs. to Solar	Top Occs. to Wind	Top Occs. to EV	Top Occs. to Renew
Sales Managers	Chief Executives	Industrial Engineers	Chief Executives
Chief Executives	General and Operations Managers	Software Developers	General and Operations Managers
General and Operations Managers	Sales Managers	Mechanical Engineers	Managers, All Other
Marketing Managers	Managers, All Other	General and Operations Managers	Marketing Managers
Managers, All Other	Marketing Managers	Chief Executives	Financial Managers
Wholesale Sales Reps	Financial Managers	Marketing Managers	Sales Managers
Office Supervisors	Industrial Engineers	Sales Managers	Arch. & Eng. Managers
Industrial Engineers	Arch. & Eng. Managers	Managers, All Other	Proj. Management Specialists
Financial Managers	Mechanical Engineers	Office Supervisors	Accountants and Auditors
Customer Service Representatives	Computer User Support Specialists	Computer User Support Specialists	Project Management Specialists
Software Developers	Production Supervisors	Production Supervisors	Life/Phys./Soc. Sci. Techs
Computer User Support Specialists	Office Supervisors	Human Resources Specialists	Office Supervisors
Proj. Management Specialists	Software Developers	Arch. & Eng. Managers	Electrical Engineers
Arch. & Eng. Managers	Mechanics Supervisors	Customer Service Representatives	Industrial Engineers
Electrical Engineers	Maint. & Repair Workers	Financial Managers	Software Developers
Retail Salespersons	Proj. Management Specialists	Electrical Engineers	Engineers, All Other
Management Analysts	Management Analysts	Management Analysts	Bus. Operations Specialists
Mechanical Engineers	Human Resources Managers	Human Resources Managers	Mkt. Research Analysts
Bus. Operations Specialists	Comp. & Info. Sys. Managers	Computer Occupations, All Other	Mechanical Engineers
Engineers, All Other	Engineers, All Other	Bus. Operations Specialists	Postsecondary Teachers

Source: Worker profile data from Lightcast.
Note: Table 1 lists the top sending occupations for each of the four green-job categories. Workers in these occupations are most likely to enter green jobs.

In summary, although some workers indeed appear to be able to make the transition from working in a carbon-intensive job to a less carbon-intensive one, the data clearly show that the majority of green jobs are not being filled by former dirty workers, at least not historically.

IV. Transitions Out of Dirty Jobs

If such a small fraction of workers who leave a dirty job enter a green one (less than 1% in our data), where do they go? From a welfare perspective, it is important to understand whether workers facing diminishing labor demand in one sector are able to make the transition out of that sector, including jobs not obviously related to green technologies. In this section, we present descriptive evidence on where workers in carbon-intensive jobs have tended to make the transition to, and how the rate of successful transition out of declining dirty industries varies by educational attainment, geography, and age.

Tables 2 and 3 show the top 30 destination occupations for workers leaving dirty jobs, broken up by workers without a bachelor's degree (BA) and workers with at least a BA. Non-BA workers formerly employed in carbon-intensive jobs appear to make the transition to a wide range of occupations—including General and Operations Managers, Sales Managers, Computer User Support Specialists, Customer Service Representatives, Heavy and Tractor-Trailer Truck Drivers, and Mechanical Engineers—highlighting the breadth of outside options potentially available to formerly carbon-intensive workers. At the same time, many of the occupational categories listed may, depending on the degree of industrial concentration in a local labor market, be directly or indirectly dependent on carbon-intensive industries. This suggests that it may be important to understand the rate of transition within carbon-intensive jobs.

As shown in table 4, which reports the most common industries that college and noncollege workers in dirty jobs enter when they leave their dirty job, a large fraction of those leaving dirty jobs enter (or remain in) the manufacturing sector. For noncollege workers, 24.5% of all transitions away from dirty jobs are to jobs in manufacturing industries.

We therefore estimate the share of workers who ever held and eventually leave a dirty job that make a transition to other dirty jobs. Specifically, we define the dirty-to-dirty transition share as the conditional probability of making a transition to a dirty job, conditional on having ever held a dirty job and moved to a new job at some point in our sample.[11] In our data, approximately 22% of workers who make the transition out of a dirty job go to another dirty job.

Table 2
Top 30 Receiving Occupations from Dirty Jobs: Less than College

Occupation	SOC	# Transitions	% Transitions
General and Operations Managers	11-1021	24,384	3.6
Chief Executives	11-1011	24,110	3.6
Supervisors of Office and Admin	43-1011	20,290	3.0
Supervisors of Prod. and Operating Work	51-1011	18,983	2.8
Sales Managers	11-2022	18,289	2.7
Managers, All Other	11-9199	17,830	2.7
Computer User Support Specialists	15-1232	14,819	2.2
Supervisors of Construction and Extract.	47-1011	13,645	2.0
Customer Service Representatives	43-4051	12,548	1.9
Supervisors of Mechanics, Inst., Repair	49-1011	11,555	1.7
Sales Reps, Wholesale and Mfg.	41-4012	11,157	1.7
Secretaries and Admin. Assistants	43-6014	10,910	1.6
Maintenance and Repair Workers, General	49-9071	10,640	1.6
Heavy and Tractor-Trailer Truck Drivers	53-3032	10,292	1.5
Business Oper. Specialists, All Other	13-1199	8,686	1.3
Marketing Managers	11-2021	8,020	1.2
Bookkeeping, Accounting, and Auditing	43-3031	7,681	1.1
Industrial Engineers	17-2112	7,623	1.1
Network and Computer Systems Admin.	15-1244	7,566	1.1
Mechanical Engineers	17-2141	6,818	1.0
Software Developers	15-1252	6,809	1.0
Inspectors, Testers, Sorters, Samplers	51-9061	6,776	1.0
Petroleum Engineers	17-2171	6,467	1.0
Financial Managers	11-3031	6,456	1.0
Service Unit Operators, Oil and Gas	47-5013	6,354	1.0
Executive Secretaries and Exec Admin.	43-6011	6,285	.9
Accountants and Auditors	13-2011	6,156	.9
Retail Salespersons	41-2031	5,965	.9
Industrial Production Managers	11-3051	5,735	.9
Project Management Specialists	13-1082	5,726	.9

Source: Worker profile data from Lightcast.
Note: Table 2 reports the most common occupations that noncollege workers in dirty jobs enter when they leave their dirty job. The first row shows that 3.6% of all transitions away from dirty are to General and Operations Managers.

This share is higher for workers without a bachelor's degree, at 27%, versus 19% for workers with at least a bachelor's degree. Workers with a high school diploma or less are 44% (8 percentage points) more likely than workers with at least an associate's degree to remain in a dirty job when making the transition out of a dirty job. Interestingly, for workers with at least an associate's degree, there do not appear to be large differences in dirty-to-dirty transition shares for workers of different levels of educational attainment.

Table 3
Top 30 Receiving Occupations from Dirty Jobs: College Grads

Occupation	SOC	# Transitions	% Transitions
Industrial Engineers	17-2112	42,499	4.0
Chief Executives	11-1011	41,439	3.9
General and Operations Managers	11-1021	37,534	3.5
Sales Managers	11-2022	35,443	3.3
Marketing Managers	11-2021	34,501	3.2
Financial Managers	11-3031	32,034	3.0
Accountants and Auditors	13-2011	31,241	2.9
Software Developers	15-1252	25,688	2.4
Managers, All Other	11-9199	24,217	2.3
Management Analysts	13-1111	22,003	2.1
Mechanical Engineers	17-2141	19,616	1.8
Supervisors of Office and Admin.	43-1011	18,259	1.7
Computer Systems Analysts	15-1211	18,248	1.7
Human Resources Managers	11-3121	18,107	1.7
Architectural and Engineering Managers	11-9041	16,967	1.6
Computer User Support Specialists	15-1232	15,107	1.4
Computer Occupations, All Other	15-1299	14,638	1.4
Business Operations Specialists	13-1199	14,087	1.3
Supervisors of Production and Op. Workers	51-1011	13,773	1.3
Computer and Information Systems Managers	11-3021	13,329	1.3
Geoscientists	19-2042	13,248	1.2
Sales Reps, Wholesale and Mfg.	41-4012	13,123	1.2
Project Management Specialists	13-1082	13,018	1.2
Customer Service Representatives	43-4051	12,729	1.2
Engineers, All Other	17-2199	11,917	1.1
Market Research Analysts	13-1161	11,898	1.1
Industrial Production Managers	11-3051	11,498	1.1
Postsecondary Teachers	25-1099	11,357	1.1
Petroleum Engineers	17-2171	10,875	1.0
Life, Physical, and Social Science Tech.	19-4099	9,887	.9

Source: Worker profile data from Lightcast.
Note: Table 3 reports the most common occupations that college workers in dirty jobs enter when they leave their dirty job. The first row shows that 4.0% of all transitions away from dirty are to Industrial Engineering occupations.

The likelihood of remaining within carbon-intensive sectors appears to be significantly higher for older workers. Workers ages 55 to 64 are approximately 25% (5 percentage points) more likely to make a transition into another dirty job compared with workers ages 18 to 34. For prime-age workers (ages 18 to 64), there appears to be a monotonically rising relationship between age and probability of remaining anchored to dirty jobs.

Consistent with previous work on the geographic concentration of fossil fuel–related jobs (Jacobsen and Parker 2016; Raimi 2021; Hanson

Table 4
Receiving Industries from Dirty Jobs

Sector	Sector Code	Total Trans	%
A: Less than College			
Manufacturing	31–33	141,180	24.5
Oil & Gas Extraction, Mining	21	81,416	14.2
Prof., Sci., and Tech. Serv.	54	51,387	8.9
Construction	23	43,872	7.6
Retail Trade	44–45	39,317	6.8
Wholesale Trade	42	37,596	6.5
Admin. and Support and Waste Mgmt.	56	23,308	4.1
Transportation and Warehousing	48–49	19,710	3.4
Finance and Insurance	52	18,329	3.2
Other Services (except Public Admin.)	81	15,264	2.7
Health Care and Social Assistance	62	14,761	2.6
Information	51	12,663	2.2
Accommodation and Food Services	72	12,552	2.2
Real Estate and Rental and Leasing	53	12,518	2.2
Public Administration	92	12,414	2.2
B: College Grads			
Manufacturing	31–33	289,329	29.5
Prof., Sci., and Tech. Serv.	54	129,995	13.2
Oil & Gas Extraction, Mining	21	75,452	7.7
Educational Services	61	64,740	6.6
Wholesale Trade	42	63,116	6.4
Retail Trade	44–45	55,922	5.7
Finance and Insurance	52	43,923	4.5
Construction	23	38,247	3.9
Information	51	28,779	2.9
Health Care and Social Assistance	62	28,476	2.9
Admin. and Support and Waste Mgmt.	56	27,365	2.8
Other Services (except Public Admin.)	81	22,183	2.3
Public Administration	92	19,835	2.0
Utilities	22	18,111	1.8
Transportation and Warehousing	48–49	17,473	1.8

Source: Worker profile data from Lightcast.
Note: Panel A reports the most common industries that noncollege workers in dirty jobs enter when they leave their dirty job. The first row shows that 24.5% of all transitions away from dirty are to the manufacturing sector. Panel B reports the same for college workers.

2023), we find that the share of dirty-to-dirty transitions varies significantly across geographies. Table 5 shows the average dirty-to-dirty transition shares for the top 15 cities and states. States such as Delaware, Oklahoma, Wyoming, Texas, Colorado, and Louisiana appear to feature high degrees of persistence of employment within dirty industries. In some cities, such as Oklahoma City, Oklahoma, Denver, Colorado, or

Table 5
Top Dirty-to-Dirty Cities and States

Top Cities	Dirty Trans Rate	Top States	Dirty Trans Rate
San Ramon	.920	Delaware	.552
Sugar Land	.845	Oklahoma	.533
The Woodlands	.691	Wyoming	.406
Oklahoma City	.681	Texas	.398
Midland	.635	Colorado	.369
Denver	.598	Louisiana	.335
Wilmington	.594	North Dakota	.299
Irving	.482	Pennsylvania	.242
Houston	.443	West Virginia	.235
Cleveland	.416	South Carolina	.205
Memphis	.410	Ohio	.192
Tulsa	.399	New Mexico	.185
Pittsburgh	.394	Tennessee	.180
San Antonio	.368	Alaska	.176
Philadelphia	.342	Kansas	.171

Source: Worker profile data from Lightcast.
Note: Table 5 provides the 15 cities and states with the highest dirty-to-dirty transition rates. These numbers are from all transitions in our sample. The maps in figure 5 report results only for years 2020–22. Cities are only included if there are more than 50,000 dirty jobs reported over the entirety of our sample. City definitions are self-reported in the data. Many "cities" in our data, such as Sugar Land and The Woodlands, are suburbs located inside large metropolitan areas like Houston.

Wilmington, Delaware, nearly two-thirds of transitions out of a dirty job are into another dirty job. As seen in figure 5, workers in states such as Kansas and Alaska appear to be less likely to remain in dirty jobs, despite relatively low population density. This suggests that simply discerning whether labor markets are geographically isolated (or not) or feature many existing carbon-intensive jobs (or not) may be of limited value in identifying the workers most likely to experience adverse labor-market shocks due to climate policy.

One way to measure the potential labor-market impacts of the transition away from fossil fuels would be to estimate the change in the set of outside options associated with ensuing reductions in labor demand. The extent to which the clean-energy transition affects a worker's labor-market prospects will depend in part on how labor demand in other jobs that she might be likely to make the transition to is affected. An informative hypothetical therefore would be to assess, for dirty workers in different local labor markets, how the menu of available job options changes in a world with dramatically reduced labor demand in other carbon-intensive sectors, and to do so in a way that accounts for local differences in the degree of thickness in historical job-to-job transition flows.

Our data allow something close to this, as we can empirically estimate the relevant outside options by job type and location (e.g., city, state), and do so separately for workers with higher and lower levels of human capital. We follow Schubert et al. (2021) to estimate outside-option wages for each occupational category in our data, with modifications to allow for different occupation-to-occupation transition shares by industry and state.[12]

Figure 6 shows how the set of outside options changes in a hypothetical world in which other local dirty jobs are no longer available. For illustrative purposes, we make the admittedly extreme assumption that the wages associated with all other local dirty jobs go to zero in this scenario. For workers both with and without a college degree, we can see that there are reductions in the set of available jobs across the wage distribution. This provides visual evidence regarding the extent to which such reductions in outside options may prove problematic for workers in different local labor markets. As shown in figure 7, some states, including Texas, Louisiana, Oklahoma, and West Virginia, appear to experience a much greater reduction in the total wage bill associated with remaining local outside options for dirty workers, compared with states such as Washington, Massachusetts, Oregon, Illinois, and Florida.

We note that, in our data, it is not possible to systematically distinguish between transitions that arise from moving up the job ladder or moving to firms that provide better match quality (pull factors) and those due to involuntary dislocations (push factors). We therefore interpret these

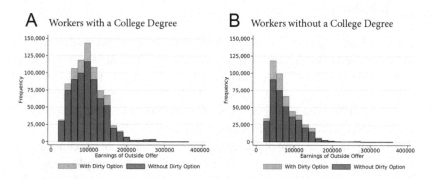

Fig. 6. Outside transition option with and without dirty option. (*A*) Workers with a college degree. (*B*) Workers without a college degree. Color version available as an online enhancement.

Notes: Figure 6 shows the difference in our measure of outside earnings option for workers in dirty industries/occupations when they are not allowed to transition to another dirty industry.

Source: Worker profile data from Lightcast.

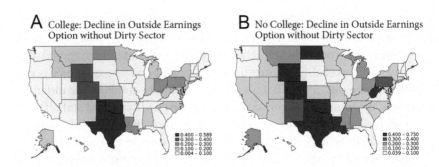

Fig. 7. Outside earnings difference without dirty option. (*A*) College: Decline in outside earnings option without dirty sector. (*B*) No college: Decline in outside earnings option without dirty sector. Color version available as an online enhancement.

Notes: Figure 7 shows the difference in our measure of outside earnings option for workers in dirty industries/occupations when they are not allowed to transition to another dirty industry.

Source: Worker profile data from Lightcast.

findings with the understanding that there may be selection effects that limit the applicability to the study of acute reductions in labor demand. Moreover, to the extent that dramatic reductions in labor demand in fossil-intensive industries may generate spillover effects in other adjacent industries, our assessment of potential changes in outside wage options may be biased in unknown directions. Therefore, we caution against interpreting the absolute magnitude of decline.

V. Job Duration

Even if a high fraction of workers in dirty jobs successfully make the transition to green ones, it may be important to know how stable or transitory such employment spells are. Such possibilities are part of a broader set of concerns around the relative quality of jobs that may prevail in an economy that makes the transition away from fossil fuels, including relative wages (Vona et al. 2018; Curtis and Marinescu 2022).

One important feature of job transition for which there remains limited empirical evidence pertains to the stability of resulting employment. For instance, a recent OECD report notes that "the duration of jobs is crucial when assessing the economic and societal impacts of green policies . . . Replacing permanent mining jobs by temporary wind farm construction jobs, results in an overall loss of long-term employment."[13] However, many occupation and industry classifications historically did not include designations for many newer green jobs. Even in instances when new classification schemes have become available over time, the ability to backward-cast new classifications to previous jobs has tended to be limited, particularly for data sets that provide a longitudinal picture of job-to-job transitions. As such, there are to our knowledge few measures of job length that allow for meaningful comparisons between dirty and green jobs.

Figure A1 shows average job lengths across job categories for both green and dirty jobs. It suggests that, in the naive cross section, green jobs appear to be significantly shorter in duration than dirty ones. The average solar job lasts between 2.2 and 2.6 years (depending on whether one includes jobs that do not have an end date and are listed as "current" in our data). The average EV job lasts approximately 1.9–2.4 years. In contrast, the average dirty job has a duration of between 4.6 and 6.3 years.

However, such measures do not account for the fact that many green jobs are likely to have started relatively recently and may be held by younger workers who tend to have shorter jobs on average (Hyatt and Spletzer 2016). Indeed, controlling for start-year changes, the relative job lengths considerably. Table 6 presents the results of a series of analyses that regress job length in years on indicator variables for categories of green jobs, with the reference category being dirty jobs. As shown in column 2 of table 6, adding fixed effects for starting year reduces the job-length differences between green and dirty jobs considerably. Whereas solar, wind, and EV jobs appear 2.48, 1.30, and 2.89 years shorter than dirty jobs in the cross section (col. 1), adjusting for start date reduces the differences dramatically, such that solar jobs appear to last 0.26 fewer years than dirty jobs, wind jobs do not appear to be significantly different in length than dirty jobs, and EV jobs actually appear to be 0.24 years longer than dirty jobs. These are novel descriptive facts that may have important implications for how policy makers weigh the costs and benefits of making the transition away from carbon-intensive production.

Including additional controls for the number of prior jobs by the worker (col. 3); worker-level demographic controls, including gender, age, education, and state (col. 4); and broad occupation category in the form of two-digit SOC fixed effects (col. 5) does not change the qualitative finding that green jobs do not appear to be dramatically shorter in duration than dirty jobs that they may replace, though solar and wind jobs do appear to be statistically significantly shorter in duration, by approximately 3 months (col. 5: 0.28 years and 0.24 years, respectively). If anything, EV jobs appear to last slightly longer (col. 5: 0.046 years) than the average dirty job. Column 6 adds company fixed effects, which focuses on variation in job length across green and dirty jobs within the same firm. Our identifying

Table 6
Job Duration: Are Green Jobs Short-Lived?

	(1)	(2)	(3)	(4)	(5)	(6)
	Job Length	Job Length	Job Length	Job Length	Job Length	Job Length
Solar job	-2.476***	-.256***	-.228***	-.307***	-.280***	-.051
	(.028)	(.022)	(.022)	(.023)	(.023)	(.058)
Wind job	-1.300***	.018	.023	-.052	-.240***	-.263***
	(.048)	(.038)	(.038)	(.038)	(.038)	(.069)
EV job	-2.891***	.238***	.266***	.047*	.046*	.472
	(.031)	(.025)	(.025)	(.028)	(.028)	(.635)
Renewable job	-1.749***	-.131***	-.080***	.032	.037	.329***
	(.037)	(.029)	(.029)	(.029)	(.029)	(.075)
Job start date FEs	N	Y	Y	Y	Y	Y
Job number FEs	N	N	Y	Y	Y	Y
Age, educ, gender, state FEs	N	N	N	Y	Y	Y
2-digit SOC FEs	N	N	N	N	Y	Y
Company FEs	N	N	N	N	N	Y
Observations	1,960,074	1,960,074	1,960,074	1,960,074	1,960,074	1,960,074

Source: Worker profile data from Lightcast.

Note: Table 6 regresses job length in years on indicator variables for categories of green jobs. The excluded category is dirty jobs. The sample consists of only dirty and green categories and jobs that have both a start and end date. Table A6 reports results when including current jobs in the sample and setting 2023 as the end date. Column 1 is a naive specification that mirrors the results in figure A1. Column 2 includes only a set of starting year fixed effects (FEs). Controlling for the year the job began dramatically changes the green-job coefficients. Column 3 also controls for the number of prior jobs held by a worker. Column 4 controls for worker demographics (age, education, gender, state). Column 5 controls for the broad occupation category of the worker by including two-digit Standard Occupational Classification (SOC) fixed effect. Column 5 is our preferred specification. We also report results that include company FEs in column 6. By including company FEs, we are absorbing much of the variation used to identify the differences in job length; nonetheless, these inform of the within-company differences in job length for those companies where this variation is present.

*p < .10.
***p < .01.

variation in this instance shrinks considerably, as variation across companies is absorbed by the fixed effects, making the coefficient on solar and EV jobs no longer significant. Nevertheless, it is instructive that, adjusting for start date, the differences in job duration between green and dirty jobs do not appear to be smaller than suggested in the cross section.

How externally valid are our measures of job length? One concern with these findings pertains to possible selection into our worker profile database. According to BLS data, median employee tenure in 2022 was 4.3 years for men and 3.8 years for women. We hesitate to make direct comparisons of absolute job tenure given the selection in our sample.[14] It is worth noting that a significant fraction of observations in our data may have been missing information on the month of the year in which a job started, leading to what appears to be bunching in January. To the extent that this is the result of mechanically assigning January as a start date to some fraction of jobs that actually began in later months in the same calendar year, this would lead our measures of job tenure to be shorter across the board. To the extent that our sample underrepresents certain blue-collar occupations (e.g., construction), the external validity of these findings may be limited for some subgroups for whom shorter job duration may be especially problematic. We note also that emerging work on alternative work arrangements and the "gig economy" suggest that shorter jobs may play an important role in the labor market, either as sources of supplementary income or in providing flexible work arrangements that are valued in themselves, and so caution against interpreting relative job duration as an indicator of job quality or welfare.

VI. Discussion and Conclusion

This paper explores the potential labor-market implications of making the transition away from fossil fuels and toward less carbon-intensive energy sources. Previous research suggests that policy-induced shifts in labor demand can have highly localized and unequal labor-market consequences: for instance, in the context of trade liberalization and import competition from China (Autor, Dorn, and Hanson 2013, 2021).

In this paper, we provide novel descriptive evidence regarding how the shift away from carbon-intensive industries might affect workers. Our findings highlight the importance of understanding the outside options available to workers, including in cleaner industries and in other local industries where their skills may be a good match.

We provide evidence that although the number of workers transitioning from carbon-intensive dirty jobs to non–carbon-intensive "green" jobs is still relatively small, the rate of dirty-to-green transition appears to be rising rapidly. The observed increase in this rate corresponds with the increase in the number of available green jobs. If this continues, we will expect to see a sizable number of workers currently employed in dirty jobs make the transition to green jobs. Moreover, green jobs appear to offer similar opportunities for longer-term employment as many existing dirty jobs, as evidenced by roughly similar average job lengths.

At the same time, our data suggest that, if past trends continue, the clean-energy transition may have important distributional consequences that could exacerbate underlying trends in labor-market inequality. We find that workers without a college degree and older workers are significantly less likely to transition into green jobs and more likely to remain in carbon-intensive jobs. The high rate of employment persistence within dirty jobs in some localities suggests that there may be limits to the extent to which local labor markets are able to absorb the workers who will be displaced by the move away from fossil fuels.

Appendix

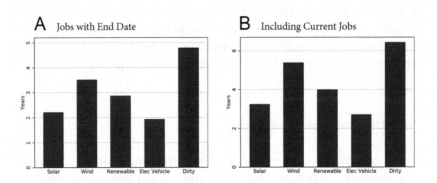

Fig. A1. Naive estimates of average job length by dirty/green. (*A*) Jobs with end date. (*B*) Including current jobs. Color version available as an online enhancement.

Notes: Figure A1 shows the average length of different brown-/green-job categories. Green jobs, which largely did not exist 20 years ago, will by construction have a shorter job length than dirty jobs, which have been prominent for decades. Table 6 reports regressions that control for the job start date and worker demographics. Those regressions show that the difference in job length shrinks considerably or disappears after controlling for these differences.

Source: Worker profile data from Lightcast.

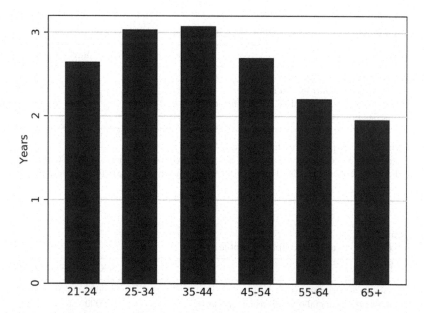

Fig. A2. Expected job length by worker age at start of job. Color version available as an online enhancement.

Source: Worker profile data from Lightcast.

Table A1
Job Profile versus BLS Industry Profile

	NAICS 2	BLS%	Profile%
Agriculture, forestry, fishing, and hunting	11	.13	.42
Mining, quarrying, and oil and gas extraction	21	.37	.65
Utilities	22	.49	.79
Construction	23	5.52	3.57
Manufacturing	31	9.08	12.3
Wholesale trade	42	4.63	4.05
Retail trade	44	12.15	9.06
Transportation and warehousing	48	4.45	2.67
Information	51	2.67	5.16
Finance and insurance	52	5.26	8.18
Real estate and rental and leasing	53	1.71	2.51
Professional, scientific, and technical services	54	7.37	12.2
Management of companies and enterprises	55	2.73	.47
Administrative and support and waste management and remediation services	56	9.73	3.54
Educational services	61	2.72	11.55
Health care and social assistance	62	16.13	9.45

Table A1
(Continued)

	NAICS 2	BLS%	Profile%
Arts, entertainment, and recreation	71	1.45	1.6
Accommodation and food services	72	9.43	4.23
Other services (except public administration)	81	3.98	3.4
Industries not classified			4.2

Source: Worker profile data from Lightcast.
Note: Table A1 compares the industry distribution of the worker profile data with Bureau of Labor Statistics (BLS). NAICS = North American Industry Classification System.

Table A2
Job Profile versus BLS Occupation Profile

	SOC 2	BLS%	Profile%
Management occupations	11-0000	7.39	23.55
Business and financial operations occupations	13-0000	6.32	8.88
Computer and mathematical occupations	15-0000	3.13	7.71
Architecture and engineering occupations	17-0000	1.62	3.04
Life, physical, and social science occupations	19-0000	.91	1.78
Community and social service occupations	21-0000	1.8	2.48
Legal occupations	23-0000	.87	1.18
Educational instruction and library occupations	25-0000	5.79	5.22
Arts, design, entertainment, sports, and media occupations	27-0000	1.76	4.74
Healthcare practitioners and technical occupations	29-0000	5.84	4.02
Healthcare support occupations	31-0000	4.44	1.14
Protective service occupations	33-0000	2.2	1.18
Food preparation and serving related occupations	35-0000	7.44	1.87
Building and grounds cleaning and maintenance occupations	37-0000	3.42	.39
Personal care and service occupations	39-0000	2.45	1.16
Sales and related occupations	41-0000	9.31	6.59
Office and administrative support occupations	43-0000	12.39	9.64
Farming, fishing, and forestry occupations	45-0000	.68	.08
Construction and extraction occupations	47-0000	4.44	.87
Installation, maintenance, and repair occupations	49-0000	3.82	1.34
Production occupations	51-0000	5.56	1.95
Transportation and material moving occupations	53-0000	8.44	1.82
Other			9.22

Source: Worker profile data from Lightcast.
Note: Table A2 compares the occupation distribution of the worker profile data to Bureau of Labor Statistics (BLS). SOC = Standard Occupational Classification.

Table A3
Top Green Entering Occupations: Noncollege

Top Occs. to Solar	Top Occs. to Wind	Top Occs. to EV	Top Occs. to Renew.
Sales Managers	Chief Executives	General and Operations Managers	Chief Executives
General and Operations Managers	General and Operations Managers	Office Supervisors	General and Operations Managers
Chief Executives	Computer User Support Specialists	Computer User Support Specialists	Managers, All Other
Wholesale Sales Reps	Maint. and Repair Workers	Production Supervisors	Sales Managers
Managers, All Other	Mechanics Supervisors	Customer Service Representatives	Office Supervisors
Office Supervisors	Production Supervisors	Auto Service Techs	Computer User Support Specialists
Customer Service Representatives	Office Supervisors	Managers, All Other	Mechanics Supervisors
Computer User Support Specialists	Managers, All Other	Chief Executives	Production Supervisors
Retail Salespersons	Sales Managers	Sales Managers	Marketing Managers
Mechanics Supervisors	Customer Service Representatives	Industrial Engineers	Construction Supervisors
Marketing Managers	Auto Service Techs	Software Developers	Construction Managers
Electricians	Electricians	Mechanics Supervisors	Wind Turbine Service Technicians
Production Supervisors	Construction Supervisors	Maint. and Repair Workers	Proj. Management Specialists
Construction Supervisors	Industrial Engineers	Mechanical Engineers	Customer Service Representatives
Services Sales Reps.	Marketing Managers	Retail Salespersons	Secretaries and Admin. Assistants
Maint. and Repair Workers	Mechanical Engineers	Wholesale Sales Reps.	Financial Managers
Proj. Management Specialists	Proj. Management Specialists	Human Resources Specialists	Software Developers
Construction Managers	Electrical and Electronic Eng.	Marketing Managers	Bus. Operations Specialists
Bus. Operations Specialists	Financial Managers	Bus. Operations Specialists	Network and Comp Sys Admins
Financial Managers	Software Developers	Network and Comp Sys Admins	Maint. & Repair Workers

Source: Worker profile data from Lightcast.
Note: Table A3 lists the top sending occupations for each of the four green-job categories for workers without a college degree.

Table A4

Top Green Entering Occupations: College

Top Occs. to Solar	Top Occs. to Wind	Top Occs. to EV	Top Occs. to Renew
Sales Managers	Chief Executives	Industrial Engineers	Chief Executives
Chief Executives	General and Operations Managers	Software Developers	General and Operations Managers
Marketing Managers	Marketing Managers	Mechanical Engineers	Financial Managers
General & Operations Managers	Sales Managers	General and Operations Managers	Marketing Managers
Managers, All Other	Financial Managers	Marketing Managers	Managers, All Other
Industrial Engineers	Industrial Engineers	Chief Executives	Sales Managers
Financial Managers	Arch. and Eng. Managers	Sales Managers	Arch. and Eng. Managers
Software Developers	Managers, All Other	Managers, All Other	Management Analysts
Arch. and Eng. Managers	Mechanical Engineers	Arch. and Eng. Managers	Life/Phys./Soc. Sci. Techs
Electrical Engineers	Software Developers	Human Resources Specialists	Accountants and Auditors
Management Analysts	Management Analysts	Financial Managers	Electrical Engineers
Mechanical Engineers	Engineers, All Other	Electrical Engineers	Engineers, All Other
Office Supervisors	Human Resources Managers	Office Supervisors	Proj. Management Specialists
Proj. Management Specialists	Proj. Management Specialists	Management Analysts	Industrial Engineers
Comp. and Info. Sys. Managers	Comp. and Info. Sys. Managers	Human Resources Managers	Mkt. Research Analysts
Accountants and Auditors	Accountants and Auditors	Computer Occupations, All Other	Software Developers
Wholesale Sales Reps	Office Supervisors	Computer User Support Specialists	Postsecondary Teachers
Mkt. Research Analysts	Postsecondary Teachers	Production Supervisors	Mechanical Engineers
Customer Service Representatives	Production Supervisors	Accountants and Auditors	Bus. Operations Specialists
Bus. Operations Specialists	Electrical Engineers	Engineers, All Other	Postsecondary Teaching Assts.

Source: Worker profile data from Lightcast.

Note: Table A4 lists the top sending occupations for each of the four green-job categories for workers with a college degree.

Table A5

Countries Sending Most Green Workers to the United States

Country	Green Transitions
Denmark	7,803
United Kingdom	2,604
Spain	2,325
Canada	1,794
Italy	1,326
Germany	1,163
France	1,142
India	768
South Korea	763
Netherlands	528

Source: Worker profile data from Lightcast.
Note: Table A5 lists the countries sending the highest number of workers to US green jobs. Denmark is a world leader in wind energy.

Table A6
Job Duration: Are Green Jobs Short-Lived? Including Current Jobs

	(1)	(2)	(3)	(4)	(5)	(6)
	Job Length	Job Length	Job Length	Job Length	Job Length	Job Length
Solar job	-3.007***	-.611***	-.523***	-.605***	-.539***	-.227***
	(.030)	(.026)	(.025)	(.026)	(.026)	(.063)
Wind job	-1.164***	.271***	.252***	.041	-.114***	-.191***
	(.050)	(.042)	(.041)	(.040)	(.041)	(.072)
EV job	-3.764***	.084***	.187***	.019	.060**	.893
	(.031)	(.026)	(.026)	(.029)	(.029)	(.723)
Renewable job	-2.213***	-.359***	-.171***	.119***	.102***	.216***
	(.039)	(.032)	(.032)	(.032)	(.032)	(.080)
Job start date FEs	N	Y	Y	Y	Y	Y
Job number FEs	N	N	Y	Y	Y	Y
Age, educ, gender, state FEs	N	N	N	Y	Y	Y
2-Digit SOC FEs	N	N	N	N	Y	Y
Company FEs	N	N	N	N	N	Y
Observations	2,505,967	2,505,967	2,505,967	2,505,967	2,505,967	2,505,967

Source: Worker profile data from Lightcast.

Note: Table A6 mirrors the regression results in table 6 but includes current jobs in the sample. Current jobs are assumed to have an end date of January 1, 2023. Column 1 is a naive specification that mirrors the results in figure A1. Column 2 includes only a set of starting year fixed effects (FEs). Controlling for the year the job began dramatically changes the green-job coefficients. Column 3 also controls for the number of prior jobs held by a worker. Column 4 controls for worker demographics (age, education, gender, state). Column 5 controls for the broad occupation category of the worker by including two-digit Standard Occupational Classification (SOC) fixed effect. Column 5 is our preferred specification. We also report results that include company FEs in column 6. By including company FEs, we are absorbing much of the variation used to identify the differences in job length; nonetheless, these inform of the within-company differences in job length for those companies where this variation is present.

**$p < .05$.

***$p < .01$.

Endnotes

Author email addresses: Curtis (curtisem@wfu.edu), Park (rjpark@upenn.edu). We thank Tatyana Deryugina, Matt Kotchen, Ioana Marinescu, Al McGartland, Catherine Wolfram, and the participants of the NBER EEPE Conference. We thank Wilson Wang for helpful research assistance. We are especially grateful to Bledi Taska and Lightcast for providing access to the data. Computing resources were provided by Wake Forest University's Distributed Environment for Academic Computing. This research was made possible through the generous support of a grant from the Washington Center for Equitable Growth. For acknowledgments, sources of research support, and disclosure of the authors' material financial relationships, if any, please see https://www.nber.org/books-and-chap ters/environmental-and-energy-policy-and-economy-volume-5/workers-and-green-energy -transition-evidence-300-million-job-transitions.

1. Terms including "green-energy transition" and "clean-energy transition" have been used to describe a wide range of phenomena, including the transition away from fossil fuels, improvements in air, soil, and water quality, and changes in sustainable management practices. We focus specifically on the expected shift in labor demand arising from correcting the carbon externality, which, though taking many possible forms (carbon tax, cap-and-trade, renewable portfolio standards, etc.), will likely have the effect of reducing labor demand in carbon-intensive industries. As discussed below, this informs our arguably conservative definition of green and dirty jobs and transitions between them.

2. For instance, Autor, Dorn, and Hanson (2013, 2019, 2021) find that trade liberalization and China's ascension to the World Trade Organization resulted in adverse wage and employment impacts for the US commuting zones most exposed to import competition, particularly for less-educated workers, and that such trade shocks had significant adverse impacts on a range of nonmarket outcomes, including family formation, the number of children raised in poverty, and mortality from drug and alcohol abuse.

3. For instance, if one assumes a social cost of carbon estimate of $190 per ton at a 2% discount rate (Rennert et al. 2021), and that annual global emissions flows of approximately 3.5 gigatons add only marginally to the stock of total greenhouse gas emissions, the implied discounted present value of global damages associated with annual emissions may be on the order of $6 trillion.

4. Lightcast has continuously updated worker profile data and newly created profiles. Because workers can report their full employment and educational history, the data go back to the earliest reported jobs, some of which are before 1970. The data we use were most recently updated at the end of 2022.

5. The timeline of most profiles lists jobs chronologically, with the start of one job occurring simultaneously with or immediately after the end date of the next. However, by defining transitions this way, we are not capturing new jobs acquired by multiple job holders. Also, this definition of a transition does not require the new job to have started immediately after the end of the previous job.

6. We decided not to define dirty jobs on the basis of company names because there are companies, such as British Petroleum, which historically had petroleum in the company name but likely included a mix of dirty and green workers.

7. Our measure of green jobs is likely a conservative one compared with some existing definitions. For instance, the International Labour Organization defines green jobs as follows: "Green jobs are decent jobs in any economic sector (e.g., agriculture, industry, services, administration) which contribute to preserving, restoring and enhancing environmental quality. Green jobs reduce the environmental impact of enterprises and economic sectors by improving the efficiency of energy, raw materials and water; decarbonizing the economy and bringing down emissions of greenhouse gases; minimizing or avoiding all forms of waste and pollution; protecting or restoring ecosystems and biodiversity; and supporting adaptation to the effects of climate change." We focus primarily on jobs that directly benefit from an implicit or explicit price on carbon, as opposed to a wider set of environmental externality-correcting policies (e.g., water- or soil-quality enhancement).

8. For instance, Solar Energy Systems Engineers (17-2199.11) and Wind Energy Operations Managers (11-9199.09).

9. We take company names from the following sources. For solar: https://www
.zippia.com/advice/largest-solar-companies. For wind: https://www.fool.com/invest
ing/stock-market/market-sectors/energy/wind-energy-stocks.
10. Although we report data from 2022 in all results, it is likely that not all workers had
reported 2022 job changes when our data were scraped. As such, we generally refrain
from comparing results in 2022 to the years immediately preceding it.
11. Workers who took a dirty job and kept it for their entire careers to date are therefore
not included in the denominator.
12. For example, this allows Oil and Gas Derrick Operators in Houston to have thicker
or thinner transition shares into nondirty jobs than other Oil and Gas Derrick Operators in
the rest of Texas, where the concentration of jobs in the oil industry may be relatively lower on
average.
13. See https://www.oecd.org/environment/Employment-Implications-of-Green
-Growth-OECD-Report-G7-Environment-Ministers.pdf.
14. From BLS 2022: https://www.bls.gov/news.release/pdf/tenure.pdf.

References

Autor, David H. 2014. "Skills, Education, and the Rise of Earnings Inequality
among the 'Other 99 Percent.'" *Science* 344 (6186): 843–51.
Autor, David H., David Dorn, and Gordon H. Hanson. 2013. "The China Syn-
drome: Local Labor Market Effects of Import Competition in the United
States." *American Economic Review* 103 (6): 2121–68. https://www.aeaweb.org
/articles?id=10.1257/aer.103.6.2121.
———. 2019. "When Work Disappears: Manufacturing Decline and the Falling
Marriage Market Value of Young Men." *American Economic Review: Insights*
1 (2): 161–78.
———. 2021. "On the Persistence of the China Shock." Working Paper no. 29401,
NBER, Cambridge, MA.
Autor, David H., Frank Levy, and Richard J. Murnane. 2003. "The Skill Content of
Recent Technological Change: An Empirical Exploration." *Quarterly Journal of
Economics* 118 (4): 1279–333. https://doi.org/10.1162/003355303322552801.
Bistline, John, Neil Mehrotra, and Catherine Wolfram. 2023. "Economic Impli-
cations of the Climate Provisions of the Inflation Reduction Act." Working Pa-
per no. 31267, NBER, Cambridge, MA.
Carleton, Tamma, and Michael Greenstone. 2022. "A Guide to Updating the US
Government's Social Cost of Carbon." *Review of Environmental Economics and
Policy* 16 (2): 196–218.
Curtis, E. Mark. 2018. "Who Loses under Cap-and-Trade Programs? The Labor
Market Effects of the NOx Budget Trading Program." *Review of Economics and
Statistics* 100 (1): 151–66. https://doi.org/10.1162/REST_a_00680.
Curtis, E. Mark, and Ioana Marinescu. 2022. "Green Energy Jobs in the US: What
Are They, and Where Are They?" Working Paper no. 30332, NBER, Cam-
bridge, MA. http://www.nber.org/papers/w30332.
Goos, Maarten, Alan Manning, and Anna Salomons. 2009. "Job Polarization in
Europe." *American Economic Review* 99 (2): 58–63.
Greenstone, Michael. 2002. "The Impacts of Environmental Regulations on In-
dustrial Activity: Evidence from the 1970 and 1977 Clean Air Act Amend-
ments and the Census of Manufactures." *Journal of Political Economy* 110 (6):
1175–219. https://www.journals.uchicago.edu/doi/full/10.1086/342808.
Hamermesh, Daniel S. 1999. "Changing Inequality in Markets for Workplace
Amenities." *Quarterly Journal of Economics* 114 (4): 1085–123.

Hanson, Gordon H. 2023. "Local Labor Market Impacts of the Energy Transition: Prospects and Policies." Working Paper no. 30871, NBER, Cambridge, MA.

Hyatt, Henry R., and James R. Spletzer. 2016. "The Shifting Job Tenure Distribution." *Labour Economics* 41:363–77. SOLE/EALE conference issue 2015. https://www.sciencedirect.com/science/article/pii/S0927537116300227.

Jacobsen, Grant D., and Dominic P. Parker. 2016. "The Economic Aftermath of Resource Booms: Evidence from Boomtowns in the American West." *Economic Journal* 126 (593): 1092–128.

Katz, Lawrence F., and Alan B. Krueger. 2017. "Documenting Decline in US Economic Mobility." *Science* 356 (6336): 382–83.

Lehr, Ulrike, Christian Lutz, and Dietmar Edler. 2012. "Green Jobs? Economic Impacts of Renewable Energy in Germany." *Energy Policy* 47:358–64. https://www.sciencedirect.com/science/article/pii/S0301421512003928.

Maestas, Nicole, Kathleen J. Mullen, David Powell, Till von Wachter, and Jeffrey B. Wenger. 2018. "The Value of Working Conditions in the United States and Implications for the Structure of Wages." Working Paper no. 25204, NBER, Cambridge, MA.

Manning, Alan. 2021. "Monopsony in Labor Markets: A Review." *ILR Review* 74 (1): 3–26. https://doi.org/10.1177/0019793920922499.

Raimi, Daniel. 2021. "Mapping County-Level Exposure and Vulnerability to the US Energy Transition." Working Paper 21-36 (December), Resources for the Future, Washington, DC.

Rennert, Kevin, Brian C. Prest, William A. Pizer, Richard G. Newell, David Anthoff, Cora Kingdon, Lisa Rennels, et al. 2021. "The Social Cost of Carbon: Advances in Long-Term Probabilistic Projections of Population, GDP, Emissions, and Discount Rates." *Brookings Papers on Economic Activity* (2): 223–305.

Schubert, Gregor, Anna Stansbury, and Bledi Taska. 2021. "Employer Concentration and Outside Options." Working paper. http://www.ecineq.org/wp-content/uploads/papers_EcineqLSE/EcineqLSE-351.pdf.

Vona, Francesco, Giovanni Marin, Davide Consoli, and David Popp. 2018. "Environmental Regulation and Green Skills: An Empirical Exploration." *Journal of the Association of Environmental and Resource Economists* 5 (4): 713–53. https://www.journals.uchicago.edu/doi/full/10.1086/698859.

The Economic Determinants of Heat Pump Adoption

Lucas W. Davis, *Haas School of Business at University of California, Berkeley, Energy Institute at Haas, and NBER,* United States of America

Executive Summary

One concern with subsidies for low-carbon technologies is that they tend to go predominantly to high-income households. Previous research has shown, for example, that the top income quintile receives 60% of subsidies for rooftop solar and 90% of subsidies for electric vehicles. This paper finds that heat pumps are an important exception. Using newly available US nationally representative data, the paper finds that there is remarkably little correlation between heat pump adoption and household income. Nationwide, 14% of US households have a heat pump as their primary heating equipment, and adoption levels are essentially identical for all income levels ranging from the bottom of the income distribution (<$30,000 annually) to the top ($150,000+). Instead, the paper shows that heat pump adoption is strongly correlated with geography, climate, and electricity prices.

JEL Codes: H23, L51, Q41, Q42, Q48, Q54

Keywords: low-carbon technologies, carbon emissions, distributional impacts, efficiency vs. equity

I. Introduction

Increased deployment of heat pumps plays a central role in most envisioned pathways for US decarbonization (National Academies 2021; Princeton University 2021; Williams et al. 2021). US electricity generation has become much less carbon intensive (Holland et al. 2020), so moving away from natural gas or other fossil fuels for home heating and toward electric heat pumps offers the potential for large-scale reductions in carbon emissions.

Environmental and Energy Policy and the Economy, volume 5, 2024.
© 2024 National Bureau of Economic Research. All rights reserved. Published by The University of Chicago Press for the NBER. https://doi.org/10.1086/727881

Policy makers are increasingly introducing subsidies for heat pumps in an effort to accelerate this substitution. For example, US households can now receive a federal income tax credit of up to $2,000 for purchasing and installing a heat pump. This marks a considerable increase compared with the $300 tax credit that was available previously. Many states, cities, and utility districts offer additional subsidies.

One concern that is often raised with regard to subsidies for low-carbon technologies is that they tend to go predominantly to higher-income households. Previous research on US federal clean energy tax credits, for example, finds that the top income quintile receives 60% of tax credits for solar panels and 90% of tax credits for electric vehicles (Borenstein and Davis 2016).

This paper finds that heat pumps are an important exception. Using newly available US nationally representative data, the paper shows that there is remarkably little correlation between heat pump adoption and household income. Nationwide, 14% of US households have a heat pump as their primary heating equipment, and heat pump adoption is essentially identical for all levels of household income, ranging from the bottom of the income distribution (<$30,000 annually) to the top ($150,000+).

This lack of correlation contrasts sharply with the pattern for other low-carbon technologies. Using these same data, the paper documents a sharp gradient with regard to income for electric vehicles, solar panels, LED light bulbs, and energy-efficient clothes washers. Households in the top income category ($150,000+) are, for example, 10 times more likely than households in the bottom income category (<$30,000 annually) to have an electric vehicle and five times more likely to have solar panels.

These findings have potentially large policy implications. Probably most importantly, the lack of correlation between heat pump adoption and income suggests that the distributional impacts of heat pump subsidies are likely to be quite different from the distributional impacts of subsidies for other low-carbon technologies, upending the standard "efficiency-versus-equity" trade-off that has tended to characterize adoption patterns in this context.

Instead, heat pump adoption is shown to be strongly correlated with geography, climate, and energy prices. The correlation between heat pump adoption and electricity prices, for example, is shown to be negative, statistically significant, and robust even in regressions that control for other variables. These patterns are of considerable independent interest and point to where heat pump adoption is likely to occur in the future.

Finally, the paper performs a series of back-of-the-envelope calculations aimed at better understanding the cost-effectiveness of heat pump and electric vehicle subsidies (the latter for comparison purposes). These calculations rely on many strong assumptions, but overall, it appears that these two subsidies yield a similar amount of carbon abatement per dollar. Thus, these two subsidies appear to be quite similar from an efficiency perspective despite having very different distributional implications.

This study contributes to a growing literature on the economics of decarbonization through electrification. Whereas most of the literature has focused on the electrification of transportation (Holland et al. 2016; Li et al. 2017; Li 2019; Burlig et al. 2021; Springel 2021; Xing, Leard, and Li 2021; Muehlegger and Rapson 2022), the electrification of buildings has received relatively less attention (Borenstein and Bushnell 2022b; Davis, forthcoming).

The study is also related to a literature on the distributional impacts of energy policies. Previous papers have examined, for example, gasoline taxes (Poterba 1991; Bento et al. 2009), carbon taxes (Cronin, Fullerton, and Sexton 2019), fuel economy standards (Davis and Knittel 2019), building codes (Bruegge, Deryugina, and Myers 2019), utility rates (Borenstein 2012; Borenstein, Fowlie, and Sallee 2021), and solar panel subsidies (Borenstein 2017; Feger, Pavanini, and Radulescu 2022).

Although the paper focuses on the United States, it has implications for heat pump adoption elsewhere. A recent report by the International Energy Agency argues that heat pumps will play a critical role in global decarbonization efforts. According to the report, 10% of space heating needs worldwide are currently being met with heat pumps, but this would need to increase to approximately 24% by 2030 to meet the carbon abatement goals outlined by the Paris Agreement (IEA 2022).

The paper proceeds as follows. Section II documents the lack of correlation between heat pump adoption and household income, and it contrasts this with correlations for electric vehicles and other low-carbon technologies. Section III provides additional background about heat pumps and a summary of relevant US federal subsidies. Section IV examines geography, climate, energy prices, and other determinants of heat pump adoption. Section V performs back-of-the-envelope calculations aimed at understanding cost-effectiveness, and Section VI concludes.

II. Technology Adoption and Income

A. Heat Pumps

Figure 1 plots US heat pump adoption rates by household income. Nationwide, 14% of US households have a heat pump as their primary

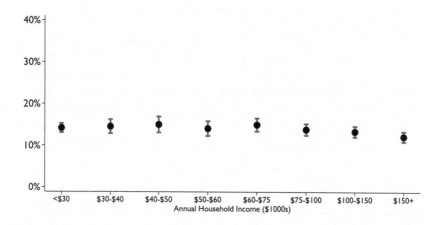

Fig. 1. Heat pump adoption by household income. Color version available as an online enhancement.

Notes: This figure shows how the percentage of US households with a heat pump varies with annual household income. These data come from RECS (2020). Households are weighted using RECS sampling weights. Brackets indicate 95% confidence intervals.

heating equipment. As the figure illustrates, the percentage of households with a heat pump is essentially the same for all levels of household income, ranging from the bottom of the income distribution (<$30,000 annually) to the top ($150,000+).

This figure was constructed using household-level microdata from the 2020 iteration of the *Residential Energy Consumption Survey* (RECS; U.S. Department of Energy, Energy Information Administration 2022). Conducted approximately every five years by the US Department of Energy, Energy Information Administration, RECS collects rich data about household energy–related durable goods and behaviors as well as information about household income and other characteristics. The underlying income variable in RECS has 16 categories, but some categories were combined when making this figure; for example, $30–$35 and $35–$40 were combined to make the single category $30–$40.

RECS is a nationally representative survey of the United States. The target population for RECS is all occupied housing units in the 50 states and District of Columbia. The RECS sample is selected using stratified sampling by state to ensure sufficient coverage even in states with relatively small populations. Accordingly, RECS sampling weights are used in all calculations throughout the analysis. An attractive feature of the 2020 RECS is its relatively large sample size. The total sample for the 2020 RECS is 18,496 households, including more than 2,600 households with heat pumps.

As with all surveys, a potential concern is nonresponse bias. The 2020 RECS had a 39% response rate, down sharply compared with the 51% response rate with the 2015 RECS and the 79% response rate with the 2009 RECS. Survey documentation attributes this lower response rate to the 2020 RECS being entirely self-administered.[1] The RECS sampling weights attempt to correct for nonresponse by balancing observable household characteristics, but it is impossible to rule out concerns about unobserved differences between responders and nonresponders.

B. Other Technologies

Figure 2 plots US adoption rates by household income for electric vehicles, solar panels, LED light bulbs, and energy-efficient clothes washers. There is a sharp gradient with regard to income for all four low-carbon technologies. Relative to the lowest income category, households in the

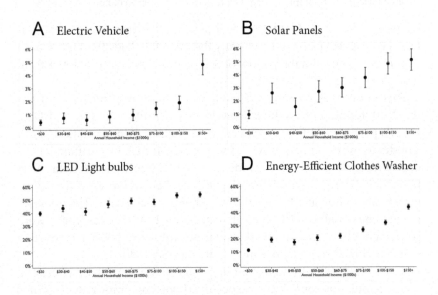

Fig. 2. Adoption of other low-carbon technologies by household income. (A) Electric vehicle. (B) Solar panels. (C) LED light bulbs. (D) Energy-efficient clothes washer. Color version available as an online enhancement.

Notes: This figure shows how the percentage of US households with low-carbon technologies varies with annual household income. These data come from RECS (2020). Brackets indicate 95% confidence intervals. The category "LED light bulbs" is defined as having "mostly" or "all" LEDs. Energy-efficient clothes washers are defined as being front-loading rather than top-loading.

highest income category are, for example, 10 times more likely to have an electric vehicle and five times more likely to have solar panels.

Baseline adoption levels vary widely across technologies. Electric vehicles and solar panels are relatively rare, with adoption rates in the single digits. LEDs and efficient washers are much more common, with adoption rates ranging from 40% to 55% for LEDs and from 10% to nearly 50% for efficient washers. LEDs, in particular, are much less expensive up front than these other technologies, which helps explain the higher adoption rates.

Previous economic analyses have posited that signaling to others may be an important driver of adoption decisions for low-carbon technologies.[2] If higher-income households derive more utility from this type of signaling, it could help explain the correlation between adoption and income. Interestingly, however, a sharp income gradient is observed both for technologies that are highly visible to other households, such as electric vehicles, and for less visible technologies like clothes washers.

Table 1 summarizes the information from figures 1 and 2. Adoption rates differ little for heat pumps, ranging from 12% to 15% across income categories. In contrast, there is a clear gradient for all other low-carbon technologies. For example, with solar panels, adoption levels range from 1% in the lowest income category to 5% in the highest.

Table 1
Technology Adoption by Income

Income ($1,000s)	Heat Pump (%)	Electric Vehicle (%)	Solar Panels (%)	LED Lights (%)	Efficient Washer (%)
<$30	14	0	1	40	11
$30–$40	15	1	3	44	19
$40–$50	15	1	2	41	17
$50–$60	14	1	3	47	21
$60–$75	15	1	3	49	22
$75–$100	14	1	4	48	27
$100–$150	13	2	5	53	32
$150+	12	5	5	54	44
Test of equality (p value)	.14	.00	.00	.00	.00

Note: This table describes US adoption levels by annual household income for five low-carbon technologies. These data come from RECS (2020). Households are weighted using RECS sampling weights. The last row reports p values from a statistical test for which the null hypothesis is that all eight percentages are equal. Except for heat pumps, there is strong evidence against the null.

These differences across income levels are strongly statistically significant for electric vehicles, solar panels, LEDs, and washers. For each technology, a statistical test is performed for which the null hypothesis is that all eight percentages are equal.[3] The last row of the table reports p values from these tests. With heat pumps, this null hypothesis cannot be rejected (p value = .14). In the other four cases, however, the null hypothesis is firmly rejected (p value = .00 for all four).

III. Background

Before proceeding, it is helpful to provide some additional background about heat pumps. This content is not crucial for understanding figures 1 and 2, but it is valuable for motivating the exploration of other determinants of heat pumps in Section IV. Subsection III.A provides a basic introduction to heat pumps including what they are and how they work. Subsection III.B describes how much heat pumps cost to purchase and operate. Subsection III.C explains US federal subsidies for heat pumps.

A. What Is a Heat Pump?

Put simply, a heat pump is an air conditioner that can be operated in reverse. Whereas an air conditioner provides cooling, a heat pump provides both heating and cooling. Moreover, because electric heat pumps operate using electricity, they can be substituted for natural gas furnaces and other forms of heating equipment and thus offer the potential to significantly reduce on-site consumption of natural gas, propane, and other fossil fuels used for heating. Heat pumps are widely deployed in both residential and nonresidential settings, though this paper focuses entirely on the former.

Electric heat pumps provide heating using a completely different approach from electric resistance heating. Whereas electric resistance heating converts electricity into heat, a heat pump uses electricity to move heat between the inside and outside of the home. Similar to refrigerators, freezers, air conditioners, and other compressor-based appliances, heat pumps move heat by compressing a refrigerant and then releasing it again. As the refrigerant evaporates (i.e., turns from a liquid into a gas), it absorbs heat, which then can be moved and released as the refrigerant turns back into a liquid.

The advantage of this approach is that heat pumps are considerably more energy efficient than electric resistance heating. Electric resistance heating, with 1 kilowatt-hour (kWh) of electricity, delivers approximately 1 kWh of heat. In contrast, a heat pump, with 1 kWh of electricity, can deliver 2, 3, or even 4 kWh of heat. Again, this is because with a heat pump, electricity is not converted into heat but is used to move heat. Heat pump energy efficiency for heating is typically measured using the coefficient of performance (COP), which is the ratio of the energy delivered to the energy consumed. Heat pump COP typically ranges from 2 to 4.

The energy efficiency of a heat pump depends on the outdoor temperature. Heat pumps are most efficient at relatively high outdoor temperatures (e.g., 60°F) because there is more warmth in the outside air to be moved. Energy efficiency decreases at lower outdoor temperatures because there is less heat outside to be moved, so a heat pump uses more electricity for each unit of heat that it delivers. For this reason, heat pumps are particularly well suited to locations with relatively mild winters.[4]

Heat pump capacity also decreases at lower temperatures. That is, the total amount of heat that can be supplied decreases when outdoor temperatures are low, sometimes making it impossible to sufficiently heat a home. Consequently, in colder locations, heat pumps are often combined with some other form of backup heating. In Kaufman et al. (2019), for example, heat pumps are assumed to be equipped with a backup electric resistance heater that provides additional heat when the building's heating demands exceed the compressor's capabilities.

B.   Up-Front and Operating Costs

Table 2 reports up-front costs for selected residential heating and cooling equipment. This information comes from the US Department of Energy and includes purchase and installation costs but not operating costs.

According to these estimates, an air-source heat pump has an up-front cost of $6,900–$8,600, which is $1,600–$2,600 more than a central air conditioner. This incremental cost is less than the up-front cost of a natural gas furnace and, in some cases, less than the up-front cost of electric resistance heating. Thus, heat pumps are particularly attractive for households that are already installing or replacing central air conditioning. This up-front cost for a heat pump does not include any backup heating system for very cold days.

Ground-source heat pumps are considerably more expensive. Whereas air-source heat pumps transfer heat to and from the air, ground-source heat pumps transfer heat to and from the ground, with refrigerant lines running through holes drilled underground. Air-source heat pumps represent 90%

Table 2
Up-Front Costs for Selected Residential Equipment

Natural gas furnace	$4,100–$4,300
Electric resistance furnace	$1,500
Electric resistance baseboard heaters	$2,300
Central air conditioner	$5,300–$6,000
Air-source heat pump	$6,900–$8,600
Ground-source heat pump	$23,100–$24,200

Note: This table presents up-front costs for selected residential heating and cooling equipment. These cost estimates come from US DOE (2023) and include purchase and installation costs. The table reports estimates for 2022 for equipment with a "typical" or "high" level of energy efficiency. In cases where equipment costs vary between "typical" and "high" or vary by region, this table reports the range. For electric resistance baseboard heaters, the assumed installation size is 6 units, and for ground-source heat pumps, the assumed installation size is 4 tons. Cost estimates have been rounded to the nearest $100.

of US residential heat pumps in the RECS 2020 and 85% of heat pumps worldwide (IEA 2022). Ground-source heat pumps have certain advantages but tend to have considerably higher initial purchase and installation costs.

In addition to these up-front costs, all heating systems also have operating costs. In the United States, natural gas heating tends to have lower operating cost than electric resistance heating. Based on US average residential prices for electricity and natural gas in 2021, for example, the price per million British thermal units (MMBtu) of heating was $13 for natural gas and $40 for electric resistance heating.[5] Operating costs can be considerably lower for heat pumps, depending on the COP. For a COP of 3.0, for example, the price per MMBtu of heating would be $13, equivalent to natural gas.[6]

These up-front and operating costs illustrate why there would be a regional pattern to heating choices. In warmer states like Florida, households tend to prefer electric heating because of its lower up-front costs. In colder states, however, the low operating costs associated with natural gas tend to make it attractive relative to electric heating. Moreover, where natural gas is not available, a heat pump will often be preferred relative to electric resistance heating based on its considerably lower operating costs.[7]

C. US Federal Subsidies for Heat Pumps

The US Inflation Reduction Act provides income tax credits and direct point-of-sale rebates for heat pumps.[8] Both types of subsidies have various requirements, but there is no specific restriction preventing a household from receiving both a tax credit and direct rebate.

The tax credit is equal to 30% of the up-front cost of a heat pump, up to a maximum of $2,000. For example, if a household spends $6,000 purchasing and installing a heat pump, it can receive a tax credit of $1,800. Available since January 1, 2023, this tax credit was implemented by extending and amending the Energy Efficient Home Improvement Credit, formerly known as the Non-Business Energy Property Credit (Internal Revenue Code Section 25C), which was originally established by the Energy Policy Act of 2005 and subsidizes certain investments that reduce energy consumption in homes. Heat pumps have long been included under this tax credit, but at much lower subsidy levels. For example, as of 2022, a qualifying heat pump could qualify for a maximum tax credit of only $300.

The Inflation Reduction Act also created a grant program called the High-Efficiency Electric Home Rebate Program, which awards grants to states for point-of-sale rebates of up to $8,000 for heat pumps. These rebates are subject to income requirements: (1) households with annual income below 80% of median local income are eligible for a 100% rebate, up to $8,000, (2) households with annual income between 80% and 150% of median local income are eligible for a 50% rebate, up to $8,000, and (3) households with annual income above 150% of median local income are ineligible. In addition to heat pumps, these rebates are available for electric load service upgrades and other electrification investments, up to a total household maximum of $14,000.

As of May 2023, federal and state agencies are finalizing the procedures for distributing rebates. States have some discretion in how they implement these rebates, so there is likely to be variation across states with regard to when these rebates are first available and how income requirements are enforced. Rewiring America, an electrification nonprofit, is reporting that funding for these rebates will likely be distributed to state agencies in 2023, with rebates available to consumers by late 2023 or 2024.

Tax credits and point-of-sale rebates are likely to be used by different types of households. Probably most importantly, the maximum income requirements for the rebates mean that they are supposed to go only to low- and middle-income households. At the same time, there are also subtle factors affecting take-up of tax credits. As emphasized by Borenstein and Davis (2016), these are nonrefundable tax credits. Consequently, there are millions of mostly lower-income taxpayers who are ineligible because they have insufficient tax liability. Moreover, tax credits require households to wait many months before receiving the credit, which also tends to tilt take-up toward higher-income households that are less liquidity constrained.

IV. Other Determinants of Heat Pump Adoption

This section explores other determinants of heat pump adoption. If not income, then what other factors are correlated with heat pump adoption? Guided by the background provided in the previous section, most of the factors considered in this section have implications for the operating costs and overall effectiveness of heat pumps.

Subsections IV.A, IV.B, and IV.C examine geography, climate, and energy prices, respectively. All three are shown to strongly predict heat pump adoption by US households. Subsection IV.D summarizes these findings and presents evidence on several additional factors that turn out not to be important. Subsection IV.E describes a regression analysis aimed at better disentangling the various factors.

These additional findings are interesting because they point to heat pump adoption having a very different pattern from electric vehicles, solar panels, and other low-carbon technologies. These patterns also have implications about where the tax credits and other subsidies for heat pumps are likely to go.

A. Geography

Figure 3 maps heat pump adoption by state. As with the previous analyses related to household income, this information comes from the RECS 2020. This is the first wave of RECS for which such a state-level analysis is possible. Previous waves identified households in large states, such as Texas and California, but state of residence was not identified for most respondents, so a map like this would not have been possible with the 2015 or 2009 RECS.

As the figure reveals, there is a pronounced regional pattern to heat pump adoption. Heat pumps are most common in Alabama, North Carolina, and South Carolina. In those three states, about 40% of households have a heat pump as their primary heating equipment. Throughout the rest of the South, heat pump adoption rates range between 20% and 36%. In Texas and Florida, for example, 20% and 32% of households have heat pumps, respectively. See table A1 for the complete list of states.

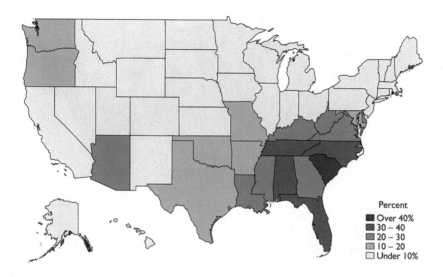

Fig. 3. Heat pump adoption by state. Color version available as an online enhancement.
Notes: This map plots the percentage of households in each state that have a heat pump as their primary heating equipment. These data come from RECS (2020). Households are weighted using RECS sampling weights.

Another region with increased heat pump adoption is the Pacific Northwest. Heat pump adoption is 13% in Washington and 15% in Oregon. This higher rate of adoption is not a coincidence. As will be explored in more detail later, electricity prices are negatively correlated with heat pump adoption, and these two states have lower electricity prices than most other states due to the availability of low-cost hydroelectric power.

Heat pumps are rare throughout the rest of the country. This includes most of the West, the Midwest, and the Northeast, as well as Hawaii and Alaska. Perhaps surprisingly, California also has relatively low heat pump adoption. Again, this is not a coincidence. California has unusually high electricity prices, as has been highlighted by several recent economic analyses (Borenstein et al. 2021; Borenstein and Bushnell 2022a, 2022b).

B. Climate

Figure 4 plots annual average heating degree days (HDDs) by state. HDDs are a widely used measure of heating demand that reflects the number of days with cold weather as well as the intensity of cold on those days. HDDs are calculated as the sum of daily mean temperatures

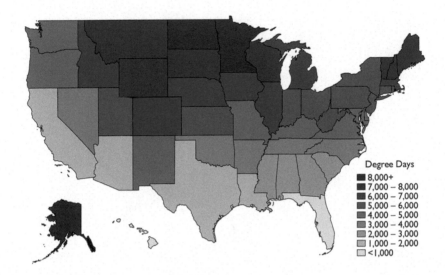

Fig. 4. Heating degree days by state. Color version available as an online enhancement.
Notes: This map plots heating degree days (HDDs) by state. HDDs are a widely used measure of heating demand that reflects the number of days with cold weather as well as the intensity of cold on those days. These data come from RECS (2020) and are 30-year annual averages from 1981 to 2010, relative to a base temperature of 65°F. Households are weighted using RECS sampling weights.

in Fahrenheit below 65°F. For example, a day with an average temperature of 55°F contributes 10 HDDs, whereas a day with an average temperature above 65°F contributes zero.

HDDs range widely across the United States. Warmer states like Hawaii, Florida, Arizona, Louisiana, and Texas experience fewer than 2,000 HDDs annually. Colder states like Maine, Vermont, Minnesota, North Dakota, and Alaska experience 7,000 or more HDDs annually.

This measure of HDDs is a 30-year annual average. Heat pumps tend to be used for many years before they are replaced. For example, the US Department of Energy's National Energy Modeling System assumes that heat pumps have a minimum lifetime of 9 years and a maximum lifetime of 22 years. Thus, it makes sense to think about heating-choice decisions as responding to a location's climate rather than to year-to-year weather variation.

Figure 5 presents a scatterplot of heat pump adoption versus HDDs. There is a pronounced negative correlation. For example, all 16 states with heat pump adoption above 20% have HDDs below or right at median HDDs. The correlation between the two variables is negative (−0.64) and strongly statistically significant.

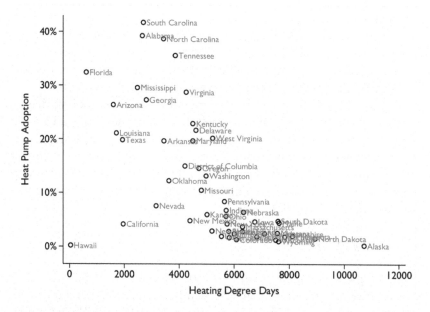

Fig. 5. Heat pump adoption versus heating degree days. Color version available as an online enhancement.

Notes: This scatterplot shows the percentage of households with heat pumps versus annual heating degree days. Both variables come from RECS (2020). Households are weighted using RECS sampling weights. The correlation between the two variables is negative (−0.64) and strongly statistically significant (*p* value = .00).

Hawaii is a fascinating outlier. Households in Hawaii experience virtually no HDDs, yet heat pump adoption is near zero. There is so little need for heating in Hawaii that most households choose not to have any heating equipment whatsoever. At the same time, Hawaii also has surprisingly little air conditioning. Only 57% of households in Hawaii have air conditioning, compared with a national average above 90%. In part, this lack of air conditioning reflects that Hawaii has the highest residential electricity prices in the United States. The average residential electricity price in Hawaii in 2020 was 30 cents per kWh, compared with a national average of 14 cents per kWh. The lack of air conditioning in Hawaii is also likely related to the housing stock. Because it tends not to get very cold in Hawaii, homes are built with less insulation, making air conditioning less effective and more expensive.

Interestingly, for European countries there is a positive correlation between heat pump adoption and HDDs (Rosenow et al. 2022). This positive correlation is largely due to three countries—Finland, Norway, and

Sweden—that all experience high levels of HDDs and have heat pump adoption rates above 40%. Heat pump popularity in these Scandinavian countries reflects many factors, including low electricity prices, high taxes for fossil fuel alternatives, lack of natural gas infrastructure, and government subsidies for heat pumps (Gross and Hanna 2019).

Figures A1 and A2 present analogous evidence for cooling degree days (CDDs). Whereas HDDs measure demand for heating, CDDs measure demand for cooling. As discussed earlier, heat pumps are, essentially, air conditioners operating in reverse, so the incremental cost of a heat pump is smaller for a household that already has or is planning to install central air conditioning. Heat pump adoption is positively correlated with CDDs (0.55).

C. *Energy Prices*

Figure 6 plots average residential electricity prices as of 2020. US electricity prices vary widely, from less than 10 cents per kWh in Louisiana, Washington State, and Idaho to more than 20 cents per kWh in California, Massachusetts, Rhode Island, Alaska, Connecticut, and Hawaii.

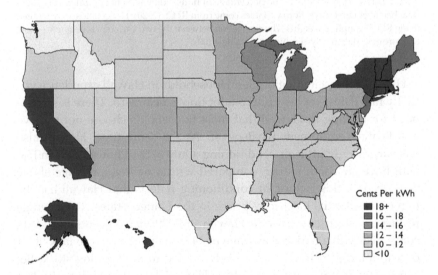

Fig. 6. Average residential electricity prices. Color version available as an online enhancement.

Notes: This map plots average residential electricity prices in 2020. These data come from the US Department of Energy, *Energy Information Administration, Electricity Data Browser* and include all relevant taxes and delivery charges.

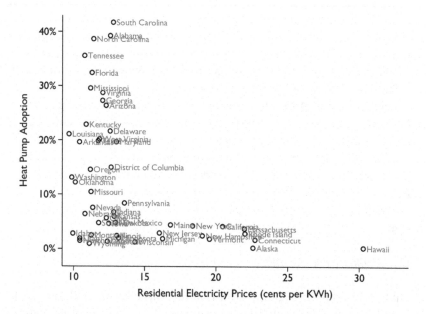

Fig. 7. Heat pump adoption versus electricity prices. Color version available as an online enhancement.

Notes: This scatterplot shows the percentage of households with heat pumps versus residential electricity prices. The percentage of households with heat pumps by state comes from RECS (2020) and was calculated using RECS sampling weights. Average residential electricity prices by state come from the US Department of Energy, *Energy Information Administration, Electricity Data Browser* and include all relevant taxes and delivery charges. The correlation between the two variables is negative (–0.41) and strongly statistically significant (p value = .00).

Figure 7 plots heat pump adoption versus electricity prices. The correlation between the two variables is negative (–0.41) and strongly statistically significant. All of the states with adoption rates above 20% have electricity prices below 13 cents per kWh, and adoption rates are below 10% for all states with prices above 15 cents per kWh.

The states with high electricity prices are very different from the states with low electricity prices, so it is hard to make a strong causal statement about this relationship. Still, the negative relationship makes sense given that electricity prices determine operating costs for heat pumps, consistent with an existing literature documenting the responsiveness of electricity demand to prices. See, for example, Reiss and White (2005, 2008) and Ito (2014).

To the extent that lower electricity prices cause increased heat pump adoption, this underscores the importance of pricing electricity efficiently.

A key theme in recent economic analyses of US electricity markets is that electricity is not priced efficiently (Borenstein and Bushnell 2022a, 2022b). In particular, in many parts of the country, residential electricity prices are too high (i.e., higher than social marginal cost), which would imply inefficiently low levels of heat pump adoption.

Figures A3 and A4 present analogous evidence for natural gas prices. Natural gas furnaces are a substitute for heat pumps, so this "cross-price" effect would be expected to be positive with, everything else equal, heat pumps being more attractive in states with high natural gas prices. Indeed, the correlation between heat pump adoption and natural gas prices is positive. The correlation is smaller in magnitude than the correlation with electricity prices, and not statistically significant, but it has the expected sign.

D.   Summary and Additional Evidence

Table 3 describes heat pump adoption rates and the implied total number of households for different categories of U.S households. Nationwide, 14% of households have a heat pump as their primary heating equipment, implying 17.2 million total US households with heat pumps.

The breakdown by geography, electricity prices, and climate confirms the patterns shown in the previous subsections. Heat pump adoption in the South is three times higher than in the West and six times higher than in the Midwest and Northeast. Heat pump adoption in states with low electricity prices (i.e., below median) is three times higher than heat pump adoption in states with high electricity prices (i.e., above median). And heat pump adoption in warm states (i.e., below median HDDs) is more than three times higher than in cold states (i.e., above median HDDs).

The table also presents evidence on several additional potential determinants, which turn out not to be important determinants of heat pump adoption. Interestingly, heat pump adoption is similar for homeowners and renters. This is perhaps surprising given previous evidence on the "landlord-tenant" problem—that is, the idea that landlords have too little incentive to invest in energy efficiency when their tenants pay the energy bills (see, e.g., Gillingham, Harding, and Rapson 2012). But in many cases, heat pumps are actually less expensive up front than installing separate heating and cooling systems, so the analogy to the literature on energy efficiency is not so straightforward.

Heat pump adoption is also similar for single-family and multiunit homes, and for homes with different numbers of bedrooms. The lack

Table 3
Heat Pump Adoption in the United States

	Percent of Households with Heat Pumps (%)	Total Households (in Millions)
Entire United States	14	17.2
By geography:		
South	28	12.9
West	8	2.1
Northeast	5	1.0
Midwest	4	1.2
By electricity prices:		
Below median	21	12.9
Above median	7	4.3
By climate:		
Below median HDDs	21	13.3
Above median HDDs	6	3.9
Homeowner versus renter:		
Homeowner	14	11.8
Renter	13	5.4
By type of home:		
Single-family	14	13.0
Multiunit	13	4.2
By size of home:		
One or two bedrooms	13	6.1
Three bedrooms	16	7.7
Four or more bedrooms	12	3.4

Note: This table describes heat pump adoption for different categories of US households, as well as the implied total number of households in each category. These data come from RECS (2020). Households are weighted using RECS sampling weights. The four regions are as defined by the US census. Single-family homes include single-family detached homes as well as single-family attached homes (duplexes and townhouses).

of correlation with these housing characteristics is notable because one might have expected economies of scale to provide clear advantages or disadvantages for heat pumps relative to alternative technologies. Were this only a comparison between heat pumps and electric resistance heating, then one might indeed expect to see single-family homes and larger homes disproportionately choosing heat pumps. But households are also considering natural gas heating which tends to be attractive in larger homes because of the relatively low operating costs.

Regardless of the exact explanations, the lack of correlation with these other factors helps explain the lack of correlation between heat pumps and household income, and why heat pumps are so different from solar panels and other technologies. For example, one of the reasons solar

panels tend to be more frequently adopted by higher-income households is that such households are more likely to live in single-family
homes, where it is typically easier to install solar panels. Similarly,
households in single-family homes are also more likely to have a conve-
nient parking spot with a garage or driveway, which makes charging an
electric vehicle easier.

E. Regression Analysis

Table 4 reports estimates from a regression model aimed at better disentangling the various determinants of heat pump adoption. Coefficient
estimates and standard errors are reported from eight separate least-
squares regressions. In all eight regressions, the dependent variable is
an indicator variable for homes for which an electric heat pump is the
primary form of space heating.

Across all eight columns, there is a striking lack of association between household income and heat pump adoption. In column 1, without any additional variables, the coefficient on income is –0.01. Thus a
$100,000 increase in annual household income is associated with a 1.0 per-
centage point decrease in heat pump adoption, a relatively small effect.
With additional variables, the coefficient on income becomes positive
but remains small in magnitude in all specifications. Thus, whether one
controls or does not control for these other variables, there is a pronounced lack of association with household income.

Instead, heat pump adoption is strongly associated with geography,
energy prices, and climate. These patterns are largely consistent with
the results presented earlier, but it is interesting to see that these relationships tend to persist even in regressions with other variables.

• Heat pump adoption is more common in the South and less common
in the Midwest and Northeast. These regional effects attenuate somewhat but remain mostly statistically significant after controlling for additional variables. The magnitude of these effects is large. For example,
in column 5, a household in the South is 14 percentage points more likely
to have a heat pump, which is a doubling relative to the national mean of
14%.

• Heat pump adoption decreases with electricity prices. The point estimates are large. For example, the estimate in column 5 implies that a
10% increase in electricity prices decreases heat pump adoption by 2.0 percentage points. In 2020, residential electricity prices in the continental

Table 4
Heat Pump Adoption, Regression Estimates

	(1)	(2)	(3)	(4)	(5)	(6)	(7)	(8)
Household income, 100,000s	−.01**	.00	.00	.00	.00	.01	.01	.01
	(.00)	(.01)	(.01)	(.01)	(.01)	(.01)	(.01)	(.01)
South		.20**	.13**	.14**	.14**			
		(.04)	(.04)	(.05)	(.05)			
Northeast		−.03	−.01	.00	.00			
		(.03)	(.01)	(.02)	(.02)			
Midwest		−.03	−.01	.00	.00			
		(.03)	(.02)	(.03)	(.03)			
Electricity price, in logs			−.18**	−.19**	−.20**			
			(.04)	(.03)	(.03)			
Natural gas price, in logs			.15**	.14**	.14**			
			(.05)	(.05)	(.05)			
Heating degree days, 1,000s				−.01	−.01		−.02	−.02
				(.01)	(.01)		(.01)	(.01)
Cooling degree days, 1,000s				−.01	−.01		−.01	−.01
				(.03)	(.03)		(.03)	(.03)
Homeowner					.02*			.02*
					(.01)			(.01)
Single-family home					−.01			−.02
					(.02)			(.02)
Number of bedrooms					.00			.00
					(.00)			(.00)
State fixed effects	No	No	No	No	No	Yes	Yes	Yes
Observations	18,496	18,496	18,496	18,496	18,496	18,496	18,496	18,496
R^2	.00	.10	.11	.11	.11	.13	.13	.13

Note: This table reports coefficient estimates and standard errors from eight separate least-squares regressions. In all regressions, the dependent variable is an indicator variable for homes for which an electric heat pump is the primary form of space heating. The indicator variables South, Northeast, and Midwest refer to three of the four census regions, with West as the excluded variable. Electricity and natural gas prices are both state-level averages, so these variables are excluded in the regressions with state fixed effects in columns 6, 7, and 8. All regressions are estimated using RECS sampling weights. Standard errors are clustered by state.
*Significant at the 5% level.
**Significant at the 1% level.

United States ranged from 9.7 cents in Louisiana to 22.6 cents in Connecticut, a difference of 0.85 log points. The regression implies that, everything else equal, an increase in electricity prices of this magnitude would decrease heat pump adoption by 17 percentage points. One standard deviation in log electricity prices is .261, so an increase in electricity prices of 1 standard deviation decreases adoption by 5.2 percentage points, or 37%.

• Heat pump adoption increases with natural gas prices. In column 5, for example, a 10% increase in natural gas prices increases heat pump adoption by 1.4 percentage points. Thus, both the own-price and cross-price effects have the expected signs.

• Heat pump adoption decreases with HDDs and CDDs. These effects are not statistically significant, but the point estimates are large when viewed relative to the relevant range. HDDS, for example, range within the continental United States from 600 in Florida to 8,400 in Minnesota, so the −.015 estimate in column 8 implies that an increase in HDDs of this magnitude would decrease heat pump adoption by 12 percentage points. One standard deviation in HDDs is 2,300, so an increase in HDDs by 1 standard deviation decreases adoption by 3.5 percentage points, or 25%.

• Homeowners are modestly more likely than renters to have a heat pump, but there is little association between heat pump adoption and the type of home (i.e., single-family versus multiunit) or the number of bedrooms. This is not unexpected given the lack of correlation with these factors in table 3, but it is interesting to see that this lack of correlation persists even in a regression with other variables.

The main takeaways from the regression analysis are as follows: (1) there is very little association between heat pump adoption and household income; (2) instead, heat pump adoption is strongly associated with geography, climate, and energy prices; and (3) these patterns are similar whether one examines simple correlations or estimates from a regression framework. The following section switches gears and considers the question of cost-effectiveness of subsidies, but the conclusion returns to this evidence and offers additional broader lessons with regard to potential policy implications.

V. Cost-Effectiveness of Subsidies

This section performs back-of-the-envelope calculations aimed at better understanding the cost-effectiveness of heat pump subsidies. As discussed previously, there is growing enthusiasm about heat pumps as a means to reduce carbon emissions from residential heating. In the United States, 56 million households (46%) heat their homes with natural gas, 5 million households (4%) heat their homes with propane, and 5 million households (4%) heat their homes with heating oil.[9]

The goal of this section is to calculate how much carbon abatement occurs per dollar spent on heat pump subsidies in the United States. Then, as a point of comparison, a similar calculation is performed for electric vehicles. These calculations require many strong assumptions. Where possible, existing data and previous estimates in the literature are used as points of comparison. Nonetheless, these should be viewed as preliminary rough calculations and interpreted with considerable caution.

The focus is on carbon abatement. In future research, it would be interesting to expand the analysis to incorporate other externalities. For example, on the one hand, burning fossil fuels releases nitrogen oxides (NOx) and other local pollutants that are dangerous to human health. In addition, there are negative externalities from fossil fuel production, including methane leaks, water use, and water contamination. On the other hand, heat pumps use refrigerants, which are a potent greenhouse gas. Quantifying these additional externalities is challenging but also important, as they have the potential to significantly affect the trade-offs associated with heat pumps.

A. Baseline Assumptions

This section describes the baseline assumptions used to quantify the carbon abatement from heat pump subsidies. The basic thought experiment is to focus on the US federal tax credit of $2,000 for heat pumps. As discussed previously, under the US Inflation Reduction Act, low- and moderate-income households will also be able to receive point-of-sale rebates of up to $8,000, but the exact implementation of these rebates is still being finalized.

Percentage Additional

For the baseline calculation, it is assumed that 50% of subsidy recipients are induced to purchase a heat pump because of the subsidy, whereas 50% of subsidy recipients would have purchased a heat pump even without the subsidy. That is, half of recipients are "additional," and the other half are "nonadditional." This is an important assumption and, unfortunately, one about which there is no existing empirical evidence. Thus, in addition to 50%, results are also reported for 25% and 75%.

Counterfactual Heating Source

The baseline calculation assumes that households induced to use a heat pump otherwise would have heated their homes using natural gas. This is another important assumption and, again, one for which there is little existing empirical evidence. Natural gas is the most common form of residential heating in the United States, but heat pump subsidies will also lead to substitution away from other heating fuels. Accordingly, results are also reported for propane, heating oil, and electric resistance heating.

Level of Heating Demand

Households are assumed to consume 35 MMBtu of heating annually, regardless of energy source.[10] As already discussed, the United States has a wide range of climates. Thus, in addition to reporting results for 35 MMBtu, the paper also reports results for 20 MMBtu and 50 MMBtu.

Operating Efficiency

Heat pumps are assumed to deliver 3.0 MMBtu of heating for each MMBtu of electricity (i.e., 300% efficient), compared with 1-to-1 (100% efficient) for electric resistance heating and 0.9-to-1 (90% efficient) for natural gas, propane, and heating oil.[11] Based on these assumptions, 35 MMBtu of heating can be met using 3,419 kWh of electricity (via a heat pump), 10,257 kWh of electricity (via electric resistance heating), 37.4 thousand cubic feet of natural gas, 425 gallons of propane, or 281 gallons of heating oil.[12]

Emissions Factors

Standard emissions factors are used to convert electricity and fuel consumption into carbon emissions. Electricity is assumed to emit 310 pounds of carbon dioxide per MMBtu of electricity consumed.[13] Natural gas, propane, and heating oil are assumed to emit 116.65, 138.63, and 163.45 pounds of carbon dioxide per MMBtu, respectively.[14] It is perhaps surprising that electricity produces more carbon dioxide per MMBtu than fossil fuels, but this reflects that a considerable amount of energy is lost when fossil fuels are converted into electricity. On average, US natural gas power plants convert only 45% of the energy content of natural gas into electricity, whereas US coal power plants convert only 32% of the energy content of coal into electricity.[15] Although these are rough averages, even the most efficient fossil fuel power plants typically have an efficiency below 60%.

System Lifetime

Heating systems are assumed to have a 20-year lifetime, with no changes in operating efficiency or emissions factors over that period. This is a bit longer than typical assumptions in the literature. For example, the US Department of Energy's National Energy Modeling System assumes that heat pumps have a minimum lifetime of 9 years and a maximum lifetime of 22 years. But the somewhat longer lifetime is intended to reflect the inertia in heating system choices and that a heat pump subsidy could affect heating system choices even beyond the lifetime of the initial equipment.

Discount Rate

Finally, these calculations assume a 5% annual discount rate. Discounting future carbon abatement takes into account that although the costs of these subsidies are borne up front, the carbon abatement occurs over many years. Discounting has little effect on the comparison between heat pumps and electric vehicles, but it lowers the overall level of abatement from both types of subsidies. Results are also reported for discount rates of 3% and 7%.

B.   Cost-Effectiveness: Results

Table 5 presents the cost-effectiveness calculations. Under the baseline assumptions, a $2,000 heat pump subsidy reduces lifetime carbon dioxide emissions by 4 tons. Carbon abatement scales as expected in response to

Table 5
Carbon Abatement for a $2,000 Heat Pump Subsidy

Baseline assumptions	4 tons
Higher proportion of recipients additional (75% rather than 50%)	5 tons
Lower proportion of recipients additional (25% rather than 50%)	2 tons
Household otherwise would have used propane	6 tons
Household otherwise would have used heating oil	10 tons
Household otherwise would have used electric resistance heating	22 tons
Households assumed to use less heating (20 MMBtu rather than 35)	2 tons
Households assumed to use more heating (50 MMBtu rather than 35)	5 tons
Lower discount rate (3% rather than 5%)	4 tons
Higher discount rate (7% rather than 5%)	3 tons

Note: This table reports calculated lifetime carbon abatement in tons for a $2,000 heat pump subsidy. Under the baseline assumptions, 50% of subsidy recipients are additional, the household otherwise would have used natural gas, households use 35 MMBtu of heating per annually, heat pumps have a 20-year lifetime, and there is a 5% annual discount rate. Abatement is rounded to the nearest ton.

alternative assumptions about the proportion of additional recipients, level of heating demand, and discount rates. For example, carbon abatement is lower when one assumes that only 25% of recipients are additional. This makes sense. After all, from a carbon abatement perspective, the worst-case scenario would be that all recipients are "free riders," that is, getting paid for doing what they would have done otherwise.

The results for other heating fuels are interesting and merit additional discussion. Carbon abatement is higher if one assumes that household otherwise would have used propane or heating oil. This reflects that these fuels are more carbon intensive than natural gas. Interestingly, carbon abatement is much higher if the household otherwise would have used electric resistance heating. This is a bit surprising because typically heat pump subsidies are described as inducing households to substitute away from natural gas and other on-site direct consumption of fossil fuels. These calculations illustrate, however, that there are significant reductions in carbon dioxide emissions from encouraging households to switch to a much more energy-efficient form of electric heating.

It is tempting to compare the calculations in table 5 to estimates in the literature for the social cost of carbon. For example, the US government currently uses a social cost of carbon of $51 per ton (US Interagency Working Group 2021), and one recent study finds a preferred social cost of carbon of $185 per ton (Rennert et al. 2022). However, this is not an apples-to-apples comparison. Subsidies are transfers, not economic costs, and many households value subsidies at close to $1-for-$1. Nonadditional recipients, for example, value each $1 subsidy at exactly $1, so for them the subsidy should be viewed as a pure transfer from taxpayers to households. These transfers are not costless because they must be financed through distortionary taxes (i.e., the marginal cost of public funds), but this is typically thought of as imposing economic costs much lower than $1 per $1 raised.

The following section presents analogous estimates for electric vehicles. This is more of an apples-to-apples comparison because in both cases the objective is to calculate the carbon abatement that would result from a $2,000 subsidy. These comparisons can be viewed in the spirit of Hendren and Sprung-Keyser (2020) and the "marginal value of public funds" (MVPF). Intended as a metric for evaluating the desirability of government policies, the MVPF is the ratio of a policy's benefits to a policy's cost to the government. The advantage of the MVPF is that it makes it possible to easily compare the societal returns to alternative uses of government expenditure.

C. Cost-Effectiveness: Comparison to Electric Vehicles

The approach taken for the back-of-the-envelope calculations for electric vehicles is quite similar. For comparability, the basic thought experiment is to consider a $2,000 subsidy for electric vehicles. At this subsidy level, it is assumed under the baseline assumptions that 25% of subsidy recipients are additional. A lower percentage is used here than the 50% assumed for heat pumps because a $2,000 subsidy is a smaller percentage of total costs.[16]

These calculations implicitly assume that the incidence of the subsidy is at least partly on buyers. If supply were perfectly inelastic, then sellers would capture 100% of the subsidy, there would be no change in the number of electric vehicles sold, and 0% of subsidy recipients would be additional. Although this is an interesting extreme case, it makes more sense to think about suppliers having at least some ability to increase the quantity supplied, particularly over the medium and long run. Muehlegger and Rapson (2022), for example, find that buyers capture 73%–85% of electric vehicle subsidies in California.

Households are assumed to otherwise have used a gasoline-powered vehicle that gets 30 miles per gallon and is driven 10,000 miles per year, with a 15-year lifetime. These assumptions are informed by previous research and empirical data on driving behavior. Perhaps most relevantly, Xing et al. (2021) use US vehicle sales data from 2010 to 2014 and a discrete choice model to find that households with an electric vehicle otherwise would have driven a vehicle with an average fuel economy of 28.9 miles per gallon. Holland et al. (2016) assume vehicles are driven 15,000 miles per year, whereas other studies of electric vehicle driving behavior have tended to find lower levels of driving intensity (Davis 2019; Burlig et al. 2021). Finally, Bento, Roth, and Zuo (2018) find that the average lifetime for passenger vehicles in the United States is 15.6 years.

Table 6 presents the cost-effectiveness results for electric vehicles. Under the baseline assumptions, a $2,000 electric vehicle subsidy reduces lifetime carbon dioxide emissions by 5 tons. Carbon abatement scales as expected in response to alternative assumptions about the proportion of additional recipients, fuel efficiency, vehicle miles traveled, and discount rates.

These calculations suggest that heat pump and electric vehicle subsidies yield a similar amount of carbon abatement per subsidy dollar. This finding of roughly equivalent efficiency is notable given the very different

Table 6
Carbon Abatement for a $2,000 Electric Vehicle Subsidy

Baseline assumptions	5 tons
Higher proportion of recipients additional (35% rather than 25%)	10 tons
Lower proportion of recipients additional (15% rather than 25%)	3 tons
Vehicle otherwise less fuel efficient (20 mpg compared with 30)	7 tons
Vehicle otherwise more fuel efficient (40 mpg compared with 30)	3 tons
Vehicles driven less (7,500 annual miles traveled)	4 tons
Vehicles driven more (12,500 annual miles traveled)	7 tons
Lower discount rate (3% rather than 5%)	6 tons
Higher discount rate (7% rather than 5%)	5 tons

Note: This table reports calculated lifetime carbon abatement in tons for a $2,000 electric vehicle subsidy. Under the baseline assumptions, 25% of subsidy recipients are additional, households otherwise would have used a gasoline-powered vehicle that gets 30 miles per gallon and is driven 10,000 miles per year, vehicles have a 15-year lifetime, and there is a 5% annual discount rate. Abatement is rounded to the nearest ton.

patterns for distributional impacts presented earlier. Economists have pointed out that many energy-related policies involve efficiency-versus-equity trade-offs, with, for example, policy makers sometimes eschewing more efficient policies due to concerns about equity (Deryugina, Fullerton, and Pizer 2019). These results suggest, however, that heat pump subsidies achieve a similar amount of carbon abatement as electric vehicle subsidies, but with more equitable distributional impacts.

Before proceeding, it is worth reiterating that tables 5 and 6 should be viewed as preliminary back-of-the-envelope calculations. This exercise requires many strong assumptions, and as more evidence becomes available, it will be interesting to update these calculations to reflect better information about additionality, substitution patterns, usage levels, and other factors. Perhaps most importantly, these calculations assume that emissions from the US electricity sector remain constant. The argument for heat pumps and electric vehicles as a climate solution hinges on the assumption that the US grid will continue to become less carbon intensive over time. Although this would not tend to affect much the comparison between heat pump and electric vehicles, it would significantly increase the overall carbon abatement from both types of technologies.

VI. Conclusion

This paper started off by showing that heat pump adoption is remarkably similar across US households with different income levels. This surprising finding stands in sharp contrast to adoption patterns for electric vehicles, solar panels, and other low-carbon technologies, which are disproportionately adopted by high-income households. The paper showed, for example, that households with an annual income above $150,000 are twice as likely to have solar panels and six times more likely to have an electric vehicle than households with income between $50,000 and $60,000.

This lack of correlation between heat pump adoption and household income has important potential implications for the distributional impact of heat pump subsidies. Whereas subsidies for other low-carbon technologies have tended to go overwhelmingly to high-income households, heat pump subsidies are likely to be much more widely distributed across the income distribution.

Instead, geography, climate, and energy prices all were shown to strongly predict heat pump adoption. Regression evidence showed, for example, that a 1 standard deviation increase in HDDs decreases heat pump adoption by one-fourth, whereas a 1 standard deviation increase in electricity prices decreases heat pump adoption by one-third. Other factors like homeowner versus renter, single-family versus multi-unit, and the size of the home were shown to be less important.

Finally, the paper presented back-of-the-envelope calculations aimed at quantifying the carbon abatement from heat pump and electric vehicle subsidies. These calculations suggest that the two types of subsidies yield a similar amount of carbon abatement per subsidy dollar. These calculations rely on strong assumptions and should be interpreted cautiously, but they suggest that these two subsidies are quite similar from an efficiency perspective, despite having very different distributional implications.

Appendix

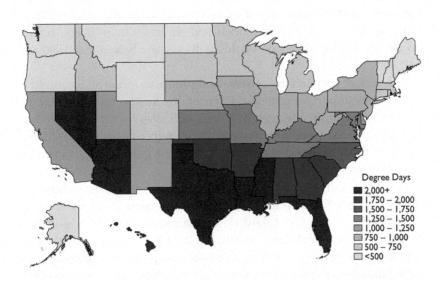

Fig. A1. Cooling degree days by state. Color version available as an online enhancement.

Notes: This map plots cooling degree days (CDDs) by state. CDDs are a widely used measure of cooling demand that reflects the number of days of hot weather as well as the intensity of heat on those days. These data come from RECS (2020) and are 30-year annual averages from 1981 to 2010, relative to a base temperature of 65°F. Households are weighted using RECS sampling weights.

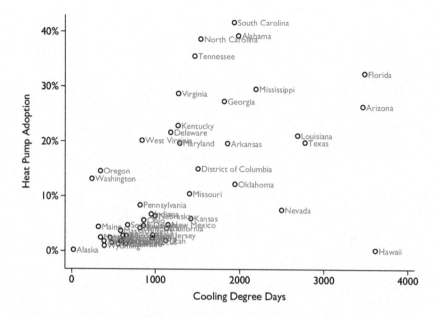

Fig. A2. Heat pump adoption versus cooling degree days. Color version available as an online enhancement.

Notes: This scatterplot shows the percentage of households with heat pumps versus annual cooling degree days. Both variables come from RECS (2020). Households are weighted using RECS sampling weights. The correlation between the two variables is positive (0.55) and strongly statistically significant (p value = .00).

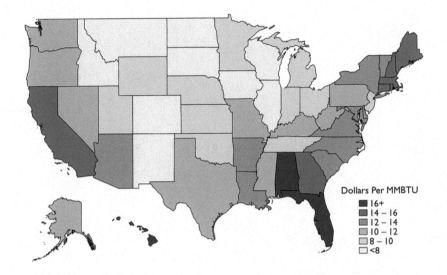

Fig. A3. Average residential natural gas prices. Color version available as an online enhancement.

Notes: This map plots average residential natural gas prices in 2020. These data come from the US Department of Energy, *Energy Information Administration* and include all relevant taxes and delivery charges. See https://www.eia.gov/dnav/ng/ng_pri_sum_a_EPG0 _PRS_DMcf_a.htm.

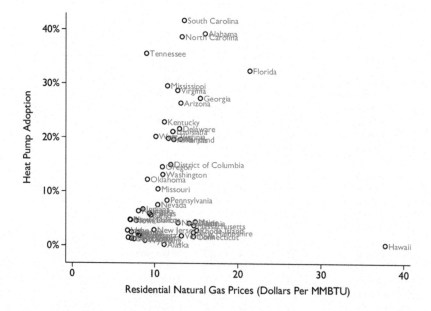

Fig. A4. Heat pump adoption versus natural gas prices. Color version available as an online enhancement.

Notes: This scatterplot shows the percentage of households with heat pumps versus residential natural gas prices. The percentage of households with heat pumps by state comes from RECS (2020) and was calculated using RECS sampling weights. Average residential natural gas prices by state come from the US Department of Energy, Energy Information Administration and include all relevant taxes and delivery charges. See https://www.eia .gov/dnav/ng/ng_pri_sum_a_EPG0_PRS_DMcf_a.htm. The correlation between the two variables is positive (0.18) but not statistically significant (*p* value = .20).

194 Davis

Table A1
Heat Pump Adoption by State, Ranked by Percentage

		Percent	Total (Millions)			Percent	Total (Millions)
1.	South Carolina	42	.8	26.	Ohio	6	.3
2.	Alabama	39	.7	27.	New Mexico	5	0
3.	North Carolina	39	1.6	28.	South Dakota	5	0
4.	Tennessee	36	.9	29.	Iowa	5	.1
5.	Florida	32	2.6	30.	Maine	4	0
6.	Mississippi	30	.3	31.	New York	4	.3
7.	Virginia	29	.9	32.	California	4	.5
8.	Georgia	27	1.1	33.	Massachusetts	4	.1
9.	Arizona	26	.7	34.	New Jersey	3	.1
10.	Kentucky	23	.4	35.	Rhode Island	3	0
11.	Delaware	22	.1	36.	Idaho	3	0
12.	Louisiana	21	.4	37.	Montana	3	0
13.	West Virginia	20	.1	38.	New Hampshire	2	0
14.	Texas	20	2.0	39.	Illinois	2	.1
15.	Maryland	20	.4	40.	Minnesota	2	0
16.	Arkansas	20	.2	41.	Utah	2	0
17.	Oregon	15	.2	42.	Michigan	2	.1
18.	Washington	13	.4	43.	Vermont	2	0
19.	Oklahoma	12	.2	44.	Connecticut	2	0
20.	Missouri	10	.3	45.	North Dakota	2	0
21.	Pennsylvania	8	.4	46.	Colorado	1	0
22.	Nevada	8	.1	47.	Wisconsin	1	0
23.	Indiana	7	.2	48.	Wyoming	1	0
24.	Nebraska	6	0	49.	Hawaii	0	0
25.	Kansas	6	.1	50.	Alaska	0	0

Note: This table reports by state the percentage of households with heat pumps and the implied total number of households with heat pumps. This information comes from RECS (2020) and was calculated using RECS sampling weights. These percentages are slightly higher than state-level percentages reported in the US Department of Energy, Energy Information Administration (EIA) report "Highlights for Space Heating in US Homes by State, 2020" (final release March 2023) because the EIA table includes only central heat pumps, whereas this table includes both central heat pumps and mini-splits. Percentages are rounded to the nearest percent, and totals are rounded to the nearest 100,000.

Endnotes

Author email address: Davis (ldavis@haas.berkeley.edu). This paper was presented at the NBER Environmental and Energy Policy and the Economy Conference, May 25, 2023, at the National Press Club in Washington, DC. I am thankful to Josh Blonz, Carl Blumstein, Severin Borenstein, Tatyana Deryugina, Justin Kirkpatrick, Matthew Kotchen, Catherine Wolfram, and conference participants at the NBER and University of California, Berkeley, for helpful feedback. I do not have any financial relationships that relate to this research. The analysis relies entirely on publicly available data, and all data and code are available on the author's website. For acknowledgments, sources of research support, and disclosure of the author's material financial relationships, if any, please see https://www.nber.org/books-and-chapters /environmental-and-energy-policy-and-economy-volume-5/economic-determinants-heat -pump-adoption.

1. That is, the 2020 RECS was implemented entirely via online and paper question-naires. Prior waves of the RECS used a combination of in-person interviews and these self-administered modes. See U.S. Department of Energy, Energy Information Adminis-tration (2022), for details.

2. Sexton and Sexton (2014), for example, find that green communities have higher market shares of the Toyota Prius relative to less conspicuous hybrids like the Toyota Camry hybrid, consistent with what they call "conspicuous conservation." This builds on earlier work showing increased registrations of hybrid vehicles like the Toyota Prius in green communities (Kahn 2007): "In green communities, social pressure may reinforce the urge to take green actions such as driving a Toyota Prius."

3. Formally, this is implemented using a regression-based statistical test. Separate re-gressions are estimated for each technology. In each case, the dependent variable is an in-dicator variable for whether the household has a particular technology, and the indepen-dent variables are indicator variables for seven of the eight income bins. Following each regression, a Wald test is performed to assess whether the seven coefficients are equal to zero; that is, equal to the value for the excluded category.

4. See, for example, *Washington Post*, "US Home Heating Is Fractured in Surprising Ways: Look Up Your Neighborhood," March 6, 2023, by John Muyskens, Shannon Osaka, and Naema Ahmed. See also US Department of Energy, Energy Information Administra-tion, "US Households' Heating Equipment Choices Are Diverse and Vary by Climate Re-gion," April 6, 2017.

5. This back-of-the-envelope calculation is based on national average residential prices of $12.18 per thousand cubic feet for natural gas and 13.7 cents per kWh for electricity. One kWh is equivalent to 3,412 Btu, or 0.003412 MMBtu, and 1,000 cubic feet is equivalent to 1.037 MMBtu. Electric resistance and natural gas heating are assumed to be 100% and 90% efficient, respectively.

6. It is hard to say whether a COP of 3.0 is representative. The US federal minimum ef-ficiency standard for air-source heat pumps was 2.40 between 2015 and 2022, before in-creasing to 2.58 in 2023. US federal minimum efficiency standards for heat pumps are measured using the heating seasonal performance factor (HSPF), which is average heating (in Btu) per watt-hour. The minimum standard was HSPF 8.2 between 2015 and 2022 and then HSPF 8.8 starting in 2023. There are 3,412 Btu per kWh of electricity, so HSPF 8.2 and 8.8 correspond to average COP of 2.4 and 2.58, respectively. Borenstein and Bushnell (2022b) assume for their calculations a COP of 2.5 (i.e., 0.4 kWh of electricity per 1 kWh of heat). Other studies report results for a range of different COP values. See, for example, Kaufman et al. (2019) and Walker, Less, and Casquero-Modrego (2022).

7. This trade-off between up-front and operating costs is a central theme in previous economic analyses of residential heating and cooling. See, for example, Hausman (1979), Dubin and McFadden (1984), Mansur, Mendelsohn, and Morrison (2008), and Rapson (2014). None of these four studies considers heat pumps, which points to their rel-atively recent rise to prominence.

8. The Inflation Reduction Act was signed into law by President Biden on August 16, 2022. See Inflation Reduction Act of 2022, HR 5376, 117th Congress, Public Law 117-169. See also Congressional Research Service, "Residential Energy Tax Credits: Changes in 2023," November 21, 2022, and Internal Revenue Service, "Frequently Asked Questions about Energy Efficient Home Improvements and Residential Clean Energy Property Credits," December 2022.

9. US Department of Energy, *Residential Energy Consumption Survey 2020*, Table HC6.1 "Space Heating in US Homes," released May 2022.

10. US Department of Energy, Energy Information Administration, 2015 Residential Energy Consumption and Expenditures Tables, Table CE3.1 "Annual Household Site End-Use Consumption in the US—Total and Averages" reports that the average US household uses 35.3 MMBtu annually for space heating. This approach of assuming a

fixed level of heating consumption implicitly ignores the potential for a "rebound effect," or the idea that lower operating costs would cause a household to consume more heating (Dubin, Miedema, and Chandran 1986), which would be a refinement worth incorporating in future research.

11. The assumption of 90% efficiency for natural gas, propane, and heating oil is based on US DOE (2023) and reflects typical efficiency for new furnaces. The current federal minimum efficiency standard for gas furnaces (including both natural gas and propane) is 80% annual fuel utilization efficiency (AFUE). Pages 8 and 9 of US DOE (2023) report "typical" and "high" efficiencies of 92% and 99% in the North, and 80% and 99% in the rest of the country. The current federal minimum efficiency standard for oil-burning furnaces is 83% AFUE, and page 12 of US DOE (2023) reports "typical" and "high" efficiencies of 83% and 97%.

12. These calculations are based on standard conversion factors from the US Department of Energy, Energy Information Administration, "Energy Units and Calculators Explained," https://www.eia.gov/energyexplained/units-and-calculators/. Electricity consumption for heating with a heat pump is calculated using the COP of 3.0 and the conversion rate 1kWh = 3,412 Btu. Electric resistance heating in kWh is calculated using the conversion rate 1 kWh = 3,412 Btu. Natural gas consumption in Mcf (thousand cubic feet) is calculated using the conversion rate 1Mcf = 1.039 MMBtu. Propane consumption in gallons is calculated using the conversion rate 1 gallon = 0.091452 MMBtu. Heating oil consumption in gallons is calculated using the conversion rate 1 gallon = 0.1385 MMBtu.

13. Holland et al. (2022) find that current marginal carbon dioxide emissions for the Western grid are about 1 pound of carbon dioxide per kWh (0.5 tons per MWh), which is equivalent to 293 pounds of carbon dioxide per MMBtu. This reflects typical emissions for electricity generation from natural gas. From this same source, the emissions factor for the entire United States is about 1.3 pounds per kWh. The lower value is used in the baseline assumptions to reflect the widespread view that the US grid will continue getting cleaner over time. Finally, these emissions are scaled up by 5% following US Department of Energy, Energy Information Administration, "How Much Electricity Is Lost in Electricity Transmission and Distribution in the United States?" to reflect that approximately 5% of electricity is lost between the power plant and the point of consumption.

14. These coefficients are from US Department of Energy, Energy Information Administration, "Carbon Dioxide Emissions Coefficients," released October 2022, https://www.eia.gov/environment/emissions/co2_vol_mass.php. These emissions factors do not account for the assumed 90% efficiency; these are emissions factors per MMBtu of energy, not MMBtu of heat.

15. See, for example, US DOE, "More Than 60% of Energy Used for Electricity Generation is Lost in Conversion," July 21, 2020.

16. The assumption that 25% of subsidy recipients is additional is probably optimistic. Muehlegger and Rapson (2022) estimate that the price elasticity of demand for electric vehicles is –2.1. Thus, a subsidy that decreases the up-front cost of electric vehicles by 10% would increase demand by 21%. In their study, the baseline price of an electric vehicle is $26,000, so a $2,000 subsidy would be an 8% decrease in up-front cost, expected to increase demand by 16%. Their study focuses on a California electric vehicle subsidy program aimed at low- and middle-income households.

References

Bento, Antonio M., Lawrence H. Goulder, Mark R. Jacobsen, and Roger H. Von Haefen. 2009. "Distributional and Efficiency Impacts of Increased US Gasoline Taxes." *American Economic Review* 99 (3): 667–99.

Bento, Antonio M., Kevin Roth, and Yiou Zuo. 2018. "Vehicle Lifetime Trends and Scrappage Behavior in the US Used Car Market." *Energy Journal* 39 (1): 159–83.

Borenstein, Severin. 2012. "The Redistributional Impact of Nonlinear Electricity Pricing," *American Economic Journal: Economic Policy* 4 (3): 56–90.

———. 2017. "Private Net Benefits of Residential Solar PV: The Role of Electricity Tariffs, Tax Incentives, and Rebates." *Journal of the Association of Environmental and Resource Economists* 4 (S1): S85–S122.

Borenstein, Severin, and James B. Bushnell. 2022a. "Do Two Electricity Pricing Wrongs Make a Right? Cost Recovery, Externalities, and Efficiency." *American Economic Journal: Economic Policy* 14 (4): 80–110.

———. 2022b. "Headwinds and Tailwinds: Implications of Inefficient Retail Energy Pricing for Energy Substitution." *Environmental and Energy Policy and the Economy* 3:37–70.

Borenstein, Severin, and Lucas W. Davis. 2016. "The Distributional Effects of US Clean Energy Tax Credits." *Tax Policy and the Economy* 30:191–234.

Borenstein, Severin, Meredith Fowlie, and James Sallee. 2021. "Designing Electricity Rates for an Equitable Energy Transition." Working paper, Energy Institute at Haas, University of California, Berkeley.

Bruegge, Chris, Tatyana Deryugina, and Erica Myers. 2019. "The Distributional Effects of Building Energy Codes." *Journal of the Association of Environmental and Resource Economists* 6 (S1): S95–S127.

Burlig, Fiona, James Bushnell, David Rapson, and Catherine Wolfram. 2021. "Low Energy: Estimating Electric Vehicle Electricity Use." *AEA Papers and Proceedings* 111:430–35.

Cronin, Julie Anne, Don Fullerton, and Steven Sexton. 2019. "Vertical and Horizontal Redistributions from a Carbon Tax and Rebate." *Journal of the Association of Environmental and Resource Economists* 6 (S1): S169–S208.

Davis, Lucas W. 2019. "How Much Are Electric Vehicles Driven?" *Applied Economics Letters* 26 (18): 1497–502.

———. Forthcoming. "What Matters for Electrification? Evidence from 70 Years of US Home Heating Choices." *Review of Economics and Statistics*.

Davis, Lucas W., and Christopher R. Knittel. 2019. "Are Fuel Economy Standards Regressive?" *Journal of the Association of Environmental and Resource Economists* 6 (S1): S37–S63.

Deryugina, Tatyana, Don Fullerton, and William A. Pizer. 2019. "An Introduction to Energy Policy Trade-Offs between Economic Efficiency and Distributional Equity." *Journal of the Association of Environmental and Resource Economists* 6 (S1): S1–S6.

Dubin, Jeffrey A., and Daniel L. McFadden. 1984. "An Econometric Analysis of Residential Electric Appliance Holdings and Consumption." *Econometrica* 52 (2): 345–62.

Dubin, Jeffrey A., Allen K. Miedema, and Ram V. Chandran. 1986. "Price Effects of Energy-Efficient Technologies: A Study of Residential Demand for Heating and Cooling." *RAND Journal of Economics* 17 (3): 310–25.

Feger, Fabian, Nicola Pavanini, and Doina Radulescu. 2022. "Welfare and Redistribution in Residential Electricity Markets with Solar Power." *Review of Economic Studies* 89 (6): 3267–302.

Gillingham, Kenneth, Matthew Harding, and David Rapson. 2012. "Split Incentives in Residential Energy Consumption." *Energy Journal* 33 (2): 37–62.

Gross, Robert, and Richard Hanna. 2019. "Path Dependency in Provision of Domestic Heating." *Nature Energy* 4 (5): 358–64.

Hausman, Jerry A. 1979. "Individual Discount Rates and the Purchase and Utilization of Energy-Using Durables." *Bell Journal of Economics* 10 (1): 33–54.

Hendren, Nathaniel, and Ben Sprung-Keyser. 2020. "A Unified Welfare Analysis of Government Policies." *Quarterly Journal of Economics* 135 (3): 1209–318.

Holland, Stephen P., Matthew J. Kotchen, Erin T. Mansur, and Andrew J. Yates. 2022. "Why Marginal CO_2 Emissions Are Not Decreasing for US Electricity: Estimates and Implications for Climate Policy." *Proceedings of the National Academy of Sciences of the United States of America* 119 (8): e2116632119.

Holland, Stephen P., Erin T. Mansur, Nicholas Z. Muller, and Andrew J. Yates. 2016. "Are There Environmental Benefits from Driving Electric Vehicles? The Importance of Local Factors." *American Economic Review* 106 (12): 3700–29.

———. 2020. "Decompositions and Policy Consequences of an Extraordinary Decline in Air Pollution from Electricity Generation." *American Economic Journal: Economic Policy* 12 (4): 244–74.

IEA (International Energy Agency). 2022. "The Future of Heat Pumps." World Energy Outlook Special Report, International Energy Agency, Paris, France.

Ito, Koichiro. 2014. "Do Consumers Respond to Marginal or Average Price? Evidence from Nonlinear Electricity Pricing." *American Economic Review* 104 (2): 537–63.

Kahn, Matthew E. 2007. "Do Greens Drive Hummers or Hybrids? Environmental Ideology as a Determinant of Consumer Choice." *Journal of Environmental Economics and Management* 54 (2): 129–45.

Kaufman, Noah, David Sandalow, Clotilde Rossi Di Schio, and Jake Higdon. 2019. "Decarbonizing Space Heating with Air Source Heat Pumps." Working paper, Columbia School of International and Public Affairs, New York, NY.

Li, Jing. 2019. "Compatibility and Investment in the US Electric Vehicle Market." Working paper, Massachusetts Institute of Technology, Cambridge, MA.

Li, Shanjun, Lang Tong, Jianwei Xing, and Yiyi Zhou. 2017. "The Market for Electric Vehicles: Indirect Network Effects and Policy Design." *Journal of the Association of Environmental and Resource Economists* 4 (1): 89–133.

Mansur, Erin T., Robert Mendelsohn, and Wendy Morrison. 2008. "Climate Change Adaptation: A Study of Fuel Choice and Consumption in the US Energy Sector." *Journal of Environmental Economics and Management* 55 (2): 175–93.

Muehlegger, Erich, and David S. Rapson. 2022. "Subsidizing Low- and Middle-Income Adoption of Electric Vehicles: Quasi-experimental Evidence from California." *Journal of Public Economics* 216:104752.

National Academies. 2021. *Accelerating Decarbonization of the US Energy System.* Washington, DC: National Academies Press.

Poterba, James M. 1991. "Is the Gasoline Tax Regressive?" *Tax Policy and the Economy* 5:145–64.

Princeton University. 2021. "Net-Zero America: Potential Pathways, Infrastructure and Impacts." Final report, Princeton University.

Rapson, David. 2014. "Durable Goods and Long-Run Electricity Demand: Evidence from Air Conditioner Purchase Behavior." *Journal of Environmental Economics and Management* 68 (1): 141–60.

Reiss, Peter C., and Matthew W. White. 2005. "Household Electricity Demand, Revisited." *Review of Economic Studies* 72 (3): 853–83.

———. 2008. "What Changes Energy Consumption? Prices and Public Pressures." *RAND Journal of Economics* 39 (3): 636–63.

Rennert, Kevin, Frank Errickson, Brian C. Prest, Lisa Rennels, Richard G. Newell, William Pizer, Cora Kingdon, et al. 2022. "Comprehensive Evidence Implies a Higher Social Cost of CO_2." *Nature* 610 (7933): 687–92.

Rosenow, Jan, Duncan Gibb, Thomas Nowak, and Richard Lowes. 2022. "Heating Up the Global Heat Pump Market." *Nature Energy* 7 (10): 901–4.

Sexton, Steven E., and Alison L. Sexton. 2014. "Conspicuous Conservation: The Prius Halo and Willingness to Pay for Environmental Bona Fides." *Journal of Environmental Economics and Management* 67 (3): 303–17.

Springel, Katalin. 2021. "Network Externality and Subsidy Structure in Two-Sided Markets: Evidence from Electric Vehicle Incentives." *American Economic Journal: Economic Policy* 13 (4): 393–432.

U.S. Department of Energy, Energy Information Administration. (2022, June). "2020 Residential Energy Consumption Survey: Household Characteristics Technical Documentation Summary." Washington, DC.

US DOE (US Department of Energy, Energy Information Administration). 2023. "Updated Buildings Sector Appliance and Equipment Costs and Efficiencies." Prepared March 2023 by Guidehouse (McLean, VA) and Leidos (Reston, VA).

US Interagency Working Group. 2021. "Technical Support Document: Social Cost of Carbon, Methane, and Nitrous Oxide, Interim Estimates under Executive Order 13990." IWG on Social Cost of Greenhouse Gases, United States Government, Washington, DC, February.

Walker, Iain S., Brennan D. Less, and Núria Casquero-Modrego. 2022. "Carbon and Energy Cost Impacts of Electrification of Space Heating with Heat Pumps in the US." *Energy and Buildings* 259:111910.

Williams, James H., Ryan A. Jones, Ben Haley, Gabe Kwok, Jeremy Hargreaves, Jamil Farbes, and Margaret S. Torn. 2021. "Carbon-Neutral Pathways for the United States." *AGU Advances* 2 (1): e2020AV000284.

Xing, Jianwei, Benjamin Leard, and Shanjun Li. 2021. "What Does an Electric Vehicle Replace?" *Journal of Environmental Economics and Management* 107:102432.

Do Red States Have a Comparative Advantage in Generating Green Power?

Robert Huang, *University of Southern California*, United States of America

Matthew E. Kahn, *University of Southern California, and NBER*, United States of America

Executive Summary

The passage of the 2022 Inflation Reduction Act will lead to a significant increase in US wind and solar power investment. Renewable power generation requires more land than fossil fuel fired power generation. The land that will be allocated to renewables depends on several demand-side and supply-side factors such as the land's renewable power potential, cost of acquisition, proximity to final power consumers, and local land use regulations. We find that Republican areas are more likely to issue interconnection permits than progressive areas. We present evidence that rural Republican areas have a cost advantage in generating wind power; however, Democratic areas have sited more solar capacity. We use our statistical model to identify Republican congressional districts that have the potential to scale up green power production.

JEL Codes: Q2, Q4, R52

Keywords: energy transition, electricity generation, land use regulations

I. Introduction

In 2021, the United States generated 21% of its electricity from renewable energy, with 9.2% from wind and 2.8% from solar.[1] To encourage utilities to purchase green power, state governments have ramped up their renewable portfolio standards (RPS). In 2010, the average RPS was 3.16%, and as of 2021, this number has jumped to 10.7%. Such green power mandates lead to greater investments in renewable power generation. The United States seeks to expand green power supply, especially

Environmental and Energy Policy and the Economy, volume 5, 2024.

wind and solar, during a time when electricity demand is likely to rise as more people rely on electricity to power homes and vehicles (Davis, Fuchs, and Gertler 2014; Rapson 2014; Cicala 2022). The passage of the August 2022 Inflation Reduction Act creates a new set of incentives intending to accelerate the decarbonization of the nation's power sector (Bistline, Mehrotra, and Wolfram 2023).

A key challenge to increasing renewable power generation is the land intensity of wind and solar capacity (Van Zalk and Behrens 2018).[2] Based on our own estimates, each megawatt (MW) of utility-scale wind capacity currently takes 55.3 acres of land, and each MW of solar capacity takes 5.97 acres.[3] These land inputs are much greater than the land inputs for generating electricity using fossil fuels. Renewable power plants also differ from conventional ones in that wind and solar cannot be shipped across space. Green electricity must be generated locally in areas with high renewable potential. Although renewable power generation reduces the global externality of climate change, its spatial concentration in specific areas raises the likelihood of local NIMBYism against renewable project development (Stokes 2016). In 2022, 47 wind projects and 75 solar projects have been blocked by local governments across the United States.[4] Brooks and Liscow (2023) have found that backlash against infrastructure projects delays their completion and inflates their costs.

As shown by Rappaport and Sachs (2003), the majority of the nation's population and an even larger share of the nation's earnings clusters close to the oceans. The sheer size of the United States means that power generation can be sited on millions of other acres of land. Mutually beneficial trade has occurred as the coastal people have purchased food from the American food belt and manufacturing goods from Southern manufacturing areas. On some level, trade in green energy represents another example of comparative advantage in a case where land prices vary across space. At the same time, the climate change challenge has raised political divisions that have not occurred in the case of producing food or manufacturing goods.

In this paper, we study whether Republican areas have an edge in siting utility-scale wind turbines and solar panels because they have fewer land use regulations, cheaper land, and more natural resources.[5] Based on voting in the 2020 election, 83% of the land area of the United States featured counties whose vote share was more than 50% for Donald Trump. In the areas with an above-median wind speed or solar radiation, 87.5% and 82% of the land area was in counties where a majority voted for Trump. For-profit developers of renewable power plants have an incentive to generate power in Republican areas. Interstate transmission capacity connects dispersed local renewable generators to coastal consumers of power (Davis, Hausman, and Rose 2023). An example is the 730-mile Anschutz power line (currently under construction) that runs through the American West.[6]

We use a project-level data set from the Berkeley Electricity Markets & Policy Lab to study the electricity generation permitting process. Generating capacity needs to wait in a queue to receive approval for commercial operation. This process is called interconnection, during which the regional transmission organization (RTO) conducts a site study to evaluate the feasibility of the project. Developers can construct power plants only if their projects are approved (see the flowchart in fig. A1). The data set we use provides information on 8,000 renewable projects that applied for interconnection between 2010 and 2020, including their capacity, status, queue time, and location. Most of the proposed capacity does not end up being built. We document that land-intensive renewable projects are less likely to withdraw from the queue in Republican areas.

We then explore the economic geography of the existing renewable capacity using a county panel data set from 2010 to 2021. We show that Republican counties feature lower population densities, lower land prices, and higher wind speeds. We also create a measure of each county's green market potential based on its neighboring states' RPS. This market potential grows faster in Republican counties. Our results show that both a state's RPS and the RPS levels from neighboring states are correlated with a developer's decision to build wind and solar capacity. We document that red states have installed more wind capacity, but blue states have built more solar farms. A border discontinuity analysis shows that solar generators are more likely to be sited on the liberal side of the border, and we interpret this as the result of policy incentives for solar in progressive states.

Rural areas tend to elect Republican congressional representatives who have opposed past environmental protection legislation (Cragg et al. 2013). The expected windfall from green power generation could change future carbon mitigation politics. The price of local land in places with high renewable power potential may be bid up as renewable power generators raise their bids for local land. This wealth effect for landowners offers local jurisdictions greater property tax revenue (Kahn 2013). Increases in federal subsidies for green power could be attractive to rural landowners in places with wind and solar generation potential. We posit that the economic interests could swing some rural area residents toward accepting renewable energy. Gaining from the rise of green power, residents will lobby their congressional representatives to support more renewable energy subsidies (Peltzman 1984). Using our empirical models on the pattern of renewable capacity deployments, we identify the subset of red districts that may be "red/green swing districts."

This paper is organized as follows. In Section II, we introduce our main data sets. In Section III, we provide conceptual reasonings on why Republican areas have an edge in generating green power and present graphical evidence. We then list our empirical hypotheses in Section IV. We study the green permitting process in Section V and the economic geography of the existing renewable capacity in Section VI. In Section VII, we identify the Republican congressional districts that may vote in favor of climate subsidies. In the concluding sections, we discuss the future land use of wind and solar power plants.

II. Data

A. Renewable Installations Data Set by County

To explore the economic geography of the installed green power plants, we compile a county/year data set including the local wind and solar capacity, sociopolitical attributes, and environmental attributes. We calculate each county's green capacity in each year from 2010 to 2021 using data from the Environmental Protection Agency's Emissions and Generation Resource Integrated Database (eGRID).[7] The eGRID data set provides detailed information on each utility-scale electricity generator in the United States, including the year built, energy source, capacity, and location. Using these generator data, we calculate the total wind capacity and total solar capacity by county/year.

We merge each state's RPS by year into our county panel.[8] Another dynamic variable in our county data set is the annual out-of-state RPS market potential for each county. It is calculated using the formula for the market potential function (Hanson 2005). This variable captures the spatial cluster of nearby aggregate demand for a county's "exports" of green power. The out-of-state RPS potential for county j in year t is given by

$$MP_{jt} = \sum_{k \in K} RPS_{kt} e^{-d_{jk}}, \tag{1}$$

where K is a set of counties in a different state but with direct electricity transmission lines to county j, and d_{jk} is the distance (in 1,000 miles) between county j and county k. This is a distance-weighted RPS from counties in nearby states. The lack of transmission capacity has led to renewables curtailment in local markets (i.e., supply > demand), which disincentivizes the construction of new generators (Davis et al. 2023). We calculate the market potential using only county pairs with direct transmission lines. In 2021, the average RPS market potential per county was 8.41 with a standard deviation of 7.65. California has an RPS of 33%. A market potential of 8.41 is roughly equivalent to having an average distance of 100 miles to 28 counties in California (and all other nearby counties have zero RPS). The RPS potential has a correlation of .185 with state RPS. The relatively low correlation indicates that many counties in states with low RPS are located close to states with high RPS.[9]

We merge in variables on county demographics and time-invariant environmental attributes. We include data on votes for Trump in the 2020 presidential election and a Republican governor dummy indicating whether a state has a Republican governor in a given year.[10] Our data on median home prices in 2010 are from Zillow.[11] We obtain the county population, population density, and area data from the American Community Survey.[12] The county-level climate change belief data are provided by the Yale Climate Change Communication program.[13] These variables (except the governor dummy) are cross-sectional.

The final component of this data set is the county-level wind and solar potential. The wind potential refers to the wind speed 100 meters above the surface level, and the solar potential refers to the global horizontal irradiance (GHI). Counties with higher wind speed and higher solar radiance are more favorable to siting green generating capacity. These environmental data are from the National Renewable Energy Laboratory (NREL) as geographic information system (GIS) files. We overlay these files with county shape files to calculate the averages by county. The average county wind speed in the United States is 6.75 m/s.[14] The average GHI is 4.48 kWh/m^2/day. On the continental United States, Arizona, Nevada, and California rank top three based on solar potential.

B. Generation Permitting Data

Developers need approval from regulators to construct and connect their generators to the grid (see fig. A1). To study the generation permitting process, we use a comprehensive project-level data set on interconnection application provided by the Berkeley Electricity Markets & Policy Lab.[15] It includes 1,500 utility-scale wind projects and 6,400 solar projects that have applied for grid connection from 2010 to 2020. For each project, the data set provides the project status (active, completed, or withdrawn), queue time, energy source, capacity, and location. Based on each project's location, we merge in the respective county's demographic and environmental attributes from the county panel.

C. Congressional Districts Data Set

Based on the county/year panel, we create a data set with the same variables by congressional district/year. The unit of analysis is a district in the 118th Congress. Our main metric of a district's political affiliation is its congressperson's DW-NOMINATE score.[16] It is a continuous measure of politicians' ideology, where 1 is the most conservative and −1 is the most progressive. If a district has multiple representatives, we average these scores from all representatives. In the 118th Congress, the average score of Democratic congresspeople is −.39, and that of Republicans is .52. We merge in DW-NOMINATE scores, population, and land area of each district in the 118th Congress.

Some congressional districts span across multiple counties. To calculate their sociopolitical and environmental attributes, we weight all county attributes (from the county/year panel) by the area intersection factor to get the averages for each district.[17] The wind and solar capacity are the only exceptions. Instead of using the weighted average, we classify each green generator into a congressional district based on its longitude and latitude. We then calculate the total renewable capacity by district/year.

III. Supplying Green Power

A. Land Requirements for Renewable Generation

Land is a key input in renewable power generation. Renewable generators have lower power density (defined as the electricity produced per unit of surface area) than conventional power plants, and solar panels occupy less land per unit of generation than wind turbines (Fthenakis and Kim 2009; Van Zalk and Behrens 2018).[18] Whereas a coal or gas power plant takes less than 1 acre per MW of capacity, our estimates suggest that for utility-scale projects, it currently takes 55 acres per MW of wind capacity and 6 acres per MW of solar capacity (including the necessary spacing between wind turbines and solar panels). Given the land intensity of renewable projects, especially wind, they have to be sited on cheap, open land.

B.   Local NIMBYism and Land Use Constraints

Unlike fossil fuels, wind and solar power cannot be shipped, which means renewable generators have to concentrate in regions with high local renewable potential and available land. These areas tend to be in rural counties with a large share of farmland. Under the current technological constraints, most crops cannot be grown under solar panels or within an acre from the base of wind turbines. The opportunity costs of converting farmland into green power plants include the forgone agricultural profits. Local farmers disproportionally bear these costs and have an incentive to oppose renewable developments.[19] Stokes (2016) has found that widely supported climate policies can fail when their benefits are dispersed but costs are concentrated in local communities. Residents also cite reasons such as declining property values and safety concerns to block local renewable projects (Gross 2020; Susskind et al. 2022).

Such NIMBYism is often bundled with stringent land use regulations. For example, in California, the Williamson Act (a.k.a. California Land Conservation Act) provides property tax relief to landowners who agree to keep their land in agricultural or open space use. The act allows local governments to penalize landowners who convert land subject to Williamson Act contracts to nonagricultural uses, which is a significant disincentive for those who consider leasing or selling their land for renewable energy development.[20] Local regulations deter renewable developers from entering the market (Djankov et al. 2002; Mulligan and Shleifer 2005).

Despite a high RPS, expensive land and strict zoning codes could disincentivize profit-maximizing developers from building land-intensive renewable capacity in liberal states like California (Carley 2009). If transmission capacity is available, neighboring states such as Nevada and Utah may have an edge in generating green power and exporting it to California. These states have cheaper land, fewer constraints on land use, and promising sun and wind potentials. However, the attempts to add transmission lines have also been met with political backlash when the lines pass through the area without financially benefiting the residents (Gross 2020). For utilities subject to rate-of-return regulations, they tend to invest in excess capitals (Averch and Johnson 1962), which implies they prefer building their own power plants instead of purchasing power from other generators. This incentivizes them to block transmission projects (Davis et al. 2023).

C. *The Spatial Distribution of the Existing Renewable Power Generators*

In 2010, there were 38,783 MW of wind capacity and 582.4 MW of solar capacity in the United States. These numbers have jumped to 133,408 MW and 61,683 MW, respectively, in 2021.[21] In this section, we present graphical evidence on the regional heterogeneity in wind and solar capacity deployment. Figure 1 shows the distribution of wind and solar capacity across congressional districts in 2021.

Districts with more conservative representatives, as measured by a higher DW-NOMINATE score (see Poole and Rosenthal 2001), are overrepresented among wind generators. Many wind farms have been built in Texas and in the midwestern states. By 2021, Texas had almost 35,000 MW of wind capacity, and the Midwest had more than 52,000 MW. They jointly accounted for roughly two-thirds of the wind capacity in the United States. Wind generators have been disproportionally built in Republican districts because these districts often feature high wind speed, low land prices, and fewer regulations such as zoning and limitations on the turbine height. These are favorable attributes that incentivize wind developers to enter the market.

The deployment of solar capacity exhibits a different pattern. Solar farms are disproportionally located along the coastline. California had built 16,000 MW of solar capacity by 2021, roughly one-fourth of the national total. Texas, North Carolina, Nevada, Georgia, and Florida also rank high in solar capacity. Coastline states feature high daily solar radiation but tend to have high land prices. Solar farms occupy less space

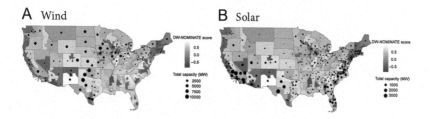

Fig. 1. Renewable capacity by congressional districts: (*A*) wind; (*B*) solar. DW-NOMINATE is a continuous measure of political ideology, with −1 being the most progressive and 1 being the most conservative. Each dot represents a congressional district with nonzero wind/solar capacity. The size of the dot is proportional to the total capacity within the district.

than wind facilities, and distributed solar panels can be installed on rooftops. Because solar farms use less land, solar developers are less responsive to the price of land per acre. Facing lower costs of building in solar capacity than wind capacity, the coastal liberal states ramp up solar to meet their ambitious RPS goals.

In figure 2, we create nonparametric plots of the total generating capacity and green power capacity per square mile with respect to each county's share of Republican votes and population density in 2020. An interesting pattern is that the total capacity density features a negative slope when plotted against Republican votes and a positive slope when plotted against population density, whereas the slope of the total green capacity has the opposite sign in both graphs. Before the ramp-up of renewable generation, due to losses of electricity during transmission, power plants locate closer to densely populated cities, which are often governed by Democrats.[22] The capacity density has been lower in

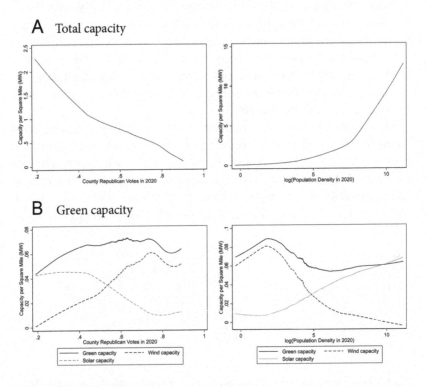

Fig. 2. Power plant density and county attributes: (*A*) total capacity; (*B*) green capacity. When the explanatory variable is Republican votes, we drop the top and bottom 1% of the data, which correspond to a vote of 89% and 19%. When the explanatory variable is logged density, we drop the bottom 1%, which corresponds to .67 person/square mile.

Republican counties, where there are fewer people and lower electricity demand.

However, green generators are more land-intensive than conventional coal or gas plants, and land prices in urban areas are high. Despite the higher power demand in cities, renewable power developers may be willing to site their generators farther from cities and bear more line losses because of the significantly lower land prices in rural areas. This could explain why we observe that green power capacity per square mile rises in counties with more Republican votes and drops in counties with a lower population density (except in counties with very high Republican votes or very high/low population density). Total green capacity density starts to rise again in the most densely populated areas as rooftop solar installations surge in cities such as Los Angeles and New York City.

The renewable power capacity density drops when Republican votes go above 70%. There could be local backlash against clean energy in highly conservative areas. These tend to be rural counties with the lowest population density, which can explain the positive slope of the green capacity density at low population density. When we plot the capacity density for wind and solar respectively, the wind density has a positive slope until Republican votes reach 70%, whereas the solar curve has a negative slope. Consistent with figure 1, Democratic areas have built in more solar panels but fewer wind turbines. These descriptive figures form the basis for our statistical analysis in the next sections.

IV. Empirical Hypotheses

In this section, we present our empirical hypotheses focused on the economic geography determinants of renewable power generation. We divide our hypotheses into the permit time, the site selection for projects, and the political implications of the growth of the green economy.

Hypothesis I: Republican areas approve more green power projects and approve them faster than Democratic-leaning areas.

A rising share of renewable electricity is produced by nonutility generators, who sell their power to local utilities in the electricity wholesale market.[23] To become commercially operable, these generators must receive approval from inspectors for interconnection to the grid. Congestion in the interconnection queue is slowing down the nation's transition to renewable generation. As of 2021, more than 1,000 GW of wind and solar generating capacity were waiting for interconnection access.[24] The completion rate of green projects has been low. Developers tend to withdraw their applications due to the unforeseen interconnection costs and the unpredictably long waiting time (Seel et al. 2023). Republican areas are more pro-business and have less stringent land use regulations (Holmes 1998). The lower level of "red tape" in Republican states gives them an edge in avoiding the land use uncertainty associated with NIMBYism in liberal states (Djankov et al. 2002; Mulligan and Shleifer 2005; Kahn 2011; Gyourko, Hartley, and Krimmel 2021). We thus hypothesize that the project withdrawal rate is lower in red counties as they grant permissions faster.

Hypothesis II: Wind and solar power plants are more likely to locate and scale up in areas featuring lax land use regulations, cheap land prices, high wind and solar potential, and proximity to areas with ambitious RPS standards.

Consider a profit-maximizing green power generator who must choose a single location within the United States for a contiguous set of solar panels or wind turbines. The firm is a price taker in the land market and the capital market. It must jointly choose a location and how many acres to "farm" for green power. The firm's cost of supplying power is an increasing function of local NIMBYism, land prices, and the transmission distance to final consumers. It is a decreasing function of wind speed or solar radiation. Each unit of capacity can produce more power in regions with higher wind/solar potentials. The demand for renewable electricity is higher in urban areas with a high RPS. The firm will seek out a location to minimize its production cost while maximizing the demand for its product. The favorable factors listed above are more likely to exist in red states. Our empirical work uses revealed preference methods to study the correlates of observed profit-maximizing choices.

Hypothesis III: Renewable power subsidies provide an incentive for elected officials from rural Republican areas to cooperate with Democrats on enacting climate change mitigation legislation.

Previous studies have found that Republicans tend to support renewable energy due to the financial benefits they offer (Gustafson et al. 2020). In the recent past, Republican representatives have consistently voted against carbon-pricing policies (Cragg et al. 2013). We hypothesize that rural Republican areas with high green power generation potential may become a new source of votes for green economy legislation going forward. Such votes would be due to economic and political interests (Peltzman 1984; Aklin and Urpelainen 2013). We identify the

Republican districts with the highest propensity to vote in favor of renewable energy bills.

V. Understanding the Correlates of Permit Approval Rates for Green Power Generation

In this section, we study the entry barriers in producing green power using interconnection data from the Berkeley Electricity Markets & Policy Lab. Among wind and solar projects proposed between 2010 and 2020, there were 4,343 active projects in the queue, 374 completed projects, and 3,144 withdrawn projects. To set up a commercially operable power plant, the developer first submits an interconnection request to the RTO, informing regulators the location, size, energy type, and other relevant characteristics of the project. The RTO then conducts site studies and grants an interconnection permit to the developer. The developer can construct the power plant after obtaining the permit. Details of this process are shown in figure A1.

In table 1, we present the characteristics of the counties where developers applied to site their projects in. We compare the unweighted average of county attributes with the weighted ones (by wind capacity and solar capacity in the queue in 2020). Both wind and solar developers send more applications to counties with higher wind speeds/solar radiation, higher RPS, greater green market potential, lower population density, and less stringent land regulations.[25] Wind capacity tends to be proposed in Republican counties with cheap land, whereas solar

Table 1
The Attributes of Counties with Proposed Wind and Solar Projects

	Unweighted	Weighted by Wind Capacity in the Queue	Weighted by Solar Capacity in the Queue
Wind speed	6.75	6.84	6.57
Solar radiation	4.48	4.51	4.82
Republican votes (%)	64.97	67.91	61.30
Median home price in 2010 ($)	133K	116K	133K
Land regulation index	2.50	2.43	2.40
Climate believers (%)	65.26	64.51	66.41
Population density	271.03	79.65	162.68
County area	1,126.21	1,460.46	2,612.09
RPS (%)	5.47	7.75	9.02
Green market potential	9.57	11.25	8.74

Note: RPS = renewable portfolio standards. In the second and third columns, capacity in the queue refers to the nonwithdrawn and noncompleted capacity by the end of 2020.

capacity is disproportionally proposed in liberal areas. These descriptive results are consistent with hypothesis II.

Among all the applications, 48% withdrew before the end of 2020 (based on projects proposed between 2010 and 2020). The high withdrawal rate is due to the uncertainties in interconnection costs and the unpredictable waiting time (Seel et al. 2023). We study the heterogeneities in the approval rate and waiting time across counties. We define the waiting time as the time since a project entered the queue (if it is still active). For completed projects, waiting time refers to the time it took from entering the queue to becoming commercially operable.[26] Based on the completed projects in our sample, the median waiting time was 1,482 days and 1,448 days, respectively, for wind and solar, and the 25th percentile was 1,007 and 701, respectively. We test whether Republican areas have higher project withdrawal rates and shorter waiting time (hypothesis I). We estimate the following linear probability model for project i in the year 2020:

$$Y_i = \beta_0 + \beta_1' \text{Republican}_i + \beta_2' X_i + \delta_{rt} + \varepsilon_i. \qquad (2)$$

In equation (2), Y is a withdrawn dummy or a waiting time dummy. The withdrawn dummy equals 1 if the project had withdrawn by December 31, 2020. This specification is estimated on all projects. The queue time dummy indicates whether the queue time exceeds a given time, which we set to 2 years when reporting results in table 1.[27] This specification is estimated only on completed and active projects. The coefficients of interest are the vector β_1. Republican is a vector including two variables: the percentage of votes for Trump in the 2020 election in the project's county and a Republican governor dummy indicating whether the project's state had a Republican governor in the year it was proposed. We control for a vector of project attributes X, such as its capacity, its county's home prices, population density, and wind/solar potential. RTOs are responsible for permitting interconnection. We include RTO/application year fixed effects (δ_{rt}). They capture spatial and temporal factors such as the renewable production tax credits (PTCs) and the congestion in the queue at a given point of time. We estimate equation (2) separately for wind and solar. Standard errors are clustered by state.

The results are reported in table 2, where the dependent variable is the withdrawn dummy in odd columns and queue time dummy in even columns. In columns 1 and 3, the coefficient on the Republican governor dummy is negative and statistically significant. In a state governed by a Republican, wind and solar projects are 7% and 11% less likely to

Table 2
The Correlates of Green Power Permit Approval "Red Tape"

	(1)	(2)	(3)	(4)
	Wind		Solar	
	Withdrawn	1 (Wait > 2 Years)	Withdrawn	1 (Wait > 2 Years)
Republican votes	−.0193	−.162	−.125**	.0272
	(.169)	(.115)	(.0622)	(.0311)
Republican governor	−.0687**	.00803	−.108***	−.00988
	(.0325)	(.0197)	(.0284)	(.0158)
Log (capacity)	.0227	.00784*	−.0397***	.0110
	(.0155)	(.00453)	(.00984)	(.00784)
State RPS	.343	.0714	.603***	.0373
	(.492)	(.232)	(.224)	(.0586)
Log (RPS market potential)	.0109	−.0675***	−.0136	−.00333
	(.0357)	(.0131)	(.0179)	(.00437)
Log (home prices)	.0227	−.0327	−.0162	−.00235
	(.0426)	(.0223)	(.0233)	(.00861)
Log (population density)	.0238	−.000646	−.00814	−.00412
	(.0218)	(.0137)	(.0101)	(.00395)
Log (wind speed)	.226	−.0104		
	(.144)	(.0844)		
Log (solar radiation)			.280	.0436
			(.262)	(.0736)
RTO/year FE	Yes	Yes	Yes	Yes
DV mean	.478	.7	.477	.36
Observations	983	389	4,233	1,318

Note: DV = dependent variable; FE = fixed effects; RPS = renewable portfolio standards; RTO = regional transmission organization. Withdrawn is a dummy indicating whether the project has withdrawn from the queue by the end of 2020. Wait refers to the time a project has been waiting in the queue (and has not withdrawn). For completed projects, it refers to the time between entering the queue and becoming commercially operable. This table shows the estimation from equation (2).
Standard errors are clustered by state.
*$p < .10$.
**$p < .05$.
***$p < .01$.

withdraw. These represent relatively large reductions given the average withdrawal rate of 48%. As shown in column 3, Republican votes have a negative and statistically significant coefficient. Conditional on the party of the state governor, solar generators' withdrawal rates are lower in red counties.[28] We attribute these differences to the stringency of land use regulations and local NIMBYism in liberal areas (Kahn 2011; Gyourko et al. 2021). Such local oppositions can slow down the interconnection process by blocking the construction of the power plant itself or the transmission lines that connect the plant to the grid (Gross 2020; Davis et al. 2023). Red states have an advantage in producing green power because it is less costly for renewable generators to acquire land there. That said, in columns 2 and 4, we find no evidence that Republican counties fast-track renewable capacity that remains in the queue.

In column 2, we find that larger wind projects take a longer time to connect to the grid, and counties with higher renewable market potentials approve wind projects faster. Column 3 shows that larger solar projects are less likely to withdraw, possibly due to the higher returns to waiting. Solar projects have higher withdrawal rates in states with high RPS. These states often feature stricter environmental regulations, which may lead to the rejection of renewable capacity due to concerns about its impact on biodiversity.[29]

VI.   Green Power Plant Site Selection and Power Generation

A.   The Natural Advantages of Republican Counties

Using our panel data set, we test whether Republican areas have lower population density, cheaper land prices, higher wind and solar potential, and higher RPS market potential than progressive areas. We estimate the following specifications for county i in state s (and year t if applicable):

$$Y_i = \beta_0 + \beta_1 \text{Votes for Republican}_i + \delta_s + \varepsilon_i, \qquad (3a)$$

$$Y_{it} = \beta_0 + \beta_1' \text{Votes for Republican}_i \times \text{Year } 2021_t + \varepsilon_{it}. \qquad (3b)$$

In equation (3a), we estimate cross-sectional regressions using several different dependent variables, including home prices in 2010, population density in 2020, wind speed, and solar radiation. We control for state fixed effects (δ_s). In equation (3b), Y is a county/year variable and refers to state RPS or RPS market potential. To construct a state's RPS market potential, we use the formula given in equation (1). We estimate this equation on data in the years 2010 and 2021. We include Republican votes, the year 2021 dummy, and their interaction term to test whether RPS and RPS market potential grow faster in red states. The standard errors are clustered by county. We weight all regressions by county area because larger counties have the potential to install more power plants.

Table 3
The Attributes of Republican Counties

	(1)	(2)	(3)	(4)	(5)	(6)
	Log (Density)	Log (Wind Speed)	Log (Radiation)	Log (Home Prices)	RPS	Log (RPS Potential + 1)
Republican	−4.811***	.0619**	.0181	−1.165***	−.0796***	.104
	(.389)	(.0254)	(.0121)	(.107)	(.0151)	(.129)
Year 2021					.123***	.555***
					(.00864)	(.0488)
Republican × Year 2021					−.121***	.317***
					(.0122)	(.0726)
State fixed effects	Yes	Yes	Yes	Yes	No	No
Observations	3,112	3,078	3,098	2,852	6,226	6,212
R^2	.565	.623	.884	.439	.131	.156

Note: Republican refers to the percentage of votes for Trump in the 2020 presidential election. Year 2021 is a dummy variable. The dependent variables in the first four columns are from 2010. In the last two columns, RPS (renewable portfolio standards) and RPS potential are data from 2010 and 2021 (the first and the last year in our full panel). RPS market potential is calculated using equation (1). Columns 1–4 show the estimation from equation (3a), and columns 5 and 6 show that from equation (3b). Standard errors are clustered by county. All regressions are weighted by county area.
*$p < .10$.
**$p < .05$.
***$p < .01$.

We report the results in table 3. We document that Republican areas feature a lower population density, a higher wind speed, and lower land prices. These are favorable conditions for land-intensive renewable power plants. These coefficients have similar significance levels and larger magnitudes when we do not include state fixed effects (not shown). We find no evidence that the solar radiation is higher in red counties.

In the last two columns, we study how RPS and RPS market potential change over time. States such as Nevada and Utah are physically close to the nation's major green state (California). They could have a low RPS but a high RPS market potential. Compared with other states with a low RPS, they have a cost edge in generating green power, given the transmission costs of electricity and the line losses over long distances. In columns 5 and 6, we estimate a negative association between a state's RPS and its share of Republican voters, and RPS in liberal states rises faster. Yet the growth rate of the market potential is higher in Republican areas, as indicated by the positive coefficient of the interaction term. A t-test on the coefficients of Republican votes and the interaction shows that Republican counties had significantly higher RPS potentials in 2021.

B. Renewable Power Incentives in Democratic Counties

Although Republican areas possess natural attributes that are conducive to renewable energy generation, liberal areas have rolled out more financial support to accelerate the green transition.[30] These incentives can compensate the natural disadvantages of blue counties and determine renewable generators' location choices. Using adjacent county pairs such that one county is located in one state and the other county is located in another state, we examine whether the more progressive county in the pair features more green power. We use the right-to-work (RTW) dummy as a proxy for a pro-business state. The unit of analysis is a county. A county can appear multiple times in this regression if it is adjacent to other counties that lie in another state. We run the following regression on county s in border pair i, using cross-sectional data from years 2010 and 2021 separately:

$$Y_{is} = \beta_0 + \beta_1 \text{RTW}_s + \beta_2' X_s + \delta_i + \varepsilon_{is}, \tag{4}$$

where Y is a wind dummy or a solar dummy indicating whether there is any wind or solar capacity in the county, RTW is a dummy indicating whether county s is on the RTW side of the border, and X is a vector of county attributes including Republican votes, home prices, land area, wind speed, and solar radiation. We include border-pair fixed effects (δ_i) so that the results are based on the difference within each border pair. The standard errors are clustered by border pair.[31] The results are reported in table 4.

In column 1, we find no evidence that the liberal and conservative sides of the border differ with respect to their wind generation capacity. Neither the RTW dummy nor the Republican vote share is statistically significant. In column 2, the RTW dummy and Republican votes are negative and statistically significant. When crossing from the liberal to the conservative side of the border, the probability of the county having solar capacity declines by 6.71%. This represents a 20% drop relative to the mean probability of 31%, implying that solar incentives in liberal states are effective in attracting developers. Because solar panels are relatively less land-intensive, the cost premium of installing each unit of capacity in liberal states is smaller for solar than for wind. The more generous solar incentive is thus likely to give liberal states a competitive advantage in siting solar power plants.

Table 4
The Effect of State Policies on the Location of Green Power Plants

	(1)	(2)	(3)	(4)
	2021		2010	
	Wind	Solar	Wind	Solar
RTW	−.0273	−.0671**	−.0157	.00868
	(.0219)	(.0264)	(.0161)	(.00950)
Republican votes	−.116	−.396***	.00276	−.0676
	(.0847)	(.129)	(.0578)	(.0761)
Log (home prices)	−.0614**	.0593	−.0229	−.0174
	(.0245)	(.0389)	(.0207)	(.0138)
Log (area)	.0742***	.173***	.0322***	.112***
	(.0156)	(.0225)	(.0110)	(.0162)
Log (wind speed)	−.00976		−.0703	
	(.258)		(.200)	
Log (solar radiation)		−1.287		−.750
		(1.095)		(.513)
Observations	4,976	4,976	4,976	4,976
DV mean	.15	.309	.068	.04

Note: DV = dependent variable. Wind and solar are two dummies indicating whether the county had any wind or solar capacity in 2021 or 2010. These results are estimated from equation (4). Standard errors are clustered by border pairs.
*$p < .10$.
**$p < .05$.
***$p < .01$.

We repeat our analysis using data from the year 2010. In columns 3 and 4, the RTW dummy is insignificant. This suggests that the solar advantages of blue states are results of the policies initiated in this recent decade.

C.   Where Is the Existing Renewable Capacity?

Based on the previous findings, we study how the natural and policy advantages jointly affect the spatial distribution of the actual generating capacity. In this section, we model whether a given county has at least one green generator and its scale of production. We study the association between these variables and county characteristics including political voting, RPS, market potential, land price, and natural environmental attributes (see hypothesis II). Using our full panel data, we estimate the following specification for county i (in state k) in year t, for wind and solar, respectively:

$$Y_{it} = \beta_0 + \beta_1 \text{Trend}_t \times \text{Republican}_i + \beta_2 \text{Republican}_i + \beta_3' X_{it} + \delta_k + \gamma_t + \varepsilon_{it}. \tag{5}$$

In equation (5), Y is a dummy indicating whether a county has any wind or solar capacity in year t in the extensive margin columns. In the intensive margin columns, it refers to the logged capacity or the share of total capacity that is wind or solar. X is a vector of county attributes, and the only time-variant variables in this vector are RPS and the RPS market potential (calculated using eq. [1]). We include state fixed effects (δ_k) and year fixed effects (γ_t). State fixed effects control for each state's time-invariant attributes (during the period we study) such as whether the electricity market is deregulated. Standard errors are clustered by state/year. The estimation results are shown in table 5. The extensive margin estimations are reported in columns 1 and 4, and the intensive margin estimations are in columns 2, 3, 5, and 6.

Republican votes are significantly positive in all columns. In the baseline year 2010, Republicans had built in more wind and solar capacity, on both the extensive and intensive margins. Compared with recent years, environmental policies varied less across states before 2010 (see table 4). We interpret this as the "business-as-usual" scenario in the absence of solar incentives. In this case, developers would locate land-intensive renewable power plants in counties that minimize the costs, which tend to be governed by Republicans.

The interaction term between Republican votes and the time trend is positive for wind but negative for solar. Over time, the gap in wind capacity keeps widening. Republicans have scaled up wind power plants, although they were not more likely to install wind turbines in new locations than Democrats. In counties with 10% more Republican votes, wind capacity increases 0.54% and 0.16% faster, as estimated in columns 2 and 3, respectively. Yet Democratic counties are overtaking Republican areas in producing solar power. A t-test of joint significance shows that Democratic areas featured significantly more solar capacity in the year 2021. A 10% increase in Republican votes is associated with a 2.3% and 0.1% slowdown in solar installations, as benchmarked by total solar capacity and the solar share. These are consistent with figures 1 and 2. Solar capacity is disproportionally installed in liberal counties, as these counties provide more fiscal incentives and as the land intensity of solar panels trends down (Van Zalk and Behrens 2018).[32]

We find some evidence supporting hypothesis II. Both wind and solar capacity tend to locate in areas with lower land prices and larger land areas, given their land-intensive nature. The magnitudes of the land prices' coefficients are larger in wind columns than in solar columns. Because wind turbines take up more space, investors' decisions are more responsive to land prices. Cheaper land prices give Republicans an edge in generating wind power. The table also shows that wind speed is significant in determining the extensive but not the intensive margin of wind capacity, and developers tend to install and scale up solar panels in places where solar radiation is higher.

We interpret the climate belief and the county's population as proxies for the demand of green power. In counties with more climate believers, developers are more likely to install green capacity. One possible reason is that residents in pro-climate areas voluntarily sacrifice some amenities to let developers install green power plants (Kotchen and Moore 2008). Population has positive coefficients in columns 1, 2, 4, and 5 but negative coefficients when the dependent variable is the share of total capacity from wind/solar. More densely populated areas tend to have a larger share of brown capacity because electricity demand in these areas is more likely to exceed the base load, which is increasingly met by renewable generation. Given this likelihood, populated areas have kept more fossil fuel capacity to fulfill the marginal demand during peak hours (Holland et al. 2022).

The coefficients on lagged RPS are positive and statistically significant in columns 4 and 5. Because we control for state fixed effects, the variations in RPS mainly come from liberal states that have increased RPS rapidly in recent years. These areas are more favorable to solar generation, so they install solar panels instead of wind turbines to meet the RPS goals. In columns 3 and 6, there is no evidence that RPS raises the share of renewable capacity. This result is consistent with the findings from Carley (2009). RPS market potential has a significantly positive coefficient in columns 1 and 3. This supports our hypothesis that wind power may be generated in rural Republican areas and shipped to nearby liberal cities. Its coefficient is significantly negative in solar columns, which could be due to the limited variations of the market potential within states.[33]

VII. Could Rising Green Power Demand Affect Congressional Carbon Mitigation Politics?

Although no Republican members of Congress voted in favor of the August 2022 Inflation Reduction Act, this bill's emphasis on expanding renewable energy subsidies raises a new possibility. Republican representatives have revealed a strong antipathy toward carbon taxes, but many rural Republican representatives may support green subsidies if their districts gain financially from the growth of the green economy (Cragg et al. 2013; Gustafson et al. 2020).

Table 5
The Economic Geography of Wind and Solar Capacity

	(1)	(2)	(3)	(4)	(5)	(6)
		Wind			Solar	
	I (Wind > 0)	Log (Capacity + 1)	Wind%	I (Solar > 0)	Log (Capacity + 1)	Solar%
Republican votes	.121***	.610***	.420***	.146***	.915***	.136***
	(.0277)	(.134)	(.0324)	(.0377)	(.117)	(.0275)
Trend × Republican votes	.00610	.0543***	.0154***	-.0651***	-.232***	-.00941***
	(.00390)	(.0182)	(.00376)	(.00573)	(.0182)	(.00363)
Lagged RPS	.0307	.219	-.0285	.446**	1.101***	.0177
	(.0401)	(.181)	(.0328)	(.176)	(.404)	(.0646)
Log (lagged RPS potential + 1)	.0227***	.0483	.0185***	-.0427***	-.262***	-.0441***
	(.00794)	(.0387)	(.00654)	(.0157)	(.0536)	(.0122)
Log (home price)	-.0778***	-.348***	-.0805***	-.0449***	-.206***	-.00733
	(.00696)	(.0359)	(.00740)	(.00986)	(.0359)	(.00998)
Log (wind speed)	.0579*	.00424	.0459			
	(.0304)	(.168)	(.0316)			

	(1)	(2)	(3)	(4)	(5)	(6)
Log (solar radiation)				.915***	4.207***	.431***
				(.0955)	(.474)	(.0662)
Climate belief	.00331***	.0173***	.0128***	−.000193	.000458	.0690***
	(.000611)	(.00332)	(.000813)	(.000621)	(.00170)	(.000634)
Log (population)	.0127***	.0218*	−.0313***	.0648***	.184***	−.0267***
	(.00256)	(.0125)	(.00296)	(.00419)	(.0168)	(.00266)
Log (area)	.0426***	.204***	.0142***	.0252***	.134***	.00178
	(.00561)	(.0277)	(.00349)	(.00683)	(.0215)	(.00330)
State fixed effects	Yes	Yes	Yes	Yes	Yes	Yes
Year fixed effects	Yes	Yes	Yes	Yes	Yes	Yes
Sample	Full	Full	Total capacity > 0	Full	Full	Total capacity > 0
DV mean in 2021	.159	43.5 (unlogged)	.157	.292	20.6 (unlogged)	.171
Observations	29,904	29,904	18,834	30,108	30,108	19,036

Note: RPS = renewable portfolio standards. The dependent variables (DVs) of columns 1 and 4 are dummies indicating whether there is any wind/solar capacity in a county in a given year. The DVs of columns 3 and 6 are proportions of the total generating capacity that is wind/solar. The lagged variables refer to their 1-year lags. These results are estimated from equation (5). Standard errors are clustered by state/year.

*$p < .10$.
**$p < .05$.
***$p < .01$.

For decades, rural areas have been centers of energy and resource extraction. There is an extensive literature studying the effects of local energy booms on the labor market. Margo (1997) documents that wages rose significantly in California during the Gold Rush in the nineteenth century, and this has left the wages in California permanently higher. Using data from the pipeline construction in Alaska in the 1970s, Carrington (1996) finds the local wage increase to be temporary. Studies on fracking show the gas and oil extraction creates job opportunities, though at the expense of local amenities (Feyrer, Mansur, and Sacerdote 2017; Bartik et al. 2019).

A growing literature studies the effect of renewable energy on the local economy and politics. It remains an open question whether the areas that welcome green power production will experience a local economic boom. Brown et al. (2012) document an increase in local income and employment following the deployments of wind turbines. Lehr, Lutz, and Edler (2012) have found similar results in Germany. In the United States, green jobs tend to locate in counties that have been offering more fossil fuel jobs (Curtis and Marinescu 2022). Once installed, wind and solar farms create tax revenues that may be used to fund public projects to improve local quality of life (Kahn 2013). These investments have positive spillover effects on neighboring counties. However, once power plants have been built, most of the jobs are for maintenance. Jacobson, LaLonde, and Sullivan (1993) and Hanson (2023) document that the shutdown of coal plants reduces local earnings and job counts. In some regions, renewable power plants have triggered electoral backlashes against governors responsible for these new installations (Stokes 2016). The logic from Peltzman (1984) suggests that local homeowners are more likely to support renewable plants if the green subsidies compensate them financially. We examine hypothesis III in this section.

Figure 3 shows the trend of renewable capacity deployment from 2010 to 2021 in blue versus red states. We normalize each category of capacity by dividing it by the total green capacity in 2010 (roughly 40,000 MW). From 2010 to 2021, the total green capacity has increased by a factor of five. Wind farms in Republican areas made up most of the renewable capacity in 2010 and still accounted for almost half of it by 2021. The figure also shows that the total wind capacity in Republican states is diverging from that in Democratic states, as Republican states have an advantage in generating wind power. Solar farms contribute to approximately 30% of the total green capacity today. Although blue states have more supportive policies toward solar installation, the difference in total solar capacity is relatively small between blue and red states.

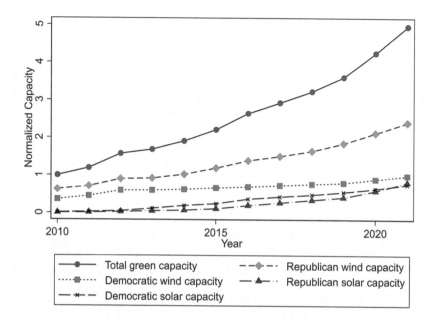

Fig. 3. The time trend for renewable power capacity. In this graph, all capacity is normalized by the total green capacity in 2010 (39,365.4 MW). A state is defined as Republican if it voted for Trump in the 2016 presidential election.

Green subsidies will disproportionally benefit rural areas that have installed or will install large-scale renewable capacity. One concern is that Republicans might have saturated their cheap land with high wind speed or solar radiation. In figure 4, using the sample of Republican districts, we calculate the average wind/solar potentials and the average land prices of the locations of renewable capacity each year. There is no evidence that new projects are built in places with lower potentials or higher land prices. This implies that diminishing returns have not kicked in. Green developers still have good land to choose from Republican districts.

There is plenty of open land in the American South and West suitable to renewable developments. Figure 5 shows the renewable potential and the DW-NOMINATE scores of representatives from these districts in the 118th Congress. A score closer to 1 indicates the representative is more conservative. The size of the dots is proportional to the district's land area. All four graphs show that Republican districts have larger land areas. In the South, Republican districts tend to have higher wind speed and solar radiation than Democratic districts. In the West, liberal districts have more solar radiation on average, but there are a few large Republican districts

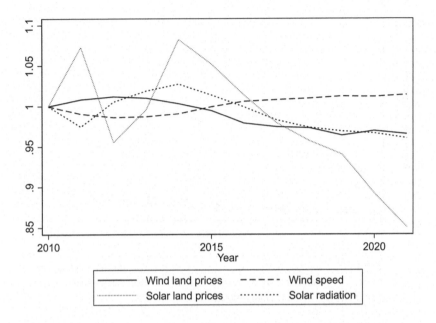

Fig. 4. Are there diminishing returns in Republican districts? We plot land prices weighted by wind and solar capacity, respectively, wind speed weighted by wind capacity, and solar radiation weighted by solar capacity. We normalize each weighted average to its value in 2010. We restrict our sample to congressional districts governed by a Republican in the 118th Congress.

with high wind and solar potentials, such as the second district of New Mexico and the fourth district of Arizona.

Political science research emphasizes that members of Congress seek to attract investment in their districts (Aklin and Urpelainen 2013). The zero-carbon transition raises the possibility that Republican districts with green power potential can get larger subsidies in the future. When voters benefit from these subsidies, they are more likely to reelect the incumbent rather than vote for an alternative candidate who is hostile to the existing policy (Peltzman 1984; Aklin and Urpelainen 2013). This "lock-in" effect incentivizes Republican congresspeople to support green legislation if they perceive economic and political gains from doing so. In this section, we present some suggestive analysis that identifies this subset of Republican districts.

In column 2 of table 5, we identify the swing Republican districts using the representatives' DW-NOMINATE scores from the 118th Congress and rank them using our specified model. We define swing districts as the Republican districts where the DW-NOMINATE score is at the lowest

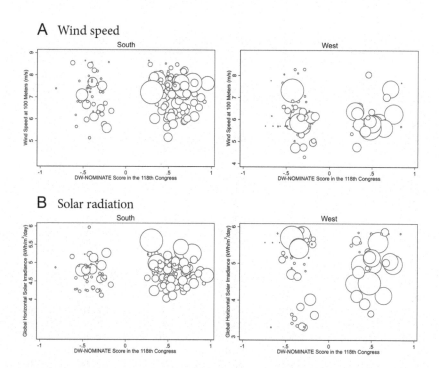

Fig. 5. Wind and solar resources across congressional districts: (*A*) wind speed; (*B*) solar radiation. Each dot represents a congressional district in the 118th Congress, and its size is proportional to its area. DW-NOMINATE score is a continuous measure of each district's representatives' political ideology. On a scale from −1 to 1, −1 is the most progressive, and 1 is the most conservative.

10th percentile (i.e., below .33). We estimate the same linear model of the time trend, sociodemographic variables, and environmental attributes (see col. 2 of table 5 for the full variable list) using the district/year panel. The only exception is that we include region fixed effects instead of state fixed effects to allow more variations. We then extrapolate each district's total wind capacity in 2025 based on our results. This extrapolation relies on the assumptions that Republicans primarily have an edge in generating wind power and have not used up the ideal land for renewable generation (see fig. 4). We rank the 21 swing districts based on their predicted capacity from high to low in table 6.

The districts at the top of the list tend to have larger land area, lower population density, and cheaper land prices. Roughly half of the swing districts have already installed wind capacity, and these districts have higher ranks than those that have not. The top district, the twenty-third district of Texas, has built more than 3,000 MW of wind capacity so far,

Table 6
Identifying Swing Republican Districts Featuring Wind Power Potential

State	District	Wind Speed (m/s)	Home Price ($10,000)	Area (10,000 mile²)	Population Density (per mile²)	Wind Capacity (MW)
TX	23	7.33	11.92	5.90	831.09	3,321.4
NY	21	8.24	12.13	1.71	84.64	1,233.3
CA	23	5.80	20.01	1.80	159.68	363.8
ID	2	6.20	16.14	4.36	157.03	974.4
IL	12	6.71	9.15	1.43	109.66	0
PA	15	6.85	11.51	1.31	87.04	159
WA	4	6.07	16.48	1.82	66.30	1,350.9
OK	4	7.83	10.99	.99	348.07	1,337.3
IA	3	6.24	14.01	1.07	553.84	2,813.4
CA	22	4.58	14.78	.43	106.25	0
IA	1	6.33	13.23	1.10	164.95	428
FL	28	8.62	18.37	.26	1,248.73	0
FL	26	8.59	20.02	.24	1,055.42	0
OH	14	5.88	12.78	.25	492.70	0
NJ	4	8.48	31.89	.07	1,063.01	0
NY	2	7.99	47.62	.04	1,736.10	0
AL	5	7.15	14.35	.35	320.06	0
OH	10	5.36	10.93	.10	908.40	0
CA	40	6.40	49.00	.04	3,670.68	0
PA	1	8.37	30.85	.07	1,138.44	0
NY	11	8.20	40.47	.01	18,427.13	0

equivalent to 2% of the national wind capacity. Given the large capacity, this district will disproportionally benefit from renewable subsidies.

We recognize that districts with higher DW-NOMINATE scores may also vote against their ideologies and turn to support renewables. Among the districts that we predict to have an above-median wind capacity in 2025, 73.5% of them are governed by Republicans, including 13 of the 21 districts in table 6. When weighted by area, Republican districts make up 83.7% of total area that would feature an above-median level of wind capacity by 2025.[34]

VIII. Future Land Use for Renewable Power Plants

A. Renewable Power Plant Productivity Growth

With our emphasis on economic geography, we have not addressed the macroeconomic issue of what will be the aggregate amount of US land that will need to be set aside for green capacity to achieve US carbon mitigation goals. The land inputs needed per unit of green power are declining.

With new techniques such as floating solar panels, it might take as little as 0.3% of the Earth's land area to meet the global electricity demand (Victoria et al. 2021). Under such optimistic assumptions, the land demand from renewables will be lower than today's estimates.

Using data at turbine and farm level, we test whether the land use per MW of capacity is declining over time. We obtain the capacity, sweep area, height, and installation year of each turbine in the United States from the US Geological Survey database.[35] This database provides the location of each turbine. We group them by wind farm and sketch out the rough boundary of each farm (see fig. A2). We then calculate the area of each farm.[36] In our sample, the median land use is 55.3 acres/MW. There is not a similar data set on the area occupied by solar farms. From the US Energy Information Administration (EIA) power plant data set, we randomly sample 150 solar farms built before 2021 and with at least 5 MW of capacity. We locate them on Google Earth and calculate their area (see fig. A3).[37] In our sample, the median area per MW is 5.97 acres.

We estimate the following specification for wind turbine or solar farm i:

$$\log (\text{MW per acre}_i) = \beta_0 + \beta_1 \text{Trend} + \beta' X_i + \varepsilon_i. \tag{6}$$

In equation (6), X is a vector of covariates including turbine count, swept area, and height when the dependent variable is wind productivity. In the wind farm regressions, we also include manufacturer fixed effects and state fixed effects. The latter controls for the state-level regulations such as turbine height limits. We estimate this equation both weighted and unweighted by total farm capacity. The results are reported in table 7.

Columns 1 and 2 show a positive but insignificant time trend of the land use productivity of wind power. The significantly negative coefficient on the turbine count suggests a trade-off between horizontality and verticality. A wind farm can produce the same amount of power using a few large turbines or many smaller ones that spread out across the land. In columns 3 and 4, we document solar generators are becoming more land-efficient. On each acre of land, 9.6% and 13.6% more capacity can be sited each year. This is consistent with existing evidence such as Van Zalk and Behrens (2018). The marginal cost of installing renewable power plants declines as their power density rises and as local oppositions diminish (Brooks and Liscow 2023).

Although only a tiny fraction of renewable capacity in the United States is offshore today, more can be sited on the ocean going forward. Currently, 40 GW of offshore wind capacity is waiting in the queue.[38] Such capacity features zero land cost, and there is no local backlash

Table 7
Productivity Time Trends for Wind Turbines and Solar Farms

	(1)	(2)	(3)	(4)
	Wind		Solar	
	Log (Capacity/Acre)			
Trend	.00141	.00118	.0959**	.136*
	(.00201)	(.00128)	(.0454)	(.0713)
Log (height)	−.0972*	−.0158		
	(.0523)	(.0381)		
Log (swept area)	.00882	−.00704		
	(.0279)	(.0180)		
Log (turbine count)	−.0808***	−.0770***		
	(.0109)	(.0103)		
Manufacturer FE	Yes	Yes	No	No
State FE	Yes	Yes	No	No
Weight	No	Total capacity	No	Total capacity
Observations	1,151	1,151	98	98
R^2	.404	.381	.031	.071

Note: FE = fixed effects. This table shows the estimation from equation (6). The unit of analysis is a wind or solar farm. In the first two columns, we include all wind farms with at least three turbines and built between 2005 and 2021. In the last two columns, we include our randomly sampled solar farms built before 2021 and with at least 5 MW of capacity. Robust standard errors are in parentheses.
*$p < .10$.
**$p < .05$.
***$p < .01$.

against these projects. Yet the lack of stable transmission capacity poses a challenge to scaling up offshore renewable generation (Ali et al. 2021).

B. Green Power Generation on Federal Lands

In the presence of backlash against renewable installation on private lands, more green capacity will be sited on federal lands. Most renewable projects have been developed on private lands, whereas public lands are almost exclusively leased to oil and gas companies. In 2021, 0.8% of the wind capacity (1.1 GW) and 7.1% of the solar capacity (4.3 GW) were located on public lands.[39] The federal government owns more than 20% of the land in the United States. Federal lands feature high lease rates and additional fees based on energy production. Due to the land intensity of renewable projects, the cost premium for siting green capacity on federal lands is higher than that for brown capacity. To reduce barrier of entry, the Bureau of Land Management has proposed to cut the costs by 80% for wind and solar developers.[40]

Only 10 counties have sited wind projects on federal lands, and 59 counties have sited solar farms. Compared with private lands, public lands have been less favorable to developers because developments on these lands often incur high costs and undergo long permitting processes with high failure rates.[41] These developments are subject to close scrutiny from environmental regulators due to concerns for issues such as biodiversity preservation. The Biden administration seeks to change this status quo and expedite the installation of green generators on public lands.[42]

In counties with more green NIMBYism, renewable capacity is more likely to be deployed on public lands. We calculate each county's proportion of federal lands and its proportion of green capacity located on federal lands. We rank them based on the ratio of the latter to the former. Out of the 66 counties with some green capacity on federal lands, 42 have a ratio greater than 1 (i.e., capacity disproportionally on federal lands). The negative correlation between this ratio and Republican votes ($r = -.26$) is statistically significantly smaller than 0 at the 5% level. This suggests that there has been less local NIMBYism in red counties so that more capacity could be sited on private lands.

IX. Conclusion

The US transition away from fossil fuel fired power plants to generating power using renewable sources will change the nation's economic geography. We document renewable projects are more likely to be permitted in Republican counties. Red rural counties also have cheaper land, lower population density, and higher wind speeds. They have added in more wind capacity but underperform Democratic counties on solar installation because solar panels are less land-intensive and blue states offer more incentives for solar developers.

The rural red state areas gaining from the emerging green power boom create the possibility of new low-carbon political coalitions forming. In the future, some rural Republican areas' elected officials may vote in favor of further increases in green power subsidies. We presented an empirical approach for identifying these districts.

In this paper, we do not explore the interdependency of developers' choices between building wind and solar capacity. Currently, wind contributes 45% of the total renewable electricity generation in the United States, and solar only contributes 10%. The PTCs for wind power will expire in 2024, whereas the investment tax credits for solar power will continue to be available.[43] Republican counties may switch from wind to solar as the PTC phases out and as Democratic counties saturate their optimal locations for solar panels.

Our paper focuses on the supply of renewable power, but the total necessary generating capacity also hinges upon the peak electricity demand. Intermittent renewables lead to resource adequacy challenges (Wolak 2022). The aggregate land use for electricity generation will increase if more backup capacity is needed. Future research can study the role of demand-side management tools such as dynamic electricity pricing in mitigating the "land rush" of renewable energy.

Appendix

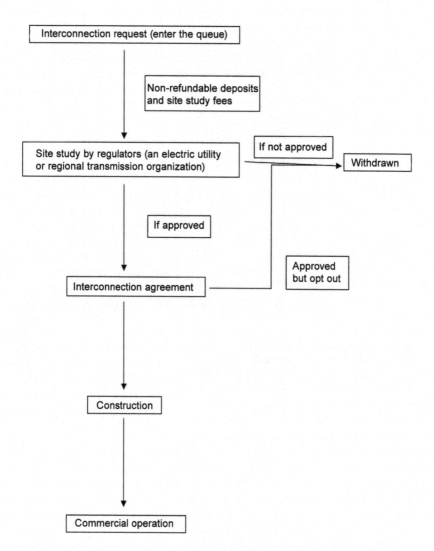

Fig. A1.   Interconnection study process

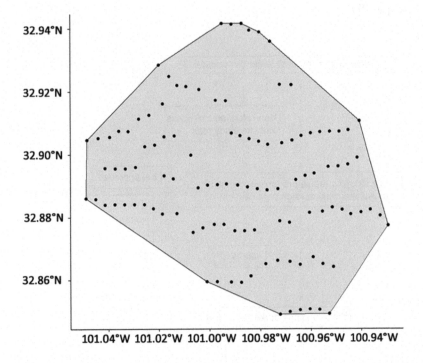

Fig. A2. Calculating the area of wind farms. We use the Amazon Wind Farm in Scurry County, Texas, as an example. Each black dot in the figure represents a wind turbine. The shaded area is generated by the st_convex_hull function, and we use the st_area function to calculate its area. We use this result as an approximation of the total wind farm area.

A   Imagery date: 5/1/21–newer. Source: Google Earth.

B   Total area=154.61+18.17+59.15=231.93 acres. Source: Google Earth.

C   Total area is coded as 0. Source: Google Earth.

Fig. A3. Calculating the area of solar farms. (*A*) One single parcel. Imagery date: 5/1/21–newer. (*B*) Multiple widely separated parcels. Total area = 154.61 + 18.17 + 59.15 = 231.93 acres. (*C*) Rooftop. Total area is coded as 0. Color version available as an online enhancement.

Source: Google Earth.

Endnotes

Author email addresses: Huang (huangrob@usc.edu), Kahn (kahnme@usc.edu). We thank Tatyana Deryugina, Erin Mansur, Catherine Wolfram, and Shaina Clorfeine for their excellent comments. For acknowledgments, sources of research support, and disclosure of the authors' material financial relationships, if any, please see https://www.nber .org/books-and-chapters/environmental-and-energy-policy-and-economy-volume-5 /do-red-states-have-comparative-advantage-generating-green-power.

1. https://www.eia.gov/tools/faqs/faq.php?id=427&t=3

2. Hydropower is another source of renewable energy, but we do not study it in this paper because hydropower depends much more heavily on local geography than do solar and wind power. Also, most hydropower plants were sited decades ago. Since 2010, only 150 utility-scale hydropower plants have been built nationwide, whereas 870 utility-scale wind generators and 5,028 solar generators have been built.

3. See Section VIII for detailed discussions. MW stands for megawatt, which measures the rate at which electricity can be generated. When we say that a power plant has a capacity of 1 MW, it means that it is capable of producing 1 million watts of electrical power at any given moment.

4. https://robertbryce.com/renewable-rejection-database/. According to the eGRID data, 74 wind projects and 517 solar projects went online in 2021. This suggests a high block rate for wind projects.

5. Utility-scale wind and solar farms are more cost-efficient than rooftop solar due to economies of scale. Relying solely on rooftop solar may not be feasible to fully decarbonize

the grid, as there may not be enough rooftops available. https://www.latimes.com/envi ronment/newsletter/2023-06-29/can-rooftop-solar-alone-solve-climate-change-heres -the-answer-boiling-point.

6. https://www.latimes.com/environment/story/2022-08-23/wyoming-clean-energy -california

7. https://www.epa.gov/egrid/download-data

8. https://emp.lbl.gov/projects/renewables-portfolio/

9. We acknowledge this measure may overstate the RPS market potential because some states require utilities to purchase renewable electricity from within-state generators to fulfill RPS requirements.

10. We access the voting data from the MIT Election Data Science Lab: https:// electionlab.mit.edu/data.

11. https://www.zillow.com/research/data/

12. https://www.census.gov/programs-surveys/acs

13. https://climatecommunication.yale.edu/visualizations-data/ycom-us/. Specifi- cally, we use the percentage of population believing climate change is real in 2021 as the measure of each county's climate belief.

14. The minimum speed to power utility-scale wind turbines is 5.8 m/s, and the aver- age wind speed of 90.6% of counties meets this standard. The maximum speed at which wind turbines can safely operate is 22.5 m/s, which is almost twice as high as the maxi- mum county wind speed. https://www.eia.gov/energyexplained/wind/where-wind -power-is-harnessed.php.

15. https://emp.lbl.gov/publications/queued-characteristics-power-plants. Data are collected from interconnection queues of all seven RTOs in the United States. The cover- age areas represent more than 85% of the US electricity load. Alaska and Hawaii are excluded.

16. https://voteview.com/data

17. If 20% of land area of district A is in county i, 50% in county j, and 30% in county k, we weight the county attributes from county i, j, and k with 2:5:3 to calculate the district attributes.

18. Solar and wind power plants require more space compared with other forms of en- ergy generation. However, they do not require any additional land for the extraction of energy. Coal-fired power plants heavily rely on mining operations to obtain fossil fuels, which necessitates a significant amount of land use. The power density calculations do not account for the land used to extract fossil fuels and may overestimate the power den- sity for brown capacity.

19. https://www.latimes.com/opinion/op-ed/la-oe-bryce-backlash-against-wind -energy-20170227-story.html; https://www.wsj.com/articles/solar-rollout-rouses-resis tance-in-europes-countryside-11665234001

20. https://www.sandiegocounty.gov/content/dam/sdc/pds/ceqa/Soitec-Docu ments/Final-EIR-Files/references/rtcref/ch2.5/2014-12-19_DOCSolarWhitePaper31111.pdf

21. These only include projects in the EIA data set, which are utility-scale projects with at least 5 MW of capacity. In 2021, there was 3.9 GW of residential solar capacity. By the data from NREL, approximately 3 GW of community solar has been installed. As of now, utility-scale solar still accounts for more than 90% of the total solar capacity in the United States.

22. https://www.eia.gov/tools/faqs/faq.php?id=105&t=3. According to the EIA esti- mates, power losses average about 5% in the transmission and the distribution process. In long-distance transmissions, the losses are 8%–14%.

23. https://www.c2es.org/content/renewable-energy/

24. https://www.energy.gov/eere/analysis/queued-characteristics-power-plants -seeking-transmission-interconnection-end-2021

25. The land regulation index is from Gyourko et al. (2021). Specifically, we use the local project approval index (LPAI). A higher value indicates more stringent regulations. One caveat is that this index is only available for 35% of the counties.

26. This is the time to secure an interconnection agreement plus the construction time. We include construction time because this is more policy relevant because developers care

about the entire duration from entering the queue to being able to commercially operate the project. Obtaining transmission access takes longer than constructing the plant.

27. We estimate the same specifications (dependent variable: 1 (wait > T years)) with $T = 1, 3, 4, 5$. The coefficients on votes for Republican and the Republican governor dummy have similar significance levels as when $T = 2$.

28. Developers do not know in advance the cost of development until local regulators conduct interconnection studies. If the application cost is low, they may have an incentive to submit multiple requests in a region as a form of price discovery, with the intent to only build one. One caveat is that we assume each developer only sends in a single request so that the project-level data are independent from each other. We will overestimate the negative effect of land use regulations on green permits if the higher withdrawal rate and the longer waiting time in progressive states are due to each developer sending in more requests.

29. https://www.nationalgeographic.com/environment/article/activists-fear-biodiversity-threat-from-renewable-energy

30. https://www.forbes.com/home-improvement/solar/solar-tax-credit-by-state/

31. There are 2,764 border pairs in our sample: 996 have green capacity on one side but not the other; 1,146 have none; 622 have green capacity on both sides.

32. As a robustness check, we estimate the models without California, Texas, or both. We also replace state fixed effects (FE) and year FE with state/year FE. In all cases, most coefficients have similar numerical values and significance levels as in table 3.

33. When we exclude state fixed effect, RPS potential is significantly positive in columns 1–3 and insignificant in columns 4–6.

34. Following the same approach, we repeat the analysis with solar capacity. Among the districts with an above-median predicted solar capacity, 72.6% are Republican (85.5% when weighted by area). Fifteen of the 22 swing Republican districts are in this subset.

35. https://eerscmap.usgs.gov/uswtdb/

36. The direct impact area of each turbine turns out to be very small (as low as 1% of the total farm area), which means the wind farmland area mainly comes from the spacing between turbines. This 99% of land can still be used for farming. However, the land between turbines cannot be used for other purposes that may offer higher returns (e.g., residential housing). Republican areas have an advantage because they have large open land that allows sufficient separations between turbines. It is thus important to analyze the total area of wind farms instead of only the direct impact area. https://css.umich.edu/publications/factsheets/energy/wind-energy-factsheet.

37. We limit the sample to solar farms built before 2021 because Google Earth has not updated information on most newly built solar farms. Among the 150 solar plants, we are able to calculate the area of 101 of them. We acknowledge there could be measurement errors in the calculation, but they are not systematically correlated with project attributes. These errors would thus not bias the productivity growth rate estimates.

38. https://windexchange.energy.gov/markets/offshore

39. We use GIS techniques to classify each green power plant into federal lands versus not based on their longitude and latitude.

40. https://grist.org/climate-energy/the-feds-move-to-speed-up-development-of-wind-and-solar-on-public-land/

41. http://eelp.law.harvard.edu/wp-content/uploads/PDaniels_EELP_Renewables-Siting_Final.pdf

42. He seeks to permit 25 GW of renewable capacity on these lands by 2025. https://www.whitehouse.gov/briefing-room/statements-releases/2022/01/12/fact-sheet-biden-harris-administration-races-to-deploy-clean-energy-that-creates-jobs-and-lowers-costs/.

43. https://www.eia.gov/todayinenergy/detail.php?id=46676

References

Aklin, Michaël, and Johannes Urpelainen. 2013. "Political Competition, Path Dependence, and the Strategy of Sustainable Energy Transitions." *American Journal of Political Science* 57 (3): 643–58.

Ali, S. W., M. Sadiq, Y. Terriche, S. A. R. Naqvi, M. U. Mutarraf, M. A. Hassan, G. Yang, C. L. Su, and J. M. Guerrero. 2021. "Offshore Wind Farm-Grid Integration: A Review on Infrastructure, Challenges, and Grid Solutions." *IEEE Access* 9:102811–27.

Averch, Harvey, and Leland L. Johnson. 1962. "Behavior of the Firm under Regulatory Constraint." *American Economic Review* 52 (5): 1052–69.

Bartik, Alexander W., Janet Currie, Michael Greenstone, and Christopher R. Knittel. 2019. "The Local Economic and Welfare Consequences of Hydraulic Fracturing." *American Economic Journal: Applied Economics* 11 (4): 105–55.

Bistline, John, Neil Mehrotra, and Catherine Wolfram. 2023. "Economic Implications of the Climate Provisions of the Inflation Reduction Act." Working Paper no. 31267, NBER, Cambridge, MA.

Brooks, Leah, and Zachary Liscow. 2023. "Infrastructure Costs." *American Economic Journal: Applied Economics* 15 (2): 1–30.

Brown, Jason P., John Pender, Ryan Wiser, Eric Lantz, and Ben Hoen. 2012. "Ex Post Analysis of Economic Impacts from Wind Power Development in U.S. Counties." *Energy Economics* 34 (6): 1743–54.

Carley, Sanya. 2009. "State Renewable Energy Electricity Policies: An Empirical Evaluation of Effectiveness." *Energy Policy* 37 (8): 3071–81.

Carrington, William J. 1996. "The Alaskan Labor Market during the Pipeline Era." *Journal of Political Economy* 104 (1): 186–218.

Cicala, Steve. 2022. "JUE Insight: Powering Work from Home." *Journal of Urban Economics* 133:103474. https://doi.org/10.1016/j.jue.2022.103474.

Cragg, Michael I., Yuyu Zhou, Kevin Gurney, and Matthew E. Kahn. 2013. "Carbon Geography: The Political Economy of Congressional Support for Legislation Intended to Mitigate Greenhouse Gas Production." *Economic Inquiry* 51 (2): 1640–50.

Curtis, E. Mark, and Ioana Marinescu. 2022. "Green Energy Jobs in the US: What Are They, and Where Are They?" Working Paper no. w30332, NBER, Cambridge, MA.

Davis, Lucas W., Alan Fuchs, and Paul Gertler. 2014. "Cash for Coolers: Evaluating a Large-Scale Appliance Replacement Program in Mexico." *American Economic Journal: Economic Policy* 6 (4): 207–38.

Davis, Lucas W., Catherine Hausman, and Nancy L. Rose. 2023. "Transmission Impossible? Prospects for Decarbonizing the US Grid." Working Paper no. w31377, NBER, Cambridge, MA.

Djankov, Simeon, Rafael La Porta, Florencio Lopez-de-Silanes, and Andrei Shleifer. 2002. "The Regulation of Entry." *Quarterly Journal of Economics* 117 (1): 1–37.

Feyrer, James, Erin T. Mansur, and Bruce Sacerdote. 2017. "Geographic Dispersion of Economic Shocks: Evidence from the Fracking Revolution." *American Economic Review* 107 (4): 1313–34.

Fthenakis, Vasilis, and Hyung Chul Kim. 2009. "Land Use and Electricity Generation: A Life-Cycle Analysis." *Renewable and Sustainable Energy Reviews* 13 (6–7): 1465–74.

Gross, Samantha. 2020. "Renewables, Land Use, and Local Opposition in the United States." Brookings Institution, January. https://www.brookings.edu/wp-content/uploads/2020/01/FP_20200113_renewables_land_use_local_opposition_gross.pdf.

Gustafson, Abel, Matthew H. Goldberg, John E. Kotcher, Seth A. Rosenthal, Edward W. Maibach, Matthew T. Ballew, and Anthony Leiserowitz. 2020. "Republicans and Democrats Differ in Why They Support Renewable Energy." *Energy Policy* 141:111448.

Gyourko, Joseph, Jonathan S. Hartley, and Jacob Krimmel. 2021. "The Local Residential Land Use Regulatory Environment across US Housing Markets: Evidence from a New Wharton Index." *Journal of Urban Economics* 124:103337.

Hanson, Gordon H. 2005. "Market Potential, Increasing Returns and Geographic Concentration." *Journal of International Economics* 67 (1): 1–24.

———. 2023. "Local Labor Market Impacts of the Energy Transition: Prospects and Policies." Working Paper no. w30871, NBER, Cambridge, MA.

Holland, Stephen P., Matthew J. Kotchen, Erin T. Mansur, and Andrew J. Yates. 2022. "Why Marginal CO_2 Emissions Are Not Decreasing for US Electricity: Estimates and Implications for Climate Policy." *Proceedings of the National Academy of Sciences of the United States of America* 119 (8): e2116632119.

Holmes, Thomas J. 1998. "The Effect of State Policies on the Location of Manufacturing: Evidence from State Borders." *Journal of Political Economy* 106 (4): 667–705.

Jacobson, Louis S., Robert J. LaLonde, and Daniel G. Sullivan. 1993. "Earnings Losses of Displaced Workers." *American Economic Review* 83 (4): 685–709.

Kahn, Matthew E. 2011. "Do Liberal Cities Limit New Housing Development? Evidence from California." *Journal of Urban Economics* 69 (2): 223–8.

———. 2013. "Local Non-Market Quality of Life Dynamics in New Wind Farms Communities." *Energy Policy* 59:800–807.

Kotchen, Matthew J., and Michael R. Moore. 2008. "Conservation: From Voluntary Restraint to a Voluntary Price Premium." *Environmental and Resource Economics* 40:195–215.

Lehr, Ulrike, Christian Lutz, and Dietmar Edler. 2012. "Green Jobs? Economic Impacts of Renewable Energy in Germany." *Energy Policy* 47:358–64.

Margo, Robert A. 1997. "Wages in California during the Gold Rush." Historical Paper no. 101, NBER, Cambridge, MA.

Mulligan, Casey B., and Andrei Shleifer. 2005. "The Extent of the Market and the Supply of Regulation." *Quarterly Journal of Economics* 120 (4): 1445–73.

Peltzman, Sam. 1984. "Constituent Interest and Congressional Voting." *Journal of Law and Economics* 27 (1): 181–210.

Poole, Keith T., and Howard Rosenthal. 2001. "D-Nominate after 10 Years: A Comparative Update to Congress: A Political-Economic History of Roll-Call Voting." *Legislative Studies Quarterly* 26 (1): 5–29.

Rappaport, Jordan, and Jeffrey D. Sachs. 2003. "The United States as a Coastal Nation." *Journal of Economic Growth* 8 (1): 5–46.

Rapson, David. 2014. "Durable Goods and Long-Run Electricity Demand: Evidence from Air Conditioner Purchase Behavior." *Journal of Environmental Economics and Management* 68 (1): 141–60. https://doi.org/10.1016/j.jeem.2014.04.003.

Seel, Joachim, Joseph Rand, Will Gorman, Dev Millstein, Ryan H. Wiser, Will Cotton, Katherine Fisher, Olivia Kuykendall, Ari Weissfeld, and Kevin Porter. 2023. "Interconnection Cost Analysis in the PJM Territory." Policy brief, Lawrence Berkeley National Lab, Berkeley, CA.

Stokes, Leah C. 2016. "Electoral Backlash against Climate Policy: A Natural Experiment on Retrospective Voting and Local Resistance to Public Policy." *American Journal of Political Science* 60 (4): 958–74.

Susskind, Lawrence, Jungwoo Chun, Alexander Gant, Chelsea Hodgkins, Jessica Cohen, and Sarah Lohmar. 2022. "Sources of Opposition to Renewable Energy Projects in the United States." *Energy Policy* 165:112922.

Van Zalk, John, and Paul Behrens. 2018. "The Spatial Extent of Renewable and Non-renewable Power Generation: A Review and Meta-Analysis of Power Densities and Their Application in the US." *Energy Policy* 123:83–91.

Victoria, Marta, Nancy Haegel, Ian Marius Peters, Ron Sinton, Arnulf Jäger-Waldau, Carlos del Cañizo, Christian Breyer, et al. 2021. "Solar Photovoltaics Is Ready to Power a Sustainable Future." *Joule* 5 (5): 1041–56.
Wolak, Frank A. 2022. "Long-Term Resource Adequacy in Wholesale Electricity Markets with Significant Intermittent Renewables." *Environmental and Energy Policy and the Economy* 3 (1): 155–220.